AUGSBURG COLLEGE & SEMINARY
George Sverdrup Library
MINNEAPOLIS 4, MINNESOTA

DUKE UNIVERSITY PUBLICATIONS

Anglophobia in France
1763-1789

Anglophobia in France
1763-1789

*An Essay in the History of
Constitutionalism and Nationalism*

FRANCES ACOMB

Duke University

Duke University Press
DURHAM, NORTH CAROLINA
1950

COPYRIGHT, 1950, BY THE DUKE UNIVERSITY PRESS

PRINTED IN THE UNITED STATES OF AMERICA
BY THE SEEMAN PRINTERY, INC., DURHAM, N. C.

To

My Mother

AND TO

The Memory of My Father

PREFACE

POLITICAL SPECULATION and controversy in France between the death of Louis XIV and the beginning of the Revolution followed three main lines, which sometimes coincided and sometimes diverged. These were the appeal to utopian rationalism, the argument from the constitutional history of the French monarchy itself, and the consideration of the example of other states. Among the latter, Great Britain easily inspired the most interest. Britain was a state large enough to merit comparison with France; small countries like the United Netherlands or Switzerland were ruled out at the start because the problems of large and small states were regarded as utterly dissimilar. Great Britain had been conspicuously successful in the international struggle for power. It was prosperous. And the English constitutional conflict of the seventeenth century, culminating in the Glorious Revolution of 1688, had awakened a host of echoes across the Channel. Some Frenchmen claimed, while others denied, that in Britain, or, more specifically, England, a solution had been found for the political problems agitating their own country. So the argument from example was chiefly in terms of the example of England—of her policies, government, history, and national character.

The fact that such a controversy over the example of the English took place has been generally but half realized. It is well understood that England furnished inspiration to French critics of the old regime, that it was the symbol of a liberalism which, derived from Locke and transmitted through Voltaire and Montesquieu particularly, had by the time of the Seven Years' War become virtually a tradition of thought. The manifestations of what contemporaries called "Anglomania" have been noted countless times, even though, to the best of the writer's knowledge, no definitive study of it exists. But comparatively little attention has been directed to the countersentiments to which the Anglophile tradition gave rise. These have attracted general interest and intensive study almost solely in connection with the constitutional controversy of 1789, when the anti-Anglophile party, opposing a bicameral legislature and a royal veto, contended sharply with those interests which, invoking the alleged example of the English constitution, demanded a government of checks and balances.[1] This episode, however, was only a late phase of a controversy that had been going on for many years.

The present study undertakes to explore that controversy, beginning some time around the close of the Seven Years' War. To

[1] There already exist two studies of French opinion on the English constitution covering the same time-span, but with extensions in both directions, as that covered by this volume. These are Gabriel Bonno, *La Constitution britannique devant l'opinion française de Montesquieu à Bonaparte* (Paris, 1932), and Richard M. Leighton, "The Tradition of the English Constitution in France on the Eve of the Revolution" (unpublished Ph.D. dissertation, Cornell University, 1941). Both of these studies take some account of the *contra* as well as the *pro*. However, it was apparent that an analysis of Anglophobe opinion could be carried much beyond what had been done in either of them. Each one differs considerably in scope and method from the present study. And it also remains true that historians generally have been much more aware of Anglomania than of Anglophobia. There are many references in works on the French Revolution to the debate of 1789 between the Anglophiles and the Anglophobes. More particularly, the matter is discussed in H. J. Laski, "The English Constitution and French Public Opinion, 1789-94," *Politica*, III (March, 1938), 27-42; David Williams, "French Opinion concerning the English Constitution in the Eighteenth Century," *Economica*, X (1930), 295-308; and Robert Redslob, *Die Staatstheorien der französischen Nationalversammlung von 1789. Ihre Grundlagen in der Staatslehre der Aufklärungszeit und in den englischen und amerikanischen Verfassungsgedanken* (Leipzig, 1912), which deals with the question at a theoretical level. Though it is of broader scope, Georges Lefebvre, *Quatre-vingt-neuf* (Paris, 1939), should also be mentioned here. For the impact of English institutions and ideas on French political thinking during the first half of the eighteenth century (a subject with which the present study is not directly concerned), there are Joseph Dedieu, *Montesquieu et la tradition politique anglaise en France. Les sources anglaises de l' "Esprit des lois"* (Paris, 1909); and Gabriel Bonno, *La Culture et la civilisation britanniques devant l'opinion française de la paix d'Utrecht aux Lettres philosophiques (1713-1734)* ("Transactions of the American Philosophical Society," New Series, Vol. XXXVIII, Part 1; Philadelphia, June, 1948). The last-named work really continues that of Georges Ascoli, *La Grande Bretagne devant l'opinion française au XVIIe siècle* ("Travaux et mémoires de l'Université de Lille. Droit-Lettres," nouvelle série, fascicule 13; 2 vols. in 1; Paris, 1930).

the conservatives who opposed the Anglophile liberals there were added, about that time, certain enemies to the left, who were eventually to wrest from the Anglophiles their ascendancy in the movement of revolutionary ideas. The emphasis in this study will be upon the anti-Anglophiles, or Anglophobes (these terms will generally be used as synonyms). It is not possible, however, to analyze Anglophobia without reference to Anglomania—without presenting, in particular, as a minor theme of the study, the decline of Anglophile liberalism. This may help, incidentally, to dispel a certain confusion which sometimes seems to exist regarding the purport of Anglophile ideas and which results from the fact that the significance of Anglomania was not at all times and in all quarters the same.

The Anglophobes of the right and those of the left assailed the constitutional concepts of the admirers of the English for very different reasons, but they resembled each other in finding the Anglophiles' admiration of foreign models and depreciation of things French (which the Anglophobes somewhat exaggerated) offensive to their nationalist sensibilities. For nationalism was a component of anti-Anglophile theory and sentiment. Moreover, one may observe in the history of the anti-Anglophile ideas that circulated in France between the Seven Years' War and the Revolution the development of a significant relation between revolutionary constitutional concepts and nationalism, a relation that the following chapters undertake to make clear. All of this somewhat subverts a rather widely held belief that French nationalism was born during the Revolution.

The reader has no doubt concluded from the foregoing remarks that what he is offered here is not a treatise on theory in the sense of something which has a detached, logical sort of existence above temporal circumstances, but an analysis of what is called, for want of a better term, "public" opinion. By definition, this term assumes that some connection exists between ideas and historical actions. But what is it? Do ideas determine events, or do events determine ideas, and in either case how much? This is a fundamental problem which the historian of ideas has to meet. One explanation, or metaphor, which seems to fit the observed phenomena pretty closely is that of two parallel lines, the one representing the evolution of ideas, the other the sequence of events, each line of development proceeding in some degree independently (in the sense that ideas produce other ideas and events produce other events), but each also extending out toward the other tentacles over which influences are transmitted. This explanation rejects on the one hand the notion that the events of an era are primarily the consequences of the ruling ideas of that era, and on the other hand the notion that ideas are only a kind of by-product in a chain of acts that would take place no matter what ideologies were prevalent. To this writer it seems that events both govern ideas and are governed by them. Perhaps the pull of the event-line is stronger than that of the idea-line. Men are quick to accommodate their theories to changes in the direction of events. Nevertheless, they are also prone to interpret events in the light of ideas which are familiar to them. Such, at any rate, are the conclusions that underlie this study in the history of ideas.

The type of source material used and the questions asked of it also deserve a brief explanation. No kind of material that might contain comment on contemporary politics or political ideas was excluded from consideration, although plays, poems, and novels as categories were not systematically explored simply because it did not seem likely that the yield would justify the effort. There was a wealth of relevant material of other kinds, including periodicals, newsletters (the *nouvelles à la main*) which circulated contemporaneously in manuscript, records of parliamentary debates and other public documents containing expressions of opinion, pamphlets on this or that question of the hour, histories, travel books and other descriptions of society and manners, dictionaries written after the fashion of Voltaire's *Dictionnaire philosophique*, satires, utopias, allegories, dialogues, moral disquisitions, political and economic theory, memoirs, and correspondence.

Much of this seems dull now, whereas some of it still makes good reading. But that is immaterial. The principal purpose of inquiry was to determine and to describe the content, or the intrinsic character, of categories of opinion, together with their variations. The stature of a writer in the eyes of posterity is thus irrelevant. His stature in his own time was a matter of consideration only in so far as he seemed to exert a kind of polarizing effect upon contemporary concepts. But no one of the greater writers of the period can be said to have created, by himself, a school of thought; and for the purpose of conveying as broad a view of public opinion as possible the more obscure writers seemed as significant as the more conspicuous. On the whole, therefore, the latter have been treated as *representatives* of this or that variety of opinion, while the question of the degree of their influence has not been argued at all.

In order to locate in the contemporary political milieu the several varieties of opinion expressed, it was desirable to identify as far as possible those who expressed them. Sometimes there was no problem about this at all. A good deal is known about most of the Physiocrats, for example—their names, social status, and occupations. On the other hand, a considerable number of sources remain completely or partially anonymous. There seemed no way of identifying the authors beyond saying that they represented such or such a viewpoint. But this fact does not make a great deal of difference inasmuch as enough is known about some of the people who subscribed to each variety of opinion to place it in its political context.

There were, indeed, certain individual cases in which the question of authorship had a special importance because the consistency of the author's views was involved. It was of some importance to know that a writer changed his mind, like Linguet, or that, like Helvétius, he was not guilty of the inconsistency which exists between the views expressed in his genuine writings and in those that are spurious.

The attempt has sometimes been made in this study to estimate the popularity or prevalence of a given point of view at a certain time, but not with any claim to scientific exactitude. It was simply not possible to obtain from the data the statistical type of information that the quantitative analyst wants. The utmost that could be said in answer to the question of popularity is something of this sort: "From the nature and quantity of such data as exist, from the paucity of contrary evidence, and from what actually happened in the realm of action, the prevailing opinion in this or that quarter appears to have been thus and so."

Finally, it should be said that the sources were interrogated not only on their own account, but also as witnesses to the opinions of their contemporaries.

The research for this study was made possible by the grant of the Dorothy Bridgman Atkinson Fellowship of the American Association of University Women for 1941-1942. To that association the writer gratefully acknowledges her indebtedness. She has to thank for their courtesy the staffs of those institutions whose collections she explored—the libraries of Chicago, Columbia, Cornell, Harvard, Princeton, and Yale universities, the Newberry and Crerar libraries in Chicago, the Boston Public Library, the New York Public Library, and the Library of Congress. Miss Katharine M. Hall of the University of Chicago Library was of much assistance in securing materials on loan. The writer wishes also to record her obligation to President Wilbur K. Jordan of Radcliffe College and to the late Professor Frances E. Gillespie of the University of Chicago for their reading of the manuscript before its final revision. Her sister, Dr. Evelyn M. Acomb, generously contributed very useful criticism of style and organization. The study was undertaken originally at the suggestion of Professor Louis Gottschalk of the University of Chicago. To his excellent advice and unfailing helpfulness in many ways the author owes most of all. But, while cognizant of her debt to these friends and critics, she alone remains responsible for any assertions of fact or any interpretations which the following pages contain. Finally, the author wishes to thank Professor William T. Laprade and Mr. Ashbel G. Brice, Director and Editor respectively of the Duke University Press, for their part in making the publication of this book possible.

Frances Acomb

Durham, North Carolina
December, 1949

CONTENTS

	PAGE
PREFACE	vii

CHAPTER

I. THE IMAGE OF ENGLAND AND THOSE WHO HELD IT	3
II. FRENCH CRITICISM OF ENGLISH INSTITUTIONS, 1763-1778: THE CONSERVATIVES	19
III. FRENCH CRITICISM OF ENGLISH INSTITUTIONS, 1763-1778: THE LIBERALS	30
IV. ANGLOPHOBIA AND FRENCH NATIONALISM BEFORE THE WAR OF AMERICAN INDEPENDENCE	51
V. THE JUSTIFICATION OF THE WAR OF AMERICAN INDEPENDENCE	69
VI. ANGLOPHOBIA AND THE FRENCH REVOLUTION	89
APPENDIX: APOCRYPHAL LETTERS OF HELVÉTIUS	124
BIBLIOGRAPHY	129
INDEX	163

Anglophobia in France
1763-1789

*Angleterre: c'est notre modèle et notre rivale,
  notre lumière et notre ennemie.*
"England is our model and our rival,
  our guiding light and our enemy."

> [J.-P.-L. de Luchet],
>   *Les Contemporains de 1789 et 1790* . . .

CHAPTER ONE

THE IMAGE OF ENGLAND AND THOSE
WHO HELD IT

WHAT WAS IT, really, that Frenchmen in the eighteenth century thought of when they thought of England? What was the image that came into their minds? For there *was* such an image, comprising a sort of common denominator of knowledge and opinion. The emotional reactions it inspired and the judgments that were based upon it varied greatly, but there was, at least until the very eve of the Revolution, quite general agreement upon its aspect. This image was not what the historian of the twentieth century sees, looking back, nor did it reflect very accurately the idea that Englishmen themselves had in the eighteenth century of their own society and government. It was less indicative of the state of English affairs than of French. It revealed not only considerable ignorance but even a lack of proper regard for the facts. There was something utopian in it. Yet England in the French mind was not primarily a utopia but a historical reality, emerging out of the same matrix of European civilization as had France. Before setting out to follow the argument that arose over the example of the English, the reader will find it desirable to have taken at least a cursory glance, first at the presuppositions that were the points of departure, then at the several groups that were the parties to the controversy.

Above all, England stood for the personal, or civil, liberties: liberty of opinion, secular or religious, of speech, petition, assembly, press, and person—liberty of person meaning the privilege of the writ of habeas corpus and public trial by jury. To be sure, there were critics who pointed out limitations and legal evasions in this system of liberties, but even when such limitations and evasions were subtracted the residue seemed impressive.

Secondarily, England was the prime exponent of the principle of the separation and balance of powers in government. This might mean any one of several things: the separation of the functions of government into legislative and executive elements, plus possibly a separate judicial element; or the division of legislative authority between the representative assembly and the executive power; or what was called contemporaneously "mixed government," that is, the distribution of legislative powers among the monarchical, aristocratic, and democratic elements of the nation. But in any case, however the concept of the balance of powers might be refined, it meant that in England authority was not concentrated in the monarch but shared in some fashion between him and a representative assembly. In the language of the time, political liberty was the end and aim of the English constitution, and the government of England was republican in a sense of the word common until near the beginning of the Revolution, a sense in which *republican* meant, not "kingless," but "antimonarchical."

After Montesquieu, who was apparently its most influential propagator if not its originator, the idea had become prevalent that government based upon the principle of the separation and balance of powers had achieved in England a certain mechanical perfection,[1] like the interior workings of a good watch. Like the workings of the watch, too, this kind of government was extremely complicated. And just as external forces like dust and dampness might alter the movement of the watch and rust its parts, so base human passions, triumphing over the political virtue of the citizens, might interfere with the operation of the government and eventually destroy it. This consideration raised the question of the survival of liberty in England, about which Montesquieu himself had had his doubts. One of the most often-quoted passages from Montesquieu relative to the English government was the prediction that liberty would be destroyed in England when the legislative power had become more corrupt than the executive.[2]

---

[1] *De l'esprit des lois*, Bk. XI, chap. vi, in Édouard Laboulaye (ed.), *Oeuvres complètes de Montesquieu avec les variantes des premières éditions, un choix des meilleurs commentaires et des notes nouvelles* (7 vols.; Paris, 1875-79), IV, 20.

[2] *Ibid.*, p. 23.

Even Anglophiles, who tended to minimize the seriousness of political corruption in England, could not deny its existence inasmuch as the English themselves publicized it.

The political behavior of the English seemed disorderly to Frenchmen. It appeared to them in fact very much as French political behavior under the Third Republic commonly appeared to Englishmen and Americans—full of notorious *affaires* and vehemently factious. "Faction" in the eighteenth century had even more invidious connotations than it has today. But whether or not Frenchmen were repelled by the factiousness of English politics, they uniformly associated with it the notion that English history had been peculiarly full of violence. They would not usually have said, as many people do today, that the English had a superior capacity for self-government. English liberty in their eyes was not an accretion of legal custom and statutory enactment, it was not freedom broadening down from precedent to precedent, but the triumph, after almost constant civil conflict, of principles laid down in the Magna Carta and consummated in the Bill of Rights. In France, moreover, the doctrine of the legislative supremacy of the King-in-Parliament was virtually unheard of. English constitutional law was read almost entirely in the light of seventeenth-century Whig political theory, and English subjects were supposed to retain a constitutional right of revolution for use whenever their liberties were seriously attacked by their own government.[3] Although Frenchmen might admire in the English their love of liberty, they nevertheless concluded that the English national character was turbulent. For this reason if for no other they were skeptical that the peace which had prevailed since 1689 in England would last indefinitely. Not only French conservatives but French liberals, Anglophile or Anglo-

[3] So strong in French minds was the impression of a fundamental law in England above Parliament that even in those few instances where French writers denied that Englishmen had a *constitutional* (as distinguished from a *moral*) right of revolution the denial was put, not upon the ground that the law was what Parliament said it was, but upon the a priori argument that revolution cannot be constitutional because it implies a reversion from the civil state to the state of nature. See Mably, *De l'étude de l'histoire, à monseigneur le prince de Parme*, in *Collection complète des oeuvres de l'abbé de Mably* (15 vols.; Paris, 1794-95), XII, 233-34; and [Saige], *Catéchisme du citoyen, ou Élémens du droit public françois, par demandes et réponses; suivi de Fragmens politiques par le même auteur* ("En France," 1788), p. 77.

phobe, were revolted by the thought of civil strife. The Puritan Revolution, with its fanaticism and regicide, they regarded with downright horror. Among scores of references to Cromwell there is not one that does not characterize him as a tyrant and a hypocrite. The Revolution of 1688 was the only one that any Frenchmen admired.[4] It was, indeed, the very core of the cult of Anglophile liberalism. It had consolidated the personal liberties of Englishmen and established the division of authority in government. It had been enlightened, bloodless, decorous, everything the Age of Reason might hope for in a revolution and fear not to find. But the character of this famous Revolution did not serve to dispel the widely held notion of the prevalence of violence in English history.

Liberty was not the only condition that marked England as a republican state. There was equality, too. Although the eighteenth century called republican some states obviously not egalitarian—the Republic of Poland, for example—its tendency was to associate republicanism with the absence of caste and with a certain middle-class tone of society, just as, conversely, it associated monarchy with the regime of privilege. England seemed preeminently republican in this sense. Was it not true in England that trade constituted no derogation of noblesse, that property was liable to taxation without distinction of noble or common, and that peasant servitudes did not exist? To be sure, Frenchmen

[4] It is true that after the close of the American Revolution, and in certain quarters, some change was noticeable. A new type of individual appeared in French politics, the professional revolutionary as distinguished from the critic or the *frondeur*. The Marquis de Lafayette and the journalist Brissot de Warville are examples. Brissot seemed exhilarated in contemplating England's stormy history, which had, he said, been the means of fabricating that country's glorious constitution. See his Preface to Oliver Goldsmith, *Lettres philosophiques et politiques sur l'histoire de l'Angleterre* (trans. from the English; 2 vols.; London and Paris, 1786), quoted in *Journal encyclopédique*, 1786, V, 412-15. Lafayette, a military leader, had his finger in revolutionary movements in half a dozen countries beside his own. See Sir Edward Newenham to Lafayette, July 5, 1784, Great Britain, Historical Manuscripts Commission, *Fourteenth Report*, Appendix, Part I, *The Manuscripts . . . Preserved at Belvoir Castle* (London, 1894), III, 119; the Duke of Rutland to Lord Sydney, May 29, 1784, *ibid.*, p. 99; Lafayette to Col. William Smith, January 16, 1787, MS in the possession of H. A. De Windt; and *Mémoires, correspondance et manuscrits du général Lafayette, publiés par sa famille* (6 vols.; Paris, 1837-38), II, 309, and III, 200. Nevertheless, Lafayette and Brissot would probably have rejected indignantly the imputation that their attitude presaged other than a peaceable revolution in France, and in any case they were exceptional.

were not unconscious of the survival of certain feudal forms and agencies of government in England. They had in mind the central government. They knew that the survival of medieval offices whose functions had become obsolete was a factor in the contemporary question of crown patronage. They understood clearly that Parliament itself had had feudal origins. A degree of privilege associated with membership in Parliament could not be overlooked. Its existence and its effects were, however, minimized. The House of Commons, not the House of Lords, appeared to be by far the more important chamber (despite the fact that the "typical" Englishman in French literature was nearly always a "milord"), and the House of Commons seemed to Frenchmen a national rather than a class assembly, comprehending the interests of all classes. The privilege of the peerage itself appeared to be political only. There was no social or legal privilege.

The reader will no doubt immediately ask: What about local government in rural England, where the gentry enjoyed a virtual monopoly of both social and political power? The answer is that the greater part of the traditional structure of English county, parish, and manor government does not appear at all in the pages of French writers, who seem to have assumed that the English citizen in his daily life was subject to no authority intermediate between himself and the government at Westminster. As late as 1788 the Marquis de Condorcet suggested that a system of provincial assemblies like those recently provided for in France might well be established in England to fill what he considered to be a void in the provincial administration of that country.[5] Such a supposition can be explained only as a rather startling example of the predisposition of contemporaries to a priori reasoning. Equality was so plainly visible to Frenchmen at the upper levels of English society and government, where the merchants were in politics and the sons of the nobility in trade, that they seem to have felt justified in assuming its existence lower down, too—especially with

---

[5] *Essai sur la constitution et les fonctions des assemblées provinciales* (1788), in A. Condorcet O'Connor and M. F. Arago (eds.), *Oeuvres de Condorcet* (12 vols.; Paris, 1847-49), VIII, 516. Cf. [P.-S. Dupont de Nemours], *Lettre à la chambre du commerce de Normandie; sur le mémoire qu'elle a publié relativement au traité de commerce avec l'Angleterre* (Rouen and Paris, 1788), p. 262.

the authority of Montesquieu behind them. Montesquieu had said, in one of his references to the government of England, that for the sake of their liberty the English had abolished all feudal jurisdictions and "intermediary powers,"[6] all authority, that is, which was based upon prescriptive right and class privilege.

With the gentry thus eliminated from local government, and in their place no visible agents of the central power like the French intendants or the *maréchaussée* (the military police), how did the English maintain public order? To this question French writers gave either of two answers. Some said in effect that the English did not maintain order. There were many derogatory allusions to the London mob and to the frequency of highway robbery in England—and no doubt there was justice in these remarks, although, as the French critics who made much of this point were not aware, the golden age of the highwaymen had been gone for some time. Other writers were disposed to discount the allegation of the prevalence of highway robbery and to maintain that in England respect for law—that is, for the rights of private property—was so general that the police were not needed. It was not supposed, exactly, that there was no crime in England, but simply that crime was no more prevalent there in the absence of a police force than it was in France, where one existed. The explanation invariably advanced as to why no military police had ever been instituted in England was, however, a purely political one. Parliament was said to have feared that the crown, if given the disposal of such a force, would use it to recover some of the powers it had lost to that body.

Liberalism, which thus characterized society and politics in England, stopped short, it seemed to French observers, at the threshold of economic policy. English mercantilism seemed more firmly established than that of France itself. It was known that there were no internal customs barriers as there were in France, but the movement for freer international trade that had begun in England about the end of the preceding century was not regarded as a continuing tendency. Frenchmen could see that commercial monopolies and guild restrictions continued to exist, but they did

---

[6] *De l'esprit des lois*, Bk. II, chap. iv, in *Oeuvres complètes de Montesquieu*, III, 115-16.

not generally observe the growth of new and freer forms of industrial enterprise. The only economic changes that they saw in England were agrarian, but they thought of England as being essentially a commercial rather than an agricultural state. They carried on a lively argument as to whether that country were a flourishing or a declining power. What they wanted to determine, of course, was the relative power of France and England, both then and in the future. In their discussion industrial potential figured only from the point of view of natural resources; but agriculture, trade, taxation, the national debt, and the general standard of living were well-worn topics. There was disagreement concerning the relative power of the two states at that time, but with respect to the future most Frenchmen believed that the pre-eminence of France was assured. They based this calculation upon her more numerous population and greater extent of territory, together with their opinion that her soil was at least as fertile at that of Britain. Colonial empire, in the contest for which England had been victorious, was not thought to be necessarily an advantage; moreover, that score was not yet settled.

The imperial conflict between France and Britain was reflected everywhere in contemporary writing. In the classical terminology of the eighteenth century England was denominated, with varying shades of opprobrium, the "modern Carthage." As the foremost imperialist power, termed unjust, proud, and grasping, she inspired in Frenchmen pretty generally a lively indignation, while on the other hand they appeared to believe that French policy was nonaggressive. The cause of British imperialism was thought to lie in the commercial spirit with which all classes of the nation were said to be imbued. From this point conservative writers would go on with disparaging remarks inspired by the idea of the ignoble nature of trade. As one such writer declared: "The English constitution is only a burghers' *(bourgeois)* government spread out over a kingdom."[7] Liberals, who admired England precisely for the middle-class features of its civilization, moralized at length about the corrupting effects of an itch for gain and the

---

[7] [Comte de Dubuat-Nançay], *Les Maximes du gouvernement monarchique, pour servir de suite aux Éléments de la politique* (4 vols.; London, 1778), III, 358.

necessity of having laws that would be conducive to good *moeurs*, either internal or international.

Frenchmen in the eighteenth century never tired of analyzing the English national character. They had no doubt that such a thing existed, and they all came to the same conclusions about it. Their feelings were mixed: the English character was admirable but disagreeable. Its more frequently encountered representative in French literature, the "milord," was a *philosophe*, as befitted the compatriot of Locke and Newton. His tastes were simple, and his thoughts were of serious things. He was a great individualist in all his actions and opinions: *singularité* was the French word for this quality. He was a woman-hater, though he practiced the domestic virtues. He had no gaiety, no social ease, but on the contrary suffered from a profound melancholy that would probably cause him sooner or later to commit suicide. Though full of a practical, public-spirited kind of charity, he was personally haughty and indifferent. He had a moral fiber and intellectual stature that came from constant participation in politics, for Parliament was a great proving-ground of a man's abilities, bringing out the best he had to offer. (To be sure, some members of that renowned assembly spent their days in slumber and their nights in debauchery, and there was a stupidly reckless species of Englishman who gambled upon everything under the sun. There was also a great deal of political corruption. The French picture no doubt had inconsistencies, but in general the typical Englishman was considered to be serious and philosophical.) Being a "republican," with a younger brother in trade, the milord could not be expected to have quite the same feeling about honor as the French gentleman, but he had instead a passion for liberty and a sense of civic duty. Unfortunately, the Englishman's love of liberty did not extend beyond the borders of his own country; he had no scruples against the enslavement of other peoples.

In the eighteenth century crowds of English travelers passed through Paris. What Frenchmen thought of these foreigners may be gauged pretty well from the following words put into the mouth of one of them (who was, needless to say, a milord), by a contemporary satirist:

We are inconstant as the element that surrounds us; there is nothing stable about us but a fund of taciturnity of which it is difficult to divest ourselves. We arrive in a city intending to remain there six months, and we leave on the following day. That is the result of a natural anxiety which torments us and which we never master despite our fanaticism for liberty. Formerly we were loved for our money but have been so often cheated that we have become as stingy *(économes)* as we are mistrustful.

We are always wanting to travel, yet ordinarily on our journeys we see only English people, a ridiculous habit that comes from too great a prejudice in our own favor and from the fear of communicating with others. We love France, and we hate the French; we compel ourselves to learn their language only never to speak it. We have a regard only for our own country, yet we cannot stay there; even our women go in quest of other places than their native soil. We are always as good as our word, but we are always fearful lest others fail us. We never leave behind us debts or causes of complaint, but we leave no regrets either.

· · · · · · · · · ·

It is rarely that we approve what does not resemble our laws and our customs; but we conform without difficulty to the ways of different countries, wishing always, nevertheless, whether in the cut of our clothes, or in our behavior, to be recognized as English.

We are rarely flattered by praise. Compliments in our eyes have something servile about them.

Patriotism is our passion, liberty our element; and if we are considered fanatics on these two points, it is because we lack the art of persuasion. There is in us at all times something austere which diminishes the merit of our feelings and our tastes. . . .

We carry friendship to the uttermost limits, but only when we have made sure of a friend over a long period of years; people frequently die before winning our confidence.[8]

---

[8] L.-A. de Caraccioli, *Voyage de la raison en Europe*, in [Garnier (ed.)], *Voyages imaginaires* (39 vols.; Amsterdam and Paris, 1787-95), XXVII, 204-7. The title page wrongly attributes the work to the *Marquis* de Caraccioli. It was first published in 1771. See J.-M. Quérard, *La France littéraire, ou Dictionnaire bibliographique des savants, historiens et gens de lettres de la France, ainsi que les littérateurs étrangers qui ont écrit en français, plus particulièrement pendant les XVIIIe et XIXe siècles* (12 vols.; Paris, 1827-64), under "Caraccioli." Cf. a contemporary English translation, *The Travels of Reason in Europe*, trans. from the French of the Marquis Caraccioli (London, 1780), pp. 60-62.

The foregoing was written by an opponent of Anglomania, but even Anglophiles, who could forgive much on account of the services Englishmen had rendered to the cause of liberty and the Enlightenment, would have recognized the likeness in the portrait.

French liberalism remained predominantly Anglophile until the War of American Independence, which appears in retrospect as a kind of watershed dividing the period when a compromise solution of the problems confronting the monarchy would seem to have been possible from that during which events moved with apparent irresistibility toward revolution. The organization of this study, as the reader will observe, turns upon that event. Who were the Anglophiles? They were not a homogeneous element of opinion, but comprised several distinct groups.

One of these groups included certain of the *philosophes*, of whom Voltaire was the most conspicuous, Helvétius perhaps the most ardent and least critical.[9] They were propagandists for civil liberty (including religious toleration), humane laws, the destruction of privilege, and a good administration—the things they most admired in England as they saw that country. They did not fail to commend the role played by Parliament in English history, Parliament having led the English nation in its struggle against despotism; and they admired, or in any case did not find fault with, the concept of government by checks and balances. Nevertheless, they tended to believe that civil liberty, equality, and an enlightened administration could come to pass in France without the establishment of representative government.

Prior to the Seven Years' War there had been another philosophic group, consisting of the administrator-economist Vincent de Gournay and his followers, which especially admired contemporary English economic policy. They had observed in England such developments as the abolition of agricultural export duties, the removal of many other duties both on imports and on exports, the rise of the interloper in foreign trade, the decline of state industrial regulation, and the absence of internal customs barriers (this

---

[9] Certain letters of a strongly Anglophobe temper hitherto attributed to Helvétius are in the opinion of the writer apocryphal. They were written, clearly, during the constitutional controversy of 1788-89, nearly twenty years after the death of the supposed author. This problem of authenticity is discussed at length in the Appendix.

last not a new or recent development, to be sure). These things, together with certain writings of late seventeenth-century English theorists, had inspired the school of Gournay with the desire to loosen up French economic policy in the same way. After the Seven Years' War, however, this school disintegrated. The followers of Gournay, as economic liberals, were obscured by or went into the camp[10] of the more doctrinaire Physiocrats, who were Anglophobes, although, like the Abbé Morellet, the remnants of the school of Gournay might so far as their political principles were concerned retain their admiration for the English.

Different in many respects from the Anglophile *philosophes* was the *frondeur* party, which included the legal aristocracy and their allies among the great court nobles. The purpose of this party was to obtain for the aristocracy, who already had a virtual monopoly of the higher administrative and judicial posts, a share of the crown's political power. To this end the so-called sovereign law-courts, the parlements, headed by the Parlement of Paris, were attempting to transform their recognized right of remonstrance against royal edicts into a power of judicial review that would give them a final veto upon all legislation. They had won a popular following by their occasional championship of popular causes, like the reduction of taxes and the suppression of the Jesuit Order, more or less against royal policy. In 1771 the king deprived the members of the Parlement of Paris of their offices because they had in effect challenged his power, exercised in the ceremony of the *lit de justice*, to override their remonstrances; and he reconstituted the court with personnel who were not hostile to royal absolutism.[11] The new body, termed the "Maupeou parlement" after the chancellor who carried through the reform, was shortlived. Louis XVI, who desired upon his accession in 1774 to

---

[10] See Edgard Depitre's introduction to Dupont de Nemours, *De l'exportation et de l'importation des grains (1764)* and L.-P. Abeille, *Premiers opuscules sur le commerce des grains (1763-64)*, ed. Edgard Depitre (Paris, 1911), pp. vi-vii, xxv-xxvi, *et passim*.

[11] A. Esmein, *Cours élémentaire d'histoire du droit français à l'usage des étudiants de première année*, ed. R. Génestal (15th ed.; Paris, 1925), pp. 522-24; E. Glasson, *Le Parlement de Paris. Son rôle politique depuis le règne de Charles VII jusqu'à la Révolution* (2 vols.; Paris, 1901), II, 349-58; Henri Carré, *Le Règne de Louis XV (1715-1774)*, Vol. VIII, Part II of *Histoire de France depuis les origines jusqu'à la Révolution*, ed. Ernest Lavisse (9 vols.; Paris, 1900-[1911]), pp. 396-99.

conciliate all parties, recalled the former members of the Parlement of Paris to their positions and restored all the parlements (the provincial parlements had also suffered somewhat under the Maupeou reform) to the status they had formerly possessed. The result was that the constitutional controversy was restored, too.

The parlements claimed that the constitution of France had formerly been and now rightfully was that of a limited monarchy, wherein they themselves were both the depositary of the "fundamental laws" and the spokesmen for the Estates-General during intervals when the latter body was not in session.[12] There was thus a certain parallel between their position and that of the English Parliament in the seventeenth century. They naturally did not themselves adduce English precedents but found their precedents in the history of their own country, and, accused of Anglomania, they or rather their spokesmen among the pamphleteers sometimes actually denied that their doctrine contained Anglophile principles or that they believed English institutions to be superior to those of France. It seems likely, however, that such denials were more indicative of the political necessity of countering the charge of being un-French, than of the real views of the judiciary.[13] Although the latter were not Anglophile in the same sense as the *philosophes*, who stood above all for intellectual liberty, they indubitably favored checks and balances.

[12] Esmein, *Cours élémentaire*, pp. 509-10 and 521-22.
[13] Anon., *Lettre sur l'état actuel du crédit du gouvernement en France* (1771), pp. 15, 19, *et passim*; [Blonde?], *Le Parlement justifié par l'impératrice reine de Hongrie, et par le roi de Prusse; ou Seconde lettre, dans laquelle on continue à répondre aux écrits de M. le Chancelier* [1771], in *Les Efforts de la liberté et du patriotisme, contre le despotisme du sieur de Maupeou, chancelier de France, ou Recueil des écrits patriotiques publiés pour maintenir l'ancien gouvernement français* [ed. M. F. Pidansat de Mairobert] (6 vols.; London, 1775), IV, 209-18. The second pamphlet, dated 1771 by its author, is attributed here to Blonde inasmuch as it is said by Barbier to be a continuation of another written by Blonde. See Ant.-Alex. Barbier, *Dictionnaire des ouvrages anonymes* (3d ed. rev.; 4 vols.; Paris, 1882). Saige, *Catéchisme du citoyen*, cited in n. 3 above, is another pro-parlement pamphlet that repudiates Anglophile principles, but is exceptional in basing its position on the allegation that in the government of England the will of the nation could not be adequately expressed. This was much too advanced for most of the parliamentary pamphleteers at that time, who did not conceive of any more radical political theory than that of the Anglophile liberals. Saige's work, republished in 1788, first appeared in 1775, according to [Louis Bachaumont *et al.*], *Mémoires secrets pour servir à l'histoire de la république des lettres en France, depuis MDCCLXII jusqu'à nos jours* . . . (36 vols.; London, 1784-89), VIII, 107.

If the parlements were averse to calling their Anglophile principles by that name, the court nobility with whom they were associated had no such inhibition. These people openly envied a constitution under which English nobles and English gentlemen were in a sense the equals of their sovereign. As one of them, the Comte de Ségur, later recollected:

> Montesquieu had opened our eyes to the advantages of English institutions . . . [and] the brilliant but frivolous life of our nobility at court and in the city could not satisfy our vanity, when we thought about the dignity, the independence, the useful and important existence of a peer of England, of a member of the House of Commons, and of the liberty, as tranquil as it was proud, of all the citizens of Great Britain.[14]

The political opinions of the *frondeurs* imparted a seditious tinge even to the court fashion of imitating the English in dress, equipages, and manners. The Anglomania of the fashionables angered Louis XV.[15] It also angered his grandson, Louis XVI, who told the Duc de Lauzun, a leading spirit of this group, that if one were so fond of the English one ought to go live among them. It was rumored that the Duc de Lauzun's Anglomania was likely to cost him the command of the regiment of the Gardes Françaises, which had been destined for him.[16]

It may be objected that, while the *frondeurs* talked a great deal about liberty, their point of view was only a quasi liberalism. They were indeed less concerned to defend the rights of individuals against authority than to assert the privileges of their own class in the face of any reforms that might undermine their special status. In the egalitarian aspects of the liberal doctrine they had at most only a romantic interest. There seems not to have been any appreciable genuinely liberal element among the nobility prior to the American war,[17] unless the aristocratic sub-

---

[14] Comte de Ségur, *Mémoires ou Souvenirs et anecdotes* (3d ed.; 3 vols.; Paris, 1827), I, 134.

[15] F. C. Green, *Eighteenth-Century France. Six Essays* (London and Toronto [1929]), p. 49.

[16] [Métra, J. Imbert, et al.], *Correspondance secrète, politique et littéraire, ou Mémoires pour servir à l'histoire des cours, des sociétés et de la littérature en France, depuis la mort de Louis XV* (18 vols.; London, 1787-89), I, 55 (Aug. 25, 1774).

[17] This conclusion is supported by the studies of Louis Gottschalk on Lafayette

scribers to the tenets of Physiocratic liberalism be excepted. Nevertheless, the influence of the *frondeur* movement in this early period was, when all is said, more in the direction of liberal objectives than against them. Some, at least, of the *philosophes* thought so. If Voltaire denounced the parlements for their social and legal conservatism,[18] Diderot and Morellet were willing to admit that they had a function in the struggle against "despotism."[19]

In the period following the War of American Independence there appeared another Anglophile group that was essentially a conservative party. Its place in the political milieu is described in the final chapter of this study. Although the views of this party were foreshadowed by the aspirations of the *frondeur* Anglophiles of the earlier period, they occupied a position with reference to the rest of public opinion that was somewhat different from that of their precursors.[20]

Most prominent among the anti-Anglophiles in the period before the War of American Independence were the conservative defenders of the absolute monarchy. Most of these also upheld economic regulation, corporate privilege, and censorship in favor of the Catholic religion. Such conservatives were convinced that the principle of limited monarchy, if established in France, would become the most effective single solvent of the old regime. Others who must be classified as conservatives might not wish to see the old order continue entirely unchanged, or they might not display a fanatical regard for it, while they nevertheless refrained from adopting the viewpoint of the liberals. Traditionalists by inclina-

---

—*Lafayette Comes to America* (Chicago [1935]), *Lafayette Joins the American Army* (Chicago [1937]), and *Lafayette and the Close of the American Revolution* (Chicago [1942])—which are studies in the emergence of a liberal nobility. The same impression is conveyed by Henri Carré, *La Noblesse de France et l'opinion publique au XVIIIe siècle* (Paris, 1920), pp. 311-12, 390-92, *et passim*, although Carré does not distinguish clearly between decades.

[18] *Les Peuples aux parlements* [Paris and Geneva, 1771], in *Oeuvres complètes de Voltaire* (new ed.; 52 vols.; Paris, 1877-85), XXVIII, 413-20; *L'Équivoque* [Paris, 1771], *ibid.*, pp. 421-24.

[19] Diderot to the Princess Dashkoff, April 3, 1771, in J. Assézat (ed.), *Oeuvres complètes de Diderot* . . . (20 vols.; Paris, 1875-77), XX, 28; Diderot, *Réfutation suivie de l'ouvrage d'Helvétius intitulé l'Homme* [written 1774], *ibid.*, II, 275; Morellet to Lord Shelburne, Feb. 25, 1773, in Lord Edmond Fitzmaurice (ed.), *Lettres de l'abbé Morellet de l'Académie française à Lord Shelburne depuis marquis de Lansdowne, 1772-1803* (Paris, 1898), p. 28.

[20] See below, pp. 104-6.

tained, and such were the several groups who were parties to the controversy over the validity, for France, of that country's example. The next three chapters will take up the opinions of the Anglophobes during the interval between the Seven Years' War and the War of American Independence.

tion and devoted to the monarchy, they did not like the iconoclasm of the liberals or the "republican" overtones of their doctrine.

According to the conservatives, *Anglomane, philosophe,* and *novateur* were interchangeable terms: all liberals were Anglophiles. But this idea was mistaken. Already in existence before the War of American Independence were two anti-Anglophile liberal schools of thought, namely, the forerunners of the school of Rousseau, and the Physiocrats. The former included such eminent philosophic writers as the Abbé de Mably, Baron d'Holbach, Denis Diderot, Jean-Paul Marat, and Jean-Jacques Rousseau himself, as well as some other more obscure writers. No doubt these individuals were quite unconscious themselves of any reason why they should be grouped together thus. Rousseau was not the recognized master of any of the writers named, despite the term used to describe them. Yet they resembled each other in their criticisms of English society, politics, and government. They were the earliest exemplars and in some degree the creators of a more "republican" and more aggressive liberalism than that of the Anglophiles, a doctrine or ideology which ultimately crystallized around Rousseau's concept of the sovereignty of the general will and which became in the 1780's both the leading liberal ideology and the most significant form of Anglophobia. The term "popular school" will be used as an equivalent to "school of Rousseau," or "school of Rousseau and Mably."

Unlike the forerunners of the school of Rousseau, the Physiocrats were a self-conscious sect. That was in fact the word by which contemporaries described them. Although not numerous, they were a closely knit and aggressive coterie of economic liberals who followed the doctrines of the court physician François Quesnay and who, aspiring to make the French monarchy a "legal despotism," achieved a noteworthy if brief political ascendancy in the 1770's while Turgot was controller-general of the finances. Their doctrinaire devotion to the principle of absolute monarchy was ultimately broken. In the 1780's they divided into two groups who may be termed the orthodox Physiocrats and the Neo-Physiocrats, or revisionists. The latter at that time joined forces with the school of Rousseau.

Such, then, was the image of England that Frenchmen enter-

CHAPTER TWO

FRENCH CRITICISM OF ENGLISH INSTITUTIONS, 1763-1778: THE CONSERVATIVES

FRENCH CONSERVATIVES were generally old-fashioned divine-right political theorists. To their mind the idea that love and reverence and fidelity were due to a king as the Lord's anointed and the father of a great political family was axiomatic; it was the foundation stone of government. When they looked across the Channel, they perceived a king who was not treated like one (or so it seemed to them). Beginning with the humiliating imposition of the Magna Carta upon King John,[1] the English had always treated their kings with hostility and disrespect. This people, said one writer, had been more "unjust" to their sovereign than any other people: they respected his office but not his person; he was the object of their distrust but never of their love.[2] In horrified tones the antiphilosophic *Journal historique et littéraire* related how King George III had been greeted in the streets of London with shouts of "Long live Wilkes!"[3]— Wilkes being a demagogue who was asserted by his enemies to have uttered "seditious libel" against the king. Even the author of the not very antiphilosophic *Dictionnaire social et patriotique* found it shocking that the role of a king when played on the Lon-

---

[1] Anon., *Le Fin mot de l'affaire* [1771?], p. 21. This was an antiparlement pamphlet.
[2] [Damiens de Gomicourt], *L'Observateur françois à Londres, ou Lettres sur l'état présent de l'Angleterre* (32 vols.; London and Paris, 1769-72), quoted in *Journal des beaux-arts et des sciences*, 1769, IV, 337. The *Observateur* itself was not available to the writer.
[3] *Journal historique et littéraire*, 1774, II, 167-68.

don stage should have been permitted to compass actions which seemed unworthy of majesty.[4]

In contrast with the English, proclaimed conservatives, the French had always manifested a singular and beautiful devotion to their kings. Never, according to the *Journal de Genève*, one of the more intelligent political journals of its day, never had the French nation as a body "conspired" against the throne as, it was implied, the English had. In France the cause of civil disorders had never been sedition but simply the weakness or insanity of the monarch or else the national hatred of foreigners who seemed to be ruling the state.[5] Similarly contrasting the political attitudes of the French and the English, a monarchist magistrate averred that since the time of Jeanne d'Arc "the Frenchman has not ceased to be distinguished by his love for and his fidelity to his kings."[6] Another publicist, after observing that the English people and their monarchs had always lived in mutual fear, added: "What a [happy] contrast in France! There the sovereign is the living image of the Supreme Being; his throne cannot be shaken; the fidelity of his people is incorruptible!"[7] Upon this attitude a contemporary Anglophile publicist, assuming the guise of an English writer, commented ironically:

The French insist upon their singular and inviolable fidelity to their kings . . . [and] even with respect to those who have exceeded the limits of mildness and moderation in their government . . . they pretend that in abstaining from giving way to their resentment they have prevented consequences that would have made the remedy worse than the evil. Without determining the worth of this assertion, it suffices to

---

[4] [Pierre Lefèvre de Beauvray], *Dictionnaire social et patriotique, ou Précis raisonné de connoissances relatives à l'économie morale, civile et politique* (Amsterdam, 1770), p. 19.

[5] *Journal historique et politique des principaux événemens des différentes cours de l'Europe*, 1772, No. 2 (Oct. 20), pp. 11-12. Hereinafter cited according to its popular designation, *Journal de Genève*.

[6] [Louis] Basset de la Marelle, *La Différence du patriotisme national chez les François et chez les Anglois. Discours lu à l'Académie des Sciences Belles-Lettres et Arts de Lyon* (Lyon, 1762), p. 30. Quérard gives 1760 as the date of first publication. To judge from the reviews, the work was not generally known until 1766.

[7] Anon., *Lettre d'un jeune homme à son ami, sur les Français et les Anglais, relativement à la frivolité reprochée aux uns, et la philosophie attribuée aux autres; ou Essai d'un parallele à faire entre ces deux nations* (Amsterdam and Paris, 1779), p. 33.

say that the French are persuaded that it is of great weight, and that in virtue of this persuasion they are always ready to discuss the contrast with our conduct in similar cases, a contrast that unquestionably demonstrates, according to them, the inferiority of our honor and of our national character.[8]

Similarly, a Scottish physician who spent some time in France in the decade of the 1770's reported:

When they [the French] hear of the freedom of debate in parliament, of the liberties taken in writing or speaking of the conduct of the king or measures of government, and the forms to be observed, before the most daring abuse of either can be brought to punishment, they seem filled with indignation, and say with an air of triumph, C'est bien autrement chez nous. Si le Roi de France avoit affaire à ces Messieurs là, il leur apprendroit à vivre.[9]

It may be, indeed, that the conservatives were merely whistling to keep up their courage in the face of an unsympathetic world. On the other hand it is more than likely that, as the two writers just quoted imply, the generality of Frenchmen in the 1760's and 1770's, even apart from the unlettered masses, were sentimentally devoted to the monarchy and genuinely shocked by the disrespect for kings attributed to the English. If this is true, conservatives acted shrewdly in appealing to such a prejudice in their attempts to discredit the Anglophiles.

The strange attitude of the English toward their monarch was of course associated by conservatives with the "republican" institutions and political philosophy of that nation. As one writer put it, the King of England was merely a grandee who received public moneys, and one could expect no majesty in royalty which was based upon a cash transaction.[10]

---

[8] [James Rutledge or Rutlidge], *Essai sur le caractere et les moeurs des François comparés à ceux des Anglois* (London, 1776), pp. 134-35. The author of this work, which appeared first in English in 1770, was a French writer of Irish extraction.

[9] John Moore, M.D., *A View of Society and Manners in France, Switzerland, and Germany: with Anecdotes Relating to Some Eminent Characters* (7th ed.; 2 vols.; London, 1789), I, 43. First published in 1779, this work appears from its contents to relate to the years 1771-74.

[10] [Ange Goudar], *L'Espion chinois; ou, l'Envoye secret de la cour de Pekin, pour examiner l'état présent de l'Europe. Traduit du chinois* (6 vols.; Cologne, 1764), IV, 18. Although Goudar is best known today for having been an advocate of the English corn-law policy of the first half of the eighteenth century, permitting the free export of grain, he was in most matters strongly Anglophobe.

But conservatives did not rest content with deploring the treatment which the English accorded to their kings. As the proof of the pudding must after all be in the eating, they made a great point of examining the English constitution upon its merits. That is, they pretended to consider whether it actually had obtained for the English that liberty which according to every eighteenth-century writer after Montesquieu was its object and which depended upon the balance of powers. They concluded that the English constitution, though beautiful in theory, was a complicated mechanism that not only was in danger of breaking down under the force of selfish human passions, as Montesquieu had suggested, but actually had broken down. Or rather, it had never really worked at all. One had only to look at English history to see that the balance of powers had never been achieved but had always been tipped one way or the other, toward the king or toward the Parliament. There was some disagreement among these commentators as to which way the balance was tipped in their own time. Most conservatives thought that it was inclined toward the throne, putting the English in imminent danger of despotism. For the King of England had corrupted Parliament, which constituted the only check upon his power that the English political tradition afforded. The French had been more fortunate, for the King of France was restrained from ruling arbitrarily by the fundamental laws of the monarchy (regarding which conservative publicists were never very explicit) and by a paternalistic tradition.[11] The reader will no doubt recognize in these observations another echo of Montesquieu, who had suggested that England, where all the *corps intermédiaires* had been destroyed, stood in greater danger

---

[11] Basset de la Marelle, *La Différence du patriotisme national*, pp. 38, 60; Goudar, *L'Espion chinois*, IV, 10-12, 18-20; *ibid.*, VI, 95-96; Abbé Millot, *Élémens de l'histoire d'Angleterre, depuis la conquête des Romains, jusqu'au règne de Georges II* (3d ed.; 3 vols.; Paris, 1776 [first published in 1768]), I, xxxv-xxxvi; Damiens de Gomicourt, *L'Observateur*, quoted in *L'Année littéraire; ou, Suite des lettres sur quelques écrits de ce temps*, 1769, VI, 314-15; *Journal de Genève*, 1772, No. 2, p. 7; [P.-L.-Claude Gin], *Les Vrais principes du gouvernement françois, démontrés par la raison et par les faits, par un François* (Geneva, 1777), pp. 72, 75-77; [Comte de Dubuat-Nançay], *Les Maximes du gouvernement monarchique, pour servir de suite aux Élémens de la politique* (4 vols.; London, 1778), III, 367-68; Anon., *Réflexions d'un citoyen sur l'édit de décembre 1770* [1770 or 1771], pp. 3-8, 20-21.

of despotism than a true monarchy, where *corps intermédiaires* were the very stuff of the political fabric.[12]

Some conservatives, however, accepted the idea that the King of England had been deprived of any power to harm his subjects, which was the thesis of the Anglophile liberals. But they gave it an anti-Anglophile twist. They declared that England was still in bondage, and in greater bondage than any purely monarchical state could ever be, because now Parliament was the despot and the tyranny of several was always worse than the tyranny of one.[13] The brilliant, if erratic, journalist Linguet, who alternated between the two views of the location of tyranny in England,[14] declared, when propounding the second, that the government of England was more oppressive than the despotisms of Asia. Parliament levied onerous taxes for the profit of its members and that of the incumbents of offices, while English law permitted such barbarous practices as imprisonment for debt, procurement of seamen by the press gang, and the violation of the sanctity of private dwellings through the use of general warrants (in the search for contraband).[15] Linguet's indictment hardly supported the furiousness of his charge. Yet it must be said that he perceived, as not many Frenchmen did, that Parliament represented only the upper classes. Linguet was not a typical conservative. It is hard to say which he hated more, the aristocracy or the *philosophes,* whose doctrines collectively he dubbed *Encyclop-économie* and whom he denounced, again collectively, as Anglophiles. Although they had taken "reason" and "liberty" for their watchwords, they were, he complained, "the most furious and unjust" of all sects, being determined to crush every one who would not wear their livery.[16]

[12] *De l'esprit des lois,* Bk. II, chap. iv, in Édouard Laboulaye (ed.) *Oeuvres complètes de Montesquieu avec les variantes des premières éditions, un choix des meilleurs commentaires et des notes nouvelles* (7 vols.; Paris, 1875-79), III, 114-16; Bk. XI, chap. vi, *ibid.,* IV, 23; and Bk. XI, chap. vii, *ibid.,* IV, 24.

[13] Lefèvre de Beauvray, *Dictionnaire social et patriotique,* pp. 179, 352; S.-N. Linguet, *Du plus heureux gouvernement, ou Parallèle des constitutions politiques de l'Asie avec celles de l'Europe,* in *Oeuvres de M. Linguet* (6 vols.; London, 1774), I, xi-xii. The work by Linguet was apparently first published in this edition.

[14] For the idea of the king as the tyrant, see Linguet, *Annales politiques, civiles, et littéraires du dix-huitième siècle,* I (1777), 296-300. This periodical will be referred to hereinafter as *Annales de Linguet.*

[15] Linguet, *Du plus heureux gouvernement,* in *Oeuvres,* I, iv, xi-xii, *et passim; ibid.,* II, 147-48; *Annales de Linguet,* I (1777), 33-35, 38, 79-80, 298-300.

[16] Linguet, *Du plus heureux gouvernement,* in *Oeuvres,* I, iv-vi, and II, 118; *Annales de Linguet,* I (1777), 62-63, 250.

Linguet's defense of absolute monarchy was not typical, either, for it was based upon Hobbesian concepts, in which sovereignty is simply superior force, and not upon the divine-right notion of God-given authority.[17]

Some conservative critics were quick to dispute the commonly received notion that England was a country where freedom of conscience prevailed. From the Reformation to their own time, they said, the history of England had been marred by fanatical intolerance in religion. One writer asserted that no Catholic Inquisition had ever been as bad as the one the Puritans had established.[18] Most of this sort of criticism related to the body of anti-Catholic statutes that existed in both Britain and Ireland. In one satirical piece the goddess Reason was depicted as amazed to find, in the course of a European tour, that the English, who were always complaining of the intolerance of Catholics, had permitted themselves to incur the same charge by their treatment of the Irish.[19] Linguet observed that the anti-Catholic laws were so unjust that many of them were no longer enforced by the courts,[20] but he did not conclude from this that the prevailing public opinion must have repudiated them, too.

Sometimes conservatives took the position that the English suffered, not from a lack of liberty, but from an excess of it. In England, they said, there existed a state of affairs which the English fondly called liberty, but which was really anarchy. It was a state of chronic party struggles that were always on the verge of violence,[21] stimulated by an incendiary and libelous press. Said

---

[17] Linguet, *Théorie des loix civiles*, in *Oeuvres*, III, *passim; Du plus heureux gouvernement, ibid.*, I, xx. It was said, despite the unorthodox character of Linguet's political theory, that Louis XVI was himself a constant reader of Linguet's *Annales* and that he regretted being compelled to agree with the ministry that Linguet must be imprisoned in the Bastille. See M. de Lescure (ed.), *Correspondance secrète, inédite, sur Louis XVI, Marie-Antionette, la cour et la ville, de 1777 à 1792* (2 vols.; Paris, 1866), I, 48 (April 10, 1777), 320 (Oct. 14, 1780); [Métra, J. Imbert, *et al.*], *Correspondance secrète, politique et littéraire, ou Mémoires pour servir à l'histoire des cours, des sociétés et de la littérature en France, depuis la mort de Louis XV* (18 vols.; London, 1787-89), IX, 6 (Nov. 9, 1779), and X, 247 (Oct. 14, 1780).

[18] Lefèvre de Beauvray, *Dictionnaire social et patriotique*, p. 257.

[19] L.-A. de Caraccioli, *Voyage de la raison en Europe*, in [Garnier (ed.)], *Voyages imaginaires* (39 vols.; Amsterdam and Paris, 1787-95), XXVII, 207.

[20] *Annales de Linguet*, I (1777), 272-73.

[21] Basset de la Marelle, *La Différence du patriotisme national*, pp. 34-60; Millot, *Élémens de l'histoire d'Angleterre*, I, xiii-xx, xxxv; Lefèvre de Beauvray, *Dic-*

the Solicitor-General Séguier, when indicting certain books before the Parlement of Paris: "Is not freedom of thought the fatal abuse which has produced among our island neighbors the multitude of sects, opinions, and parties, and the independent spirit which will end by destroying the very constitution of which they are so proud?"[22] The devout, moreover, could not forget that the English were heretics, a consequence, they believed, of this same libertarian spirit. Just as the English had turned upon their kings, so they had turned upon their religion,[23] and now, said one writer, they could not make up their minds whether to be Quakers, Puritans, or Protestants![24] The English in fact were even worse than heretics, for they had tolerated writers who had directly advanced the cause of infidelity and atheism.[25]

According to the conservative thesis, the constitution of the French monarchy had preserved Frenchmen alike from the shame of slavery and the stumbling block of liberty.[26] This constitution, together with the French national character, which was stable and constant and not, as the English were fond of charging, flighty and changeable,[27] had given the country a history remarkably free from internal dissensions and permitted French citizens of the eighteenth century to enjoy an enviable existence. One had only

---

tionnaire social et patriotique, p. 179; [Contant d'Orville], *Les Nuits angloises, ou Recueil de traits singuliers, d'anecdotes, d'événements remarquables, de faits extraordinaires, de bisarreries, d'observations critiques et de pensées philosophiques, etc., propre à faire connoître le génie et le caractere des Anglois* (4 vols.; Paris, 1771 [a previous edition in 1770]), I, 165-66; Caraccioli, *Voyage de la raison*, in Garnier (ed.), *Voyages imaginaires*, XXVII, 200-201; Anon., *Réflexions d'un citoyen sur l'édit de décembre 1770*, pp. 20-21; Anon., *Extrait d'une lettre, en date de Londres, du 3 mai 1771* [1771], p. 5; *Journal de Genève*, 1772, No. 2, pp. 5-6; Gin, *Les Vrais principes du gouvernement françois*, pp. 72-75.

[22] Quoted in [Louis Bachaumont et al.], *Mémoires secrets pour servir à l'histoire de la république des lettres en France, depuis MDCCLXII jusqu'à nos jours* . . . (36 vols.; London, 1784-89), V, 159 (Aug. 29, 1770). Cf. Basset de la Marelle, *La Différence du patriotisme national*, p. 60, and Lefèvre de Beauvray, *Dictionnaire social et patriotique*, pp. 279-80.

[23] Basset de la Marelle, *La Différence du patriotisme national*, p. 58; Anon., *Lettre d'un jeune homme . . . sur les Français et les Anglais*, p. 41.

[24] Anon., *Lettre d'un jeune homme . . . sur les Français et les Anglais*, p. 41.

[25] [L.-M. Chaudon], *Anti-dictionnaire philosophique, pour servir de commentaire et de correctif au Dictionnaire philosophique, et aux autres livres qui ont paru de nos jours contre le christianisme* . . . (4th ed.; 2 vols.; Paris, 1775), II, 7.

[26] Basset de la Marelle, *La Différence du patriotisme national*, p. 31.

[27] *Ibid., passim*; Anon., *Lettre d'un jeune homme . . . sur les Français et les Anglais, passim*.

to look about one for the proof of this. "Of all the countries of Europe," asserted the *Journal de Genève*, "the kingdom of France combines the greatest number of natural and political advantages. . . . The internal administration of the kingdom, the security of its highways, the beauty of its great roads, have long been the admiration of foreigners."[28] Frenchmen were happier under their government than Englishmen under theirs, for, as everyone knew, the French were gay and cheerful whereas the English were a melancholy people. In a popular play of the period a French marquise was made to say to an English milord, who had boasted that in England even the humblest citizens participated in politics and had some influence upon Parliament:

> Trop au dessus de nous sont ces graves emplois.
>   Libres de tout soin inutile,
> Nos heureux citoyens respirent le repos:
> La surface des mers voit agiter ses flots;
> Mais la profonde arène est constante et tranquille.[29]

(These serious matters are too far above us. Free from every useless anxiety, our happy citizens breathe tranquillity. On the surface of the seas the waves are troubled, but the sandy depths are unchanging and peaceful.)

Politics were not every one's proper concern anyway, according to this thesis. Politics were only for those at the top of that hierarchy of classes that was the natural constitution of society. Otherwise the hierarchy would break down as it had broken down in England: you would have the king reduced to an equality with politicians and the upper classes shorn of that respect which they should possess in the eyes of their inferiors. Conservatives repeated with distaste an anecdote relating how an English candidate for election, a very elegant gentleman, ordered wine for one of his constituents, a cobbler who was "very disgusting in dress and appearance," and then proceeded with the greatest familiarity to sit down with him in his shop to drink it.[30] This clearly and concretely demonstrated how liberty had opened the floodgates to equality.

---

[28] *Journal de Genève*, 1772, No. 2, pp. 10-12.
[29] C.-S. Favart, *L'Anglois à Bordeaux*, in *Répertoire général du théatre français* (67 vols.; Paris, 1818), XLV, 322.
[30] *Journal des beaux-arts et des sciences*, 1769, IV, 335-36, citing Damiens de Gomicourt, *L'Observateur françois à Londres*.

The burden of the conservatives' charge against the Anglophiles, then, was that they were subversive innovators who wanted to destroy a good society and to substitute instability for order. Conservative writers fulminated roundly against the Anglomania of the *philosophes*, but were inclined to ridicule that of the courtiers, depicting these people as shallow, silly fellows. Declared the author of a leading article in the *Mercure de France*, the principal journal of belles-lettres:

One day I was present at one of those frivolous gatherings to which the impulse to be different from one's fellows brings young scatter-brains who pay in ridiculous affectations the tribute they think they owe to novelty. You imagine no doubt that they were talking of fashions, of pom-poms, of the gossip of the day? Not at all. They were discussing the most abstract questions. Bored by their metaphysical jargon, I turned to the most sensible of these gentlemen. "Tell me," said I, "is this now the tone of polite society? . . ." "Where have you been?" put in one of my neighbors. "Don't you see that these three gentlemen are just back from London? That they must, for some months anyway, parade gravity, put on the air and aspect of thinkers, and regard ourselves as mere blockheads?"[31]

It was possible, of course, for conservatives to admire the English as distinguished from the Anglophiles and to agree that specific English institutions or conditions were in advance of those of an analogous sort in France. The general tone of conservative opinion at this time was not reactionary. For example, the Catholic, absolutist, and nationalist *nouvelles à la main* which go under the name of Métra advocated that the French copy English criminal jurisprudence.[32] Another writer, who had criticized the English for their intolerance of Catholics, also affirmed that it was good to see in England that men paid taxes according to their ability to pay, implying that France compared unfavorably with England in this respect.[33] Still a third commentator, author of one of those numerous miscellanies about English life and customs current in France at the time, glowingly described the high standard

---

[31] *Mercure de France*, Aug. 1766, pp. 7-8.
[32] Métra, *Correspondance secrète*, III, 170-71 (July 8, 1776), and VI, 10 (Feb. 11, 1778).
[33] Caraccioli, *Voyage de la raison en Europe*, in Garnier (ed.), *Voyages imaginaires*, XXVII, 201, 207.

of living which prevailed, as he believed, among the English agricultural classes, and which was to be contrasted with the poverty of the French peasantry.[34] But, declared he: "I am not tainted with that modish vice which our fashionables call Anglomania. I esteem, I respect that learned nation. . . . But I do not think it useful to imitate the English in everything."[35]

His reservation was characteristic. Conservatives who consented to compliment the English did so, it is clear, only in relatively indifferent matters, where the fundamental political and social institutions of the old regime were not involved. Where, on the other hand, these institutions were in question, conservatives always pointed out that England was essentially a republic, whose institutions would naturally be unlike those of France, a monarchy. If they did not decry completely the republican customs of their neighbors, they at least maintained that the same standards of judgment could not be applied to the two countries. Thus the *Dictionnaire social et patriotique*, which was devoted to the campaign against Anglomania, displayed on its title page the following motto:

> Si Romae fueris, Romano vivito more.
> Soïés Anglois à Londre, et François à Paris.[36]

The Abbé Millot, who wrote a history of England well thought of in France in its day,[37] asserted in his preface to this work that what in England might be reckoned a deed of usurpation and violence might be in France, in all justice, a legitimate act of authority.[38] Everything depended on the laws of the country. In reviewing the *Moral and Political Essays* of David Hume the *Année littéraire,* the vehicle of Voltaire's chief antiphilosophic opponent, Fréron, cautioned readers against taking at face value Hume's discussion of the question of a free press. "Everything that he says on this subject," asserted the *Année littéraire,* "is applicable only to the government of England, and even then it is subject to many objections."[39]

---

[34] Contant d'Orville, *Les Nuits angloises*, IV, 89-90. [35] *Ibid.*, I, 2.
[36] Lefèvre de Beauvray, *Dictionnaire social et patriotique*.
[37] The *Mercure de France* for April, 1783, p. 165, said, in reviewing the fourth edition, that the success of the work had been unequivocal.
[38] Millot, *Élémens de l'histoire d'Angleterre*, I, xxvi.
[39] *L'Année littéraire,* 1767, V, 319.

Progovernment pamphleteers in the controversy of 1770-71 between the ministry and the parlements reflected the same idea. The French parlements' ambition to emulate the Parliament of England was, they said, founded upon a false analogy. Despite the orthographical similarity, which seemed to denote that the corresponding institutions should have like functions, there was no real parallel between them. For while England was a republic, in which legislative power naturally resided in a representative body, France was a monarchy. In a monarchy the legislative power resided in the king alone, and the parlements were no more than judicial bodies.[40] Besides, added one writer, "The Parliament of England is composed of the greatest noblemen of that kingdom and of the people's representatives. What a contrast with what we today call 'parlements'!" For even if the English Parliament was corrupt, it was more worthy still to be the guardian of the people's welfare than the privileged judicial aristocracy of France with its narrow, corporate outlook upon national policies.[41]

This relativism of the conservatives was a convenient weapon for parrying the arguments of Anglophile liberals without going to the length of attacking them frontally. Moreover, it enabled them to associate themselves with projects for which from the viewpoint of constitutional theory they had no sympathy but which for other reasons they desired to support, like the American Revolution. But it was an expedient. Their deepest feelings were best represented in their outright repudiation of the republican example of the English.

[40] Anon., *Le Songe d'un jeune Parisien* [ca. 1770], p. 11; Anon., *Extrait d'une lettre, en date de Londres, du 3 mai 1771*, p. 6; Anon., *Lettre de M. C** à M. de St**** à Rouen. Servant de réponse à la lettre du parlement de Normandie au roi, en date du 8 février, sur l'état actuel du parlement de Paris* [1771], pp. 8-9; Anon., *Réflexions d'un citoyen sur l'édit de décembre 1770*, pp. 3-4.

[41] Anon., *Le Songe d'un jeune Parisien*, pp. 11, 23.

CHAPTER THREE

FRENCH CRITICISM OF ENGLISH INSTITUTIONS, 1763-1778: THE LIBERALS

WHEREAS CONSERVATIVES found English institutions much too republican, some of the liberals thought them not republican enough. These liberal critics, who have already been identified as the forerunners of the school of Rousseau, or the popular school, concerned themselves above all (at least in theory) with the problem of political liberty, the limitation of the crown's legislative power by a body representative of the citizens. Rousseau always assumed, in the *Contrat social* and works written subsequently, that the question of civil liberty was secondary to that of political liberty. Holbach and Marat had a similar opinion. As early as 1758, the Abbé de Mably had favored the restoration of the Estates-General in France.[1] Diderot affirmed that liberty—and he seems to have meant any kind of liberty pertaining to political organization—depended upon the separation of the executive and legislative powers,[2] and endeavored to persuade the Czarina Catherine II to set up a representative assembly in Russia.[3] This viewpoint seems to have been a general bias of these writers which, though strengthened by their analysis of English politics, also to some extent conditioned it. Their bias distin-

[1] *Des droits et des devoirs du citoyen* [first published in 1789 but generally agreed to have been written about 1758], in *Collection complète des oeuvres de l'abbé de Mably* (15 vols.; Paris, 1794-95), XI, 304-5.
[2] "Liberté civile," *Encyclopédie, ou Dictionnaire raisonné des sciences, des arts et des métiers*, in J. Assézat (ed.), *Oeuvres complètes de Diderot* . . . (20 vols.; Paris, 1875-77), XV, 510.
[3] Diderot, *Observations sur l'instruction de S. M. I. aux députés pour la confection des lois (1774)*, ed. Paul Ledieu (Paris, 1921), p. 21.

guished them from the Anglophile liberals, that is, the Anglophile *philosophes*, who were less interested in political than in civil liberty, and admired the English above all for their pre-eminence in that respect. But the distinction went further. Neither the Anglophile *philosophes* nor the *frondeurs*, who *were* interested in the limitation of the legislative power of the crown, thought of finding fault with the character of the representatives or the functioning of the representative system in England. The incipient school of Rousseau, on the other hand, regarded Parliament with a severely critical eye. What occasioned their objections was the spectacle of parliamentary politics—specifically, the phenomenon that English writers of the time called "influence," or crown control of a working majority in Parliament through the use of pensions, titles, bribes, and the extensive apparatus of the patronage, together with the correlative phenomenon, the rise of the Whig and Radical opposition to the government of George III and the King's Friends.

The attention given by Frenchmen to these party battles was centered principally on the career of John Wilkes, the leading Radical politician of the 1760's. According to one well-informed contemporary, Wilkes interested Frenchmen more than any other English politician since Bolingbroke.[4] His fame had originated in 1763 in the notorious affair of the *North Briton*, No. 45.[5] Because this was Wilkes's paper, and No. 45 had contained statements about the king that according to the ministry constituted "seditious libel," Wilkes had been arrested and his papers seized upon the authority of general warrants made out by order of the secretaries of state. Released from custody on the ground of his privilege as a member of Parliament, Wilkes had nevertheless instituted and won a suit for damages against one of the secretaries for what the court declared to be an illegal use of general warrants. Frenchmen did not fail to point out the contrast that this case highlighted between their own liability to arbitrary search and imprisonment and the personal liberties enjoyed by English subjects. The case

---

[4] Dominique-Joseph Garat, *Mémoires historiques sur la vie de M. Suard, sur ses écrits, et sur le XVIIIe siècle* (2 vols.; Paris, 1820), II, 90.

[5] For the facts of Wilkes's career as reviewed here, see the *Dictionary of National Biography*, Vol. XXI, and Horace Bleackley, *Life of John Wilkes* (London, 1917), pp. 73-318.

indeed became the stock example among Frenchmen of the immunity of Englishmen from the arbitrary action of government.

The affair of the *North Briton*, No. 45, entailed, however, a sequel that to many Frenchmen had quite another meaning. The House of Commons having resolved that the privilege of a member did not apply in a question of seditious libel, the government began a suit against Wilkes on that charge. Next, the House expelled him, depriving him of the remainder of his parliamentary immunity along with his seat. Facing imprisonment for debt as well as prosecution on the sedition charge, he fled to the Continent. This was in 1764. During the next four years the exile spent a good deal of time in Paris in the society of his friends among the *philosophes*, especially those comprising the circle of the Baron d'Holbach, whom he had known since their student days together at the University of Leyden. In 1768 he decided to return to England in order to re-enter politics. As he had been convicted of seditious libel while abroad and outlawed for having failed to appear to receive judgment, he had to serve a term in prison, where he was during the famous Middlesex election or elections of 1769. In the course of this affair the House of Commons pronounced him incapable of election, while on the other hand it affirmed the government's candidate, who lost to Wilkes in three successive returns, to be the lawfully chosen representative of the county. Not until 1774 was Wilkes again permitted to take his seat in Parliament. Meantime he became active in London politics. As an alderman of the city, he was one of the principals in the jurisdictional controversy between the city of London and the House of Commons over the reporting of parliamentary debates in the London dailies, a controversy that ended in a victory for the city and the press. He won the mayoralty of London in the year when he re-entered Parliament.

Wilkes's running battle with the ministry and the King's Friends in the House of Commons was felt in France to have some counterpart in the contemporaneous struggle going on between the crown and the parlements. The reader will recall that the crisis that resulted in the Maupeou reform occurred in 1770-71. A journalist of proparlementary sympathies noted in August, 1768, that a shipment of very fine linen handkerchiefs *à la Wilkes*, printed, that is, with a letter from that politician to his constituents of Middlesex County, had just arrived in Paris from England. "The testimony, however frivolous," observed this journalist, referring to the handkerchiefs, "does honor to this patriotic hero and is calculated to sustain in every soul the noble enthusiasm which characterizes him."[6] French conservatives denounced the parlementary party, whose stronghold was the city of Paris and who relied on the support of the Parisian population, for "imitating" Wilkes and his party,[7] who also were supported by the population of a great capital city.

Neither the parlementary party nor those *philosophes* whose viewpoint was basically Anglophile deduced from the machinations of the ministry and the King's Friends that English liberty was dead or dying. But the publicists who are the subject of the present discussion thought otherwise. How could liberty exist when Parliament had become the servile instrument of the king's will? These writers occupied themselves with the problem of parliamentary reform. They concluded that certain structural reforms were necessary before the government of England could be a proper model for French liberals to copy. Their analysis of the problem and their constructive proposals incorporated some of the ideas of both the Whigs and the Radicals, but their views were much affected also by the archaic quality of their own concepts of the structure of English government and the issues of English politics.

From the Whigs they borrowed certain proposals for the further limitation of the crown's prerogatives: the elimination or reduction of "placemen" (officeholders appointed by the crown) in the House of Commons, the curtailment of the crown's patronage, and a more systematic supervision of the crown's expenditure of

---

[6] [Louis Bachaumont *et al.*], *Mémoires secrets pour servir à l'histoire de la république des lettres en France, depuis MDCCLXII jusqu'à nos jours; ou Journal d'un observateur* . . . (36 vols.; London, 1784-89), IV, 71 (Aug. 2, 1768).

[7] Anon., *Extrait d'une lettre, en date de Londres, du 3 mai 1771* [1771], p. 5; Anon., *La Tête leur tourne* [*ca.* 1770-71], p. 17. The Catalogue of the White Library, Cornell University, dates the second pamphlet 1788, whereas in the Harvard College Library it appears bound in a pamphlet collection dealing with the judicial crisis of 1770-71. From internal evidence, including the reference to Wilkes, it is clear that the pamphlet belongs to the earlier period.

moneys.⁸ These proposals they took at face value. While they were not so naïve as to suppose that there were no place-seekers in the Whig party,⁹ they did not perceive that the main object of the Whigs was the restoration of government by the great aristocratic "connections" of the two previous reigns. They supposed that the Whigs' purpose in reducing "influence" was simply to reduce it and restore thereby the proper balance in the government.

From the Radicals they adopted proposals designed to broaden the electorate and to strengthen its control of the House of Commons: some reform of the franchise in a democratic direction,[10] annual instead of septennial parliamentary elections,[11] and the submission of members of Parliament to instructions from their constituents.[12] Not included here were the extreme theoretical concepts of English Radicalism, such as the abstract right of every man to the franchise, an idea which in fact postdated, at least in published form, most of the writings on which the present chapter is based.[13] The proposed reforms enumerated above constituted the program of the Radical politicians of the 1760's and 1770's. To the Radicals, the main object of thus tightening up the control

---

[8] Mably, *De l'étude de l'histoire, à monseigneur le prince de Parme*, in *Oeuvres*, XII, 234-35 [first published, probably, about 1773, for although the known editions do not antedate 1775, it was reviewed in Jan., 1774, in the *Correspondance littéraire . . . par Grimm, Diderot, Raynal, Meister, etc.*, ed. Maurice Tourneux (16 vols.; Paris, 1877-82), X, 333]; [Jean-Paul Marat], *The Chains of Slavery, a Work Wherein the Clandestine and Villainous Attempts of Princes to Ruin Liberty Are Pointed Out, and the Dreadful Scenes of Despotism Disclosed: to Which Is Prefixed an Address to the Electors of Great Britain, in Order to Draw Their Timely Attention to the Choice of Proper Representatives in the Next Parliament* (London, 1774), pp. 214-15; [Baron d'Holbach], *Éthocratie ou Le Gouvernement fondé sur la morale* (Amsterdam, 1776), p. 18.

[9] Skepticism regarding the disinterestedness of the opposition is reflected in [Holbach], *Système social ou Principes naturels de la morale et de la politique. Avec un examen de l'influence du gouvernement sur les moeurs* (3 vols.; London, 1773), II, 103, and Mably, *De la législation, ou Principes des lois* [first published in 1776], in *Oeuvres*, IX, 282.

[10] Marat, *The Chains of Slavery*, pp. 199-200.

[11] Mably, *De l'étude de l'histoire*, in *Oeuvres*, XII, 235-36; Holbach, *Système social*, II, 106 n.; Rousseau, *Considérations sur le gouvernement de Pologne et sur sa réformation projetée en avril 1772* [written in 1772, first published in 1782], in C. E. Vaughan (ed.), *The Political Writings of Jean Jacques Rousseau* (2 vols.; Cambridge, 1915), II, 446.

[12] Diderot, "Représentants," *Encyclopédie*, in *Oeuvres*, XVII, 21; Rousseau, *Gouvernement de Pologne*, in *Political Writings*, II, 450; Holbach, *Système social*, II, 101, and *Éthocratie*, p. 18; Marat, *The Chains of Slavery*, pp. 202-3.

[13] C. B. Roylance Kent, *The English Radicals. An Historical Sketch* (London, 1899), pp. 67-74.

of the electorate over Parliament was to destroy parliamentary absolutism. To the French mind, however, it was still, as in the case of the Whig program, to destroy "influence." Certainly, French critics complained that Parliament could, as matters then were, enact "unconstitutional" measures with impunity.[14] But that would be rectified when "influence" was eliminated.

The French critics were not quite satisfied with the ideas of the Whig and Radical opposition. They proceeded to advance certain propositions of their own manufacture which reveal that they did not realize at all the full extent of the crown's defeat in the seventeenth century. They said, for example, that the convocation of Parliament ought not to be dependent on the royal summons.[15] They thought that the king's command of the armed forces was, despite the fact that Parliament customarily granted military supply for one year only, a potentially dangerous weapon in the hands of an ambitious monarch.[16] They assailed the crown's right to confirm the nomination of the speaker of the House of Commons.[17] They held that the king ought not to have the sole or unlimited power of creating peers, but that he should share it with Parliament or give it up to Parliament entirely.[18] They never envisaged this prerogative of the crown as a weapon with which conservative resistance in the upper house might be overcome. Mably, one of the most "republican" of these writers, opposed the king's personal exemption from prosecution under the law.[19] He also attacked the royal veto,[20] which all Frenchmen thought to be an important feature of the royal prerogative in England although in fact it had not been used since the days of Anne.

In short, all the publicists heretofore named, with the excep-

[14] Marat, *The Chains of Slavery*, pp. 180-82 n.
[15] Mably, *De l'étude de l'histoire*, in *Oeuvres*, XII, 233; Marat, *The Chains of Slavery*, pp. 212-13; Holbach, *Éthocratie*, p. 17.
[16] Marat, *The Chains of Slavery*, p. 222; Mably, *De l'étude de l'histoire*, in *Oeuvres*, XII, 232.
[17] Marat, *The Chains of Slavery*, p. 217.
[18] Diderot to Sophie Volland [Nov. 12], 1765, in André Babelon (ed.), *Lettres à Sophie Volland* . . . (3 vols.; Paris [1930]), II, 308-9; Mably, *De l'etude de l'histoire*, in *Oeuvres*, XII, 236-37; Marat to the president of the Estates-General, Aug. 23, 1789, in Charles Vellay (ed.), *La Correspondance de Marat* (Paris, 1908), p. 102.
[19] *De l'étude de l'histoire*, in *Oeuvres*, XII, 231-32.
[20] *Ibid.*, p. 232; *Des droits et des devoirs du citoyen*, in *Oeuvres*, XI, 474.

tion of Rousseau, tended to think that the royal authority should be almost, and perhaps entirely, eliminated from the legislative process. Mably went the farthest in this direction. Rousseau's own views about the division of powers in government were closer to the Anglophile tradition of checks and balances;[21] his special contribution to the development of this anti-Anglophile critique was something else that will be discussed in a later connection.

Why had the Revolution of 1688-89 stopped short of destroying the legislative power of the crown? Because, said Mably, William III would never have assented to such an outcome, and William's aid had been essential to the success of the Revolution. But while he was thus disposed to condone the inconclusive character of the revolutionary settlement, Mably thought that the occasion of the Hanoverian succession had presented a clear opportunity that the Whig party had shamefully neglected. He implied that the Whig politicans had, in failing at that time further to restrict the crown's prerogative, virtually betrayed their country so that they might pay court to the House of Hanover.[22] Another writer belonging to this group of critics blamed public opinion as well as the Whig party. The Revolution itself, he said, had been a compromise between Whig ideas of government by contract and Tory notions of a power naturally inherent in the monarch. The English people themselves possessed a long-standing prejudice in favor of monarchy. Hence, although the Whigs had managed to keep control of the government following the Revolution, they had not dared to affirm that power should reside solely in the body of the nation.[23] This notion of the monarchical predisposition of the English people was at variance with the prevailing view in France at the time the work containing it was written.

Underneath the whole problem of "influence" and considerations of structural reform, however, lay something deeper. This was the problem of party, or faction. Here the precursors of the

[21] *Contrat social*, in *Political Writings*, II, 81-82; *Gouvernement de Pologne*, ibid., pp. 446-47, 466.
[22] *De l'étude de l'histoire*, in *Oeuvres*, XII, 237.
[23] [Saige], *Catéchisme du citoyen, ou Élémens du droit public françois, par demandes et réponses; suivi de Fragmens politiques par le même auteur* ("En France," 1788 [first published in 1775—see above, chap. i, n. 13]), pp. 79-81.

popular school again departed from the Anglophile viewpoint. To Anglophiles, the clamor of party strife echoing loudly from across the Channel was, while not always to their taste, an indication that liberty was flourishing in England. Indeed, the idea of a conflict of parties seemed to them inherent in the very nature of a constitution of checks and balances as well as a natural result of laws that guaranteed free speech and a free press. For their notions of liberty were individualistic, utilitarian. As Helvétius put it: "The opposition, excited by ambition, vengeance, or the love of country, protects the people against tyranny; the court party, animated by the desire of places, favor, or money, sustains the ministry against the sometimes unjust attacks of the opposition."[24]

But for the precursors of the popular school such dissonance in English politics indicated that liberty had at best a precarious foothold there. "If the equilibrium of the several powers is fairly established," asked Mably, "why these continually recurring alarums of the nation? Why these continual complaints against the ministry, which is always being accused of betraying its duty?"[25] Holbach was even more explicit. "If factions agitate societies where liberty reigns," he said, "it is because liberty is not yet established on sufficiently solid foundations."[26] Diderot thought that English party struggles were as unedifying as those between the monarchy and the parlements in France.[27] Marat's opinion was exceptional. Marat thought English liberty in danger, and he thought that want of decency in the party press had prejudiced the public cause,[28] but he did not believe that the "great noise" malcontents could make in England signified anything but that the English were still free.[29] Mably himself was not entirely consistent. When he wished to show that England was more

[24] *De l'homme, de ses facultés intellectuelles et de son éducation*, in *Oeuvres complettes de M. Helvétius* (new ed.; 5 vols.; London, 1781), IV, 133 n. 26. *De l'homme* was first published in 1772.
[25] *De l'étude de l'histoire*, in *Oeuvres*, XII, 231.
[26] *La Politique naturelle ou Discours sur les vrais principes du gouvernement* . . . (2 vols.; London, 1773), II, 91.
[27] Diderot to Sophie Volland [Nov. 12], 1765, in *Lettres à Sophie Volland*, II, 311.
[28] Marat, *The Chains of Slavery*, p. 71.
[29] Marat, *Polish Letters*, trans. from the original unpublished MS (2 vols. [1905]), I, 187.

free than France because she had a constitution and France (so he said) had not, he took an almost Anglophile attitude toward party.[30] But his prevailing sentiments were hostile to it.

Indeed, for publicists like Mably, Holbach, Diderot, and Rousseau, political opposition could legitimately have only an *ad interim* function. It was necessary in the struggle to attain liberty, but once liberty had been secured, opposition should wither away. The republic of virtue had no room for conflicting interests. Freedom really depended on the harmony of wills. This idea, more or less implicit in Mably, Diderot, and Holbach, was explicitly and positively set forth by Rousseau in the *Contrat social* as the concept of the general will—the will of the people or nation absorbing and dominating the wills of individuals and classes. Rousseau, in fact, went still further, conferring upon this general will the attribute of political sovereignty.

The completed doctrine of the popular school, the doctrine that in the 1780's was to replace the Anglophile tradition as the dominant liberal creed, was a melange chiefly of the ideas of Rousseau and Mably. Like both of them, its adherents held the general will to be indivisible. Like Rousseau, they held it to be the sovereign. Like Mably, they assumed that its only spokesman in the government was the legislature and declared that the king should be in effect no more than the mandatory of the legislature. Above the king, in short, should be the legislature, and above the legislature the sovereign nation.

In this new Anglophobe liberalism there were echoes of the traditional Anglophile interpretation of English history. According to that interpretation the crown had been, at least prior to 1688, the antagonist of the nation. Parliament had been the nation's representative: within it the House of Commons had dwarfed the House of Lords and the Commons had been a really national assembly, some Anglophiles supposing the franchise to be much more democratic than it actually was.[31] While nothing was said

---

[30] Mably, *Observations sur l'histoire de France*, in *Oeuvres*, II, 282. The part of the *Observations* to which this citation has reference was written about 1770, though not published until 1788. See M.-W. Guerrier, *L'Abbé de Mably moraliste et politique* . . . (Paris, 1886), p. 137, and Ernest A. Whitfield, *Gabriel Bonnot de Mably* (London, 1930), pp. 16-17.

[31] Jacques Necker, *Sur la législation et le commerce des grains* [first published in 1775], in Baron de Staël (ed.), *Oeuvres complètes de M. Necker* (15 vols.;

about the sovereignty of the nation, the people had been supposed to have a constitutional right of revolution. The popular school, however, unlike the Anglophile liberals, did not think that the king had been deprived in 1688 of all real power to work harm. They also scrutinized more realistically than the Anglophiles the relationship between Parliament and the electorate and wanted the nation to possess an immediate and compelling authority in the ordinary activities of government. It did not seem to them that the right of revolution was a very effective guarantee that the general will would be carried out from day to day or even month to month. As an early pamphleteer of this school declared:

> [In England] the popular will never speaks except through representatives, that is, a small number of individuals *will* for the entire nation, which consents periodically to renounce the supervision of its own welfare in order to confide it to them without any reservation; and . . . this absurd arrangement leaves the mass of citizens with no other recourse than that of physical force, a disastrous expedient, contrary to the object of political society.[32]

Moreover, the popular school differed from the Anglophile liberals in their conception of the nature of the will of the nation. The nation in Anglophile ideology consisted of individuals, each possessed of "natural" rights; or else it consisted of groups of interests of which there might be a great many, possessed of rights analogous to the rights of individuals, and having interests that might well conflict. These separate interests would naturally be reflected in the structure of politics and government, and policy would be a resultant of their several desires, a compromise. According to the popular school, the nation was not an aggregation of individuals or interests but a collectivity. Only one opinion, one policy, was right, and the structure of government and politics should reflect this unity. Prior to the Revolution of 1789 it was assumed that the general will (in France, at least) coincided with the opinion of the majority, although essentially the general will—the will of citizens when willing the general good—was independ-

---

Paris, 1820-21), I, 133; [P.-J. Grosley], *Londres* (3 vols.; Lausanne, 1770), III, 423; [Abbé G.-F. Coyer], *Nouvelles observations sur l'Angleterre par un voyageur* (Paris, 1779), p. 113.
[32] Saige, *Catéchisme du citoyen*, p. 81.

ent of majorities. But whether the spokesmen of the general will were actually a majority or a minority, their opponents would be entitled to no consideration. This was the drift of the doctrine, even though the concept of the natural rights of individuals did not entirely disappear from the ideology of the school of Rousseau. It was a fighting doctrine, less tolerant and more militantly "republican" than the old Anglophile liberalism, and the measure of its ever-increasing hold upon public opinion was the measure of the deepening of the tensions in the society of the old regime.

The precursors of the popular school concerned themselves not only with the problem of making the government reflect the national interest, or the general will, making it "free" in other words, but also with the problem of making the citizens understand the nature of the national interest. In the opinion of these critics the English did not understand it. Preoccupied with private and material interests, suffering from a mania for imperial conquests and profits,[33] they were losing that civic virtue, that heroic character, which had formerly enabled them to defend their liberties against the tyranny of their kings.[34] The state would have to assume the duty of educating its citizens in the meaning of political virtue, but in England the state was doing just the opposite, catering to the cupidity of the subjects. Mably was fond of moralizing on this question. In one of his writings an Englishman who had been brought to understand the error of contemporary English policy was made to say:

> I begin to perceive that a state can be happy only by training its citizens in the habits which are conducive to happiness, and that there is no use in its enacting laws which direct them to be just, disinterested, and beneficent, while at the same time it carries on a policy that excites avarice and necessitates immorality.[35]

---

[33] Mably, *De l'étude de l'histoire*, in *Oeuvres*, XII, 238-240, and *De la législation, ibid.*, IX, 16; Holbach, *Système social*, II, 105-9; Diderot, *Réfutation suivie de l'ouvrage d'Helvétius intitulé l'Homme*, in *Oeuvres*, II, 422. This last-named work was written about 1773-74 but not published until its inclusion in the Assézat edition of the works of Diderot.

[34] Diderot to Sophie Volland [Nov. 12], 1765, in *Lettres à Sophie Volland*, II, 308-9; Diderot to Wilkes, April 2, 1768, in *Oeuvres*, XIX, 499; Mably, *De l'étude de l'histoire*, in *Oeuvres*, XII, 238, and *De la législation, ibid.*, IX, 18; Holbach, *Système social*, II, 105-9.

[35] *De la législation*, in *Oeuvres*, IX, 41.

Similarly, Holbach asserted that only a "moral and national" education could assure to the state subjects who would be worthy of liberty. There could be no true liberty in a nation—meaning the English—that was unjust, avaricious, venal, and corrupt.[36] One of the basic troubles with the English, it seemed to Holbach, was that in English society there were great inequalities of wealth that were becoming greater all the time. This situation had the effect, among other undesirable consequences, of predisposing the poor to welcome bribery as a feature of elections.[37]

Holbach's observation regarding the distribution of wealth in England was directly opposed to the belief that prevailed in France, especially among Anglophiles, that as a whole the people of England enjoyed a relatively high standard of living.[38] While Holbach's opinion was doubtless nearer to the truth than the contrary one, it is doubtful that it was more objectively arrived at, for Holbach had reacted violently against everything he had seen or experienced during his travels in England.[39] Perhaps the most objective reporter of conditions among the common people of England was Marat, who lived and practiced as a physician in that country for a number of years before the War of American Independence. Marat thought that the English lower classes were freer and happier than their kind in France because, he said, the laws protected them from the oppression of the great. On the other hand, their manner of life was hard, like that of the same

---

[36] *Éthocratie*, p. 22.

[37] Holbach, as cited in Diderot to Sophie Volland, Sept. 20, 1765, in *Lettres à Sophie Volland*, II, 290-91, and in Diderot to Sophie Volland, Oct. 6, 1765, *ibid.*, p. 295; *Système social*, II, 101-2.

[38] Helvétius to his wife [1764], in Antoine Guillois (ed.), "Correspondance d'Helvétius avec sa femme," *Le Carnet historique et littéraire, revue mensuelle rétrospective et contemporaine*, VI (July-Dec., 1900), 485; Helvétius, *De l'homme*, in *Oeuvres* (1781), IV, 77; Voltaire, "Blé ou bled" [first published in 1770], *Dictionnaire philosophique*, in *Oeuvres complètes de Voltaire* (new ed.; 52 vols.; Paris, 1877-85), XVIII, 12-14; "Économie" [first published in 1771], *ibid.*, pp. 460-61; "Propriété" [first published in 1771], *ibid.*, XX, 292-93; Grosley, *Londres*, I, 29-30, 114, 115-16; Marquis de Chastellux, *De la félicité publique, ou Considérations sur le sort des hommes dans les différentes époques de l'histoire* (new ed.; 2 vols.; Paris, 1822), II, 303 [first published in 1772, the edition used here being, apparently, a reprint of that of 1776]; Necker, *Sur la législation et le commerce des grains*, in *Oeuvres*, I, 131-33; Coyer, *Nouvelles observations sur l'Angleterre*, pp. 33-37, 41, 164-70, 172-77.

[39] Diderot to Sophie Volland, Oct. 6, 1765, in *Lettres à Sophie Volland*, II, 294-97.

classes elsewhere. Toiling incessantly in order to live, they had no time to acquire any education.[40] The workhouses presented some shocking scenes, he asserted. He recorded with indignation that letters of recommendation were necessary for admission to charity hospitals, that the unemployed could be forced into the army on the theory that an idle man was simply a lazy one, and that persons who had been acquitted in a court of law but could not pay the necessary fees might therefore be kept in custody.[41]

English legal procedure as a whole drew hostile criticism from these writers. Now of all things English, the practices of the courts were among those most highly rated by the Anglophiles. Some Anglophiles now and then discovered a few flaws in English justice—even Voltaire, its most ardent panegyrist;[42] but such criticisms were exceptional. Both Marat and Rousseau, however, complained that legal procedure in England, instead of being guided by the "natural" insights of equity and good sense, had become bogged down in a quagmire of conservatism and literalness and an infinity of laws, with the result that judgments were frequently iniquitous and extravagant, and swarms of lawyers were enabled to devour the litigants.[43]

Despite the severity of their indictment, the precursors of the popular school or school of Rousseau were not the most Anglophobe of the reformers of the period ending with the War of American Independence. Still more Anglophobe were the Physiocrats.

The Physiocrats did not have a good word to say for the constitution of England. Their political doctrine was, at this time, the theory of "legal despotism." This theory was founded in part upon the idea of a proprietary right of the sovereign (i.e., the monarch) to the revenues of the state and in part upon the concept of "evidence," which meant that the laws constituting the "natural and essential order" of society were, to sufficiently intelligent minds, self-evident. The legislator, the monarch, would

---

[40] *Polish Letters*, I, 203-4.   [41] *The Chains of Slavery*, pp. 208-9.
[42] "Lois" [first published in 1771], *Dictionnaire philosophique*, in *Oeuvres*, XIX, 614; *Prix de la justice et de l'humanité, par l'auteur de la Henriade, avec son portrait* [first published in 1777], *ibid.*, XXX, 537.
[43] Marat, *Polish Letters*, I, 189-92; Rousseau, *Gouvernement de Pologne*, in *Political Writings*, II, 473.

be a sort of philosopher-king who, comprehending these laws, would have the power to declare them to be in effect. Until after the War of American Independence the only dissenter from that part of Physiocratic theory which embraced absolute monarchy was Turgot.[44] As a precursor of the Neo-Physiocrats of the 1780's, Turgot professed a theory of government by the enlightened intelligence of the nation. But the concept of evidence underlay both positions: whether the legislator were one or several, the laws of the country were to be arrived at in the same way, through the divination and application of the laws of nature.

The Physiocrats declared that they were unable to see how good laws, laws conformable to the natural and essential order of society, could be formulated through the parliamentary process based upon the principle of the separation and balance of powers, or, as they called it, the principle of counterforces. Said Mercier de la Rivière, the principal systematizer of Physiocratic theory:

> Either the principles of a government are *evident*, or they are not: if they are, power and authority inhere in their *evidence*; thus counterforces can have no place. . . . If on the contrary these principles are not *evident*, the establishment of counterforces is a useless procedure; for what counterforce can be opposed to that of ignorance, if it is not evidence? How dissipate the gloom of error, if not by the light of truth? What kind of plan is it to choose a blind man to lead another blind man? People fear ignorance in the sovereign, and lest it lead him astray, they set up against him other men who are not qualified even to guide themselves; that is what is meant by counterforces.[45]

In other words, the mode of government by counterforces as in England attempted to discover political truth, which was no less absolute than any other kind, by the mere compromising of opinions. It assumed what the Physiocrats denied, that the opinion of one person was as good as that of another. To them, and indeed to most French observers of the eighteenth century, the government of England was the paradise of the ordinary citizen, who shared with his betters, directly or indirectly, in the delights of power.

[44] Gustave Schelle (ed.), *Oeuvres de Turgot et documents le concernant avec biographie et notes* (5 vols.; Paris, 1913-23), II, 29; Turgot to David Hume, March 25 [1767], *ibid.*, p. 660.
[45] Mercier de la Rivière, *L'Ordre naturel et essentiel des sociétés politiques (1767)*, ed. Edgard Depitre (Paris, 1910), p. 122.

While the Physiocrats were not the only people of their time, even among liberals, who mistrusted the influence of the opinion of the general public upon government, the close kinship of their ideas with absolutist tradition on the one hand and utopian idealism on the other made them doubly sensitive to the deficiency of political wisdom in that public.

The criticism of the English government as being quite peculiarly liable to the bad influence of common prejudices runs like a leitmotif through all the Anglophobe sentiments of the Physiocrats. The English, observed the Marquis de Mirabeau, one of the more illustrious of Dr. Quesnay's converts, were "a nation where the cries of the people frequently prevail over good reasons."[46] About the time that Turgot was inaugurating the program of reforms for which his tenure of the office of controller-general is remembered, the Physiocratic lawyer Le Trosne asserted that no English government could ever succeed in carrying out a comparable program. Their efforts would always be obstructed by party quarrels and by the prejudices of a public opinion devoted to a false and selfish economic policy.[47] Turgot himself shared this opinion about the English. He remarked, for example, that although an English ministry (he was referring no doubt to the Walpole ministry) had at one time been able to destroy a part of the fabric of abuses which constituted the mercantilist system, they had been prevented from going any further "because a republican constitution sometimes opposes obstacles to the reformation of certain abuses when these abuses can be corrected only by an authority whose exercise, however advantageous to the public, always excites its distrust."[48] Turgot further complained that English ministers sometimes frankly and openly catered to public prejudices. Thus he wrote to David Hume, himself an economic liberal, regarding the Pitt ministry of 1766-68:

[46] Marquis de Mirabeau, *L'Ami des hommes, ou Traité de la population* (2 vols.; 1758), I, Part III, 131. First published in 1757. Although this work was written before the Marquis de Mirabeau had been entirely converted to Physiocracy, the quotation nevertheless represents the Physiocratic attitude.

[47] [G.-F.] Le Trosne, *De l'administration provinciale, et de la réforme de l'impôt* (2 vols.; Basel and Paris, 1788), I, 473. Written in 1775 and first published in 1779.

[48] Turgot, *Éloge de Vincent de Gournay*, in *Oeuvres*, I, 601-2. First published in 1759.

It would be indeed desirable that Mr. Pitt and all national leaders should think like Quesnay on all points. I am in truth afraid that your famous demagogue will follow quite different principles and will believe it his interest to support in your nation the prejudice which you have called *Jealousy of trade*.[49]

Turgot was also of the opinion that "there is no greater enemy of liberty than the people," and was confirmed in this belief[50] by the Gordon riots, which occurred in June, 1780, when Parliament, removing a number of the legal disabilities of Roman Catholics, offended the religious prejudices of the London population. Because of his distrust of the untrained and ordinary intelligence, Turgot objected to that shibboleth of the Anglophiles, jury trial. Although admitting that he would in fact prefer to be tried before an English jury rather than before the Parlement of Paris, he nevertheless preferred in principle an expert and permanent to an untrained and *ad hoc* panel of judges. "It is a profession, and a difficult one, to be a good judge," he said.[51] In sum Turgot, as ardent an advocate of individual liberty in the abstract as any Anglophile, thought that the concrete liberties that Englishmen enjoyed and Anglophiles praised were in themselves, without the aid of right reason (which few possessed), a stumbling block to a good and just administration.

The charge of corruption in government, so conspicuous in the criticism of writers like Mably, existed also in Physiocratic literature,[52] but was not common. The Physiocrats were characteristically concerned with intelligence rather than with morality. Their critique of English institutions, as thus far analyzed, amounted chiefly to a contention that the form of government in England made it impossible for an intellectual elite—people like themselves, initiated into a knowledge of the laws of nature—to get and keep the reins of power.

Another element in the Physiocrats' critique of English institutions was their disapproval of "equality," in so far as this meant

---

[49] Turgot to Hume, July 23 [1766], *ibid.*, II, 495-96.
[50] Turgot to Dupont de Nemours, June 28 [1780], *ibid.*, V, 628-29.
[51] Turgot to Condorcet, Feb. 12 [1771] and May 17 [1771], *ibid.*, III, 514, 516.
[52] Comte d'Albon, *Discours sur l'histoire, le gouvernement, les usages, la littérature et les arts, de plusieurs nations de l'Europe* (4 vols.; Geneva and Paris, 1782), I, 47-63. First published in 1779.

that merchant or manufacturer and landowner were upon the same economic and political footing. Although the Physiocrats condemned those vestiges of feudal and corporate privilege that had survived in their own country, their ideal society was nevertheless characterized by what Karl Marx described as a feudal *tone*.[53] It was in some degree still a hierarchical society, dominated by the great proprietors of land and by their tenants, large-scale farmers, and governed by a sovereign whose title and authority themselves derived from proprietorship in the land. Equality was a perversion of the natural and essential order of things, and republican government, or the machinery of counterforces, was the means by which in England the perversion had been accomplished. "When the Physiocrats condemn every system of 'counterforces' in politics," remarks Georges Weulersse, "they are no doubt thinking that the English parliamentary regime permits industrial and commercial interests to counterbalance the interest of the landowners."[54]

In Physiocratic writing there was often a clear-cut antithesis between the agricultural-monarchical concept and the commercial-republican one. The founder of Physiocracy, Dr. Quesnay, who used the words *nation* and *kingdom* as equivalents for the agricultural interest,[55] had a low regard for any country like England,

... where not only the colonies, but even the provinces of the metropolis, are subjected to the laws of the carrying trade ... ; where the interests of the soil and of the state are subordinated to the interests of the merchants; where commerce in agricultural products, the ownership of the land, and the state itself are regarded merely as accessories of the metropolis, and the metropolis as composed of merchants.[56]

A tract of the Abbé Baudeau, written in 1787 but reaffirming the concepts of Physiocracy in their most classic form, declared:

We have jealous neighbors who are tradesmen, republicans essentially.

[53] Georges Weulersse, *Le Mouvement physiocratique en France de 1756 à 1770* (2 vols.; Paris, 1910), II, 711 n. 3.
[54] *Ibid.*, pp. 709-10 n. 7.
[55] [François Quesnay], *Dialogues sur le commerce*, in *Physiocratie, ou Constitution naturelle du gouvernement le plus avantageux au genre humain*, ed. Dupont de Nemours (Leyden and Paris, 1768), pp. 280, 283.
[56] *Journal de l'agriculture*, Feb. 1766, quoted in Weulersse, *Le Mouvement physiocratique*, II, 709.

An anti-monarchical doctrine was formed among them a long time ago. . . . Its fundamental principle is to confound all classes of civilized society in order to raise trade, [which is] basically republican, to the level of the nobility, the clergy, and the landed proprietors, who are, in a good monarchy, according to the eternal and imprescriptible rules of nature, much above it.[57]

To the Physiocrats, who were enthusiastic laissez-faire extremists, nothing could be said in favor of contemporary English economic policy except in regard to the existence of internal free trade. They led the reaction against the Anglomania of the school of Gournay, which had admired in England the relaxation of state controls over industry and trade during the first half of the eighteenth century.[58] The degree of economic liberty allowed under English policy was too negligible, the Physiocrats thought, to be worth any consideration. In fact, they tended to think that English policy was becoming more rather than less mercantilist. Before the Seven Years' War, said the Physiocratic organ *Éphémérides du citoyen*, English politics had been ruled by a triumvirate of merchants, fund-holders *(rentiers)*, and landed proprietors, on the basis of a fairly even balance of power.[59] But now the merchants and the fund-holders were coming out on top. It was they who were the chief promoters of mercantilism.

One of the considerations that led the Physiocrats to this conclusion about the direction of English economic policy was the fact that Parliament was abandoning the practice, established in the last quarter of the seventeenth century, of permitting the unlimited and duty-free export of grain. Beginning about 1756, it had laid temporary but annually recurring embargoes on grain exports, until finally, in 1773, it enacted that the export of grain should cease automatically whenever the domestic price should have risen above a given statutory level.[60] The Physiocrats deplored this reversal of policy not merely in the abstract but also because it was embarrassing to their own program in France, where

---

[57] *Idées d'un citoyen presque sexagénaire sur l'état actuel du royaume de France, comparées à celles de sa jeunesse* (Paris, 1787), pp. 25-26.

[58] See above, pp. 12-13.

[59] *Éphémérides du citoyen, ou Bibliothèque raisonnée des sciences morales et politiques*, 1767, VIII, 127-28; cf. *ibid.*, II, 6.

[60] Donald Grove Barnes, *A History of the English Corn Laws from 1660-1846* (London, 1930), chaps. ii and iii.

they were engaged in a violent controversy over the freedom of the grain trade with the advocates of regulation. During the period when English producers had rejoiced in freedom of export, the transportation and sale of grain in France had been subject to rigid restrictions intended to safeguard localities against famine and high prices. Then, in 1763 and 1764, royal edicts had established the freedom of the trade within the country and a qualified freedom of export. But there was a strong popular opposition to the new policy. Aided by a condition of scarcity, it was in 1770 successful, at least temporarily, in securing a reversion to the old one.[61] The Physiocrats consistently attributed to the former English policy of unlimited and duty-free export of grain that agricultural prosperity which, they agreed, had prevailed in England during the first half of the eighteenth century.[62] The Physiocrats admitted (although they admitted the superiority of the neighboring country in little else) that England had been more prosperous at that time than France.[63] They declared that the recent reversal of English policy was a sad mistake. Parliament could not prevent scarcity and stop the rising cost of living by embargoing grain exports.[64] This would only destroy the incentive

[61] H.-F. Rivière, *Précis historique et critique de la législation française sur le commerce des céréales et des mesures d'administration prises dans les temps de cherté* (Paris, 1859), chap. iii.

[62] Marquis de Mirabeau, *Théorie de l'impot* (1761), pp. 240-41, and *Philosophie rurale, ou Économie générale et politique de l'agriculture, réduite à l'ordre immuable des loix physiques et morales, qui assurent la prospérité des empires* (3 vols.; Amsterdam, 1763), II, 201 n. a; Le Trosne, *Suite de la dispute sur la concurrence de la navigation étrangère pour la voiture de nos grains; ou Lettre de M. Le Trosne, avocat du roi au bailliage d'Orléans, en réponse à la lettre datée de Quimper, insérée dans la Gazette du commerce du 11 mars 1765, et les trois suivantes* (Paris, 1765), pp. 101-2; Le Trosne, *La Liberté du commerce des grains toujours utile et jamais nuisible* (Paris, Nov. 1, 1765), pp. 48-50; *Éphémérides du citoyen*, 1767, VIII, 128, 129-30; ibid., XII, 96-97; Baudeau, *Avis au peuple sur son premier besoin* (new ed.; Amsterdam and Paris, 1774 [first ed. 1768]), pp. 53-54; [Mercier de la Rivière], *L'Intérêt général de l'état, ou La Liberté du commerce des blés, démontrée conforme au droit naturel; au droit public de la France; aux loix fondamentales du royaume; à l'intérêt commun du souverain et de ses sujets dans tous les temps: avec la Réfutation d'un nouveau système, publié en forme de Dialogues sur le commerce des blés* (Amsterdam and Paris, 1770), p. 198.

[63] The admission is generally implicit but is expressed explicitly in Baudeau, *Éclaircissements demandés à M. N.**, sur ses principes économiques, et sur ses projets de législation; au nom des propriétaires fonciers et des cultivateurs françois* (1775), p. 162, and d'Albon, *Discours*, I, 243.

[64] *Éphémérides du citoyen*, 1767, VIII, 129-30; ibid., 1768, I, 133; Baudeau, *Avis au peuple*, p. 54.

for abundant production of the staple. It would actually create scarcity. Had it not been for the old corn laws, the cost of living would have risen sooner.[65] In Physiocratic opinion this rise in the cost of living was attributable to all the restrictions of the whole mercantilist regime, and the new corn-law policy was only more of the same thing.

The Physiocrats were also unfavorably impressed by the development of British fiscal policy in the eighteenth century. They believed in only one tax, assessed as a percentage of the annual income of the proprietors of land so that a constant relation would be established between the annual agricultural yield and the income of the government.[66] All other taxes were only impediments to the production and exchange of goods. The British had a land-tax, but it was levied upon rents and assessed at a valuation of property which had not been revised since 1692.[67] Moreover, it produced but a minor share of the revenues, a fact that was the fault chiefly of the landed proprietors. A mistaken view of their own interest, as the Physiocrats termed it, had caused this class to oppose the levy of a sizable land-tax and forced the government to rely chiefly upon the customs and the excise, indirect and therefore vicious forms of taxation that had contributed in no small measure to the aforementioned rising cost of living.[68] The perpetuation of this fiscal policy reflected the vestiges of the power of the landowning interest, which, as the change in the corn laws indicated, was otherwise declining. But the injuriousness of the taxes lay not only in their incidence; it was also in their sheer weight. They were necessary in order to service a now overwhelming national debt and to maintain the class of fund-holders who battened upon it. In turn, the institution and rapid growth of the national debt had been the result of that series of commercial wars by which the English mercantile interest had attempted to acquire a monopoly of the world's trade.[69]

[65] *Éphémérides du citoyen*, 1767, VIII, 129-30.
[66] Marquis de Mirabeau, *Philosophie rurale*, II, 273-74; *Éphémérides du citoyen*, 1767, III, 194.
[67] Stephen Dowell, *A History of Taxation and Taxes in England from the Earliest Times to the Present Day* (4 vols.; London, 1884), III, 95-97.
[68] Marquis de Mirabeau, *Philosophie rurale*, II, 273; *Éphémérides du citoyen*, 1767, VIII, 126-29; *ibid.*, 1768, I, 133; *ibid.*, 1769, IV, 139; Le Trosne, *De l'administration provinciale*, I, 473.
[69] Quesnay, *Maximes générales du gouvernement économique d'un royaume agricole*, in *Physiocratie*, ed. Dupont [de Nemours], p. 121; *Éphémérides du*

That the monopolistic tendency of English commerce was now greater than ever, and the mercantile interest in England predominant, were indicated, finally, by the colonial policy adopted by the English at the close of the Seven Years' War. At this time Parliament had supplemented the Acts of Trade and Navigation and resorted to a tax levy upon the colonials for the support of the military and administrative establishment that was to enforce them.[70]

The Physiocrats could not discover in England any appreciable opposition to mercantilism. In the words of the Marquis de Mirabeau, a dominating commercial spirit had "deceived" the nation.[71] To Turgot it seemed significant that in a country where presumably any opinion might be freely expressed, Josiah Tucker, Dean of Gloucester, was "almost the only author who has known and felt the advantages of freedom of trade, and who has not been seduced by the puerile and sanguinary illusions of a would-be commercial exclusiveness."[72] Adam Smith, be it remembered, had not yet published *The Wealth of Nations*.

In short, the view of the Physiocrats about the value of England as a model for the French in economic matters may be stated somewhat as follows: The errors of English economic policy, no different in kind from those of French policy, were more and not less deeply rooted than the latter, and in fact English prosperity (which in Physiocratic theory could be derived from agriculture alone) had already reached its apogee and was probably beginning to decline. Any prejudice of economic liberals in favor of England was therefore quite unfounded.

---

citoyen, 1767, VIII, 127; Le Trosne, *De l'administration provinciale*, I, 473; Le Trosne, *De l'ordre social, ouvrage suivi d'un traité élémentaire sur la valeur, l'argent, la circulation, l'industrie et le commerce intérieur et extérieur* (Paris, 1777), p. 380 n.

[70] Le Trosne, *De l'intérêt social, par rapport à la valeur, à la circulation, à l'industrie, et au commerce intérieur et extérieur* . . . (Paris, 1777), p. 135; Turgot to Dupont de Nemours, Aug. 5 [1768], in *Oeuvres*, III, 13 and n. b; Turgot to Dr. Tucker, Sept. 12 [1770], *ibid.*, p. 422; *Éphémérides du citoyen*, 1769, X, 44 ff., 54. Cf. Morellet to Lord Shelburne, March 12, 1776, in Lord Edmond Fitzmaurice (ed.), *Lettres de l'abbé Morellet de l'Académie française à Lord Shelburne depuis marquis de Lansdowne, 1772-1803* (Paris, 1898), pp. 102-3. Morellet was politically an Anglophile but in economic matters followed the Physiocrats and resembled them in his judgments about English colonial policy.

[71] Marquis de Mirabeau, *Théorie de l'impôt*, p. 241.

[72] Turgot to Tucker, Sept. 12 [1770], in *Oeuvres*, III, 422.

CHAPTER FOUR

ANGLOPHOBIA AND FRENCH NATIONALISM BEFORE THE WAR OF AMERICAN INDEPENDENCE

THUS FAR NOTHING has been said about nationalism in the critiques of Anglomania—at least, nothing explicit. But the matter might easily have been mentioned at more than one point in the preceding chapters.

Nationalism is difficult to define. It changes color, chameleon-like, according to the garb of the wearer, while any analysis of its essential character is likely to be affected by the analyst's philosophy of history. Still, there appear to be certain fairly constant factors in its manifestations, and there will probably be general agreement that the ones included here are the minimum essentials, or among the minimum essentials, of a definition. Nationalism, then, is a mixture of ideas and sentiments about the nation. The nation is conceived in one way as a culture-group possessing certain traditional and distinctive institutions. Toward both the group and the institutions the individual feels warmly, just because he belongs to them and they to him. But the nation is also conceived as a political entity, virtually the same thing as the state. It is the object of a political allegiance which transcends narrower political loyalties to king, class, or province and which is fundamentally at variance with the universalism professed by cosmopolitans. In reality, political nationalism, or national patriotism, exists only when the cultural and political concepts of the nation are fused. The idea of the nation as a political entity would, without the feeling of belonging to the nation because it is composed of one's own people, be deprived of the greater part of its emotional concomitant. Political allegiance would be reduced in that case to what the eighteenth century called political virtue, a somewhat chilly, abstract sort of sentiment.

A good deal of attention has been centered on the problem of dating the emergence of this political nationalism—or simply nationalism, as it will henceforth be termed. The view has prevailed rather widely that it cannot be said to have existed in France until aroused by the Revolution.[1] According to this belief, before the Revolution there were both a cultural tradition involving the concept of nationality and the beginnings of a political theory of nationalism, but political sentiments were prenationalistic, that is, either cosmopolitan or else dynastic, feudal, and provincial. On the other hand, there have been those who differ with this view and who would place the emergence of French nationalism in some

[1] Several distinguished modern French historians have held this opinion. See, for example, Ernest Lavisse, *General View of the Political History of Europe* (trans. Charles Gross; New York [1891]), pp. 142-43. Alphonse Aulard and Henri Hauser later set forth a variant of the thesis in asserting that although French nationalism had come into existence long before the Revolution, before the seventeenth century in fact, it had been eclipsed in the seventeenth and eighteenth centuries by the ideas of the state (Hauser) and the absolute monarchy (Aulard). It reappeared in the eighteenth century prior to the Revolution, but it was then, as these historians describe it, only an incipient nationalism and associated entirely with political liberalism. See A. Aulard, "Patrie, patriotisme avant 1789," *La Révolution française*, LXVIII (1915), 200-224; Aulard, "Patrie, patriotisme sous Louis XVI et dans les cahiers," *ibid.*, pp. 301-39; and Henri Hauser, *Le Principe des nationalités. Ses origines historiques* (Paris, 1916), pp. 12-19. The idea that French nationalism really dates from the Revolution was given added authority and wider currency by the studies of Carleton J. H. Hayes, *Essays on Nationalism* (New York, 1926) and *The Historical Evolution of Modern Nationalism* (New York, 1931). It was accepted by Beatrice Hyslop in her monograph, *French Nationalism in 1789 according to the General Cahiers* (New York, 1934), and has been defended by her in an article, "Recent Work on the French Revolution," *American Historical Review*, XLVII (April, 1942), 506. The English historian of the Revolution, J. M. Thompson, accepts it in his *The French Revolution* (New York, 1945), p. 133. It is incorporated in the full-dress study of the history of nationalism by Hans Kohn, *The Idea of Nationalism. A Study in Its Origins and Background* (New York, 1944), which affirms that "the French nationality was born of the enthusiastic manifestation of will in 1789" (p. 15). The co-operative study by the Royal Institute of International Affairs, *Nationalism* (London, 1939), likewise accepts this view, stating: "It thus appears that, although the nation itself and national feeling can be traced back to a much earlier date, nationalism as a conscious political force was a product of the French Revolution and its sequel" (p. 31). Boyd C. Shafer, "Bourgeois Nationalism in the Pamphlets on the Eve of the French Revolution," *Journal of Modern History*, X (1938), 31, by concluding that "Frenchmen were fast becoming nationalistic in 1788 and 1789," seems to subscribe to the general view although perhaps less unreservedly.

period prior to the Revolution.² It seems to the present writer that in the manifestations of Anglophobia that are the subject of this study there is no little evidence to support such a contention. Some of the nationalism that appears during the period 1763-89 is rudimentary, but much of it is mature.

The vocabulary of nationalism at this time contained the words *nation, national, patrie, patriotique,* and *patriotisme* (or *amour de la patrie*). These terms had both general or abstract and specific or localized meanings. *Nation* in one sense meant "people" and *national* meant "popular" or "general," implying some concept of a community that was more inclusive than any one of the class strata or geographical segments into which the population of the country might be otherwise divided. In another sense, *nation* and *national* designated a community distinguished by historical traditions or by a national character that imparted to its members a sense of kinship with one another and of separateness from other such nations. Similarly, *patrie* might signify that which was the object of the political virtue or *patriotisme* of its citizens, or it might also have a distinctly historical connotation, indicating a particular *patrie*. These meanings were not essentially different from the meanings of these words today. The words *patrie* and *nation*, which in a fully developed nationalism are almost synonymous, were not infrequently used in that way in the period 1763-89.

² René Johannet, *Le Principe des nationalités* (new ed.; Paris, 1923), holds not only that French nationalism dates from the late Middle Ages but that it was not eclipsed during the seventeenth and eighteenth centuries (pp. 70-78). More recent advocates of the opinion that a genuine French nationalism existed in the eighteenth century prior to the Revolution are Robert R. Palmer, "The National Idea in France before the Revolution," *Journal of the History of Ideas*, I (1940), 95-111; Paul Hazard, *La Pensée européenne au XVIIIe siècle de Montesquieu à Lessing* (3 vols.; Paris, 1946), II, 244-47; and Philippe Sagnac, *La Formation de la société française moderne* (2 vols.; Paris, 1945-46), II, 112-14, and *La Fin de l'ancien régime et la Révolution américaine (1763-1789)* ("Peuples et civilisations," Vol. XII, ed. Louis Halphen and Philippe Sagnac; Paris, 1947), pp. 22-23, 565. Cf. Sagnac, "L'Idée de la nation in France (1788-1789)," *Revue d'histoire politique et constitutionelle*, I (1937), 158-63, which seems somewhat more reserved. In "Pacifisme et nationalisme au dix-huitième siècle," *Annales historiques de la Révolution française*, XIII (1936), 1-17, A. Mathiez finds that in a predominantly internationalist eighteenth century there were signs of a change. Lucien Febvre, "Langue et nationalité en France au XVIIIe siècle," *Revue de synthèse historique*, XLII (Dec., 1926), 31-39, sees evidence of the national idea making headway here and there during the eighteenth century against particularism and the *religion monarchique*.

There was at that time no one French word meaning "nationalism" precisely, but, when necessary, *patriotisme* did duty for it.

Those who associate the emergence of French nationalism with the Revolution itself think of that nationalism as a product of the liberal and democratic movements. Those who discover the existence of nationalism in France at an earlier date find that it was by no means exclusively the property of the liberals. Indeed, among the liberals were some of the least nationalist of Frenchmen; the Anglophile *philosophes,* for example, were cosmopolitans who found more to admire abroad than at home. The principal element among the nationalists at the close of the Seven Years' War was, by reason of probable superiority in numbers, the conservatives.

One very strong component of conservative nationalism was pride in the achievements of French civilization during the "great century" of Louis XIV. The nationalism of some conservatives was, to be sure, hardly more than this; it had little, if any, political content. Their political sentiments were dynastic and found adequate expression in the cult of allegiance to the king. But the nationalism of other conservatives included the idea of allegiance to the nation. They did not abandon the cult of monarchy entirely. What had happened was a fusion in their minds of the two cults of monarchy and of the nation. As one writer put it: "The king, the *patrie* present the same idea; to die for the ruler is to sacrifice oneself for the subjects."[3] Another writer, quoted in the *Mercure de France,* exclaimed:

> It is said that the word *patrie* is, in our language and with reference to ourselves, quite modern, and very new in our ideas. Please Heaven that it may always be so! Our *patrie* is in our king united with his subjects. France . . . is less a state than it is a family.[4]

A third writer, analyzing what he called *patriotisme national,* affirmed (albeit anachronistically) that "in France the glory of the prince and the honor of the nation constituted the great object of

---

[3] Anon., *Lettre d'un jeune homme à son ami, sur les Français et les Anglais, relativement à la frivolité reprochée aux uns, et la philosophie attribuée aux autres; ou Essai d'un parallele à faire entre ces deux nations* (Amsterdam and Paris, 1779), p. 33.

[4] *Mercure de France,* April, 1765, I, 50.

patriotism as early as the beginning of the monarchy."⁵ The first and third of these quotations are from works written with the explicit purpose of comparing the English and the French. Clearly, an important factor in the development of conservative nationalism at this time was the political rivalry of France and England, a rivalry conceived of not in dynastic or even statist terms, but in the terms of a rivalry of peoples.

This fact is more extensively illustrated in certain examples of the contemporary drama. The semiofficial play composed for the ceremonies celebrating the Peace of Paris in 1763 was a gay little comedy by Favart entitled *L'Anglois à Bordeaux*.⁶ The original title, *L'Antipathie vaincue,* changed upon the request of the English ambassador,⁷ had indicated the theme of the play: the victory of the French national character over the national character of the English—a subtle revenge for the loss of an empire. In this play a melancholy, haughty milord, bristling with convictions about the superiority of the English to all other nations, especially the French, was being held as a prisoner in the household of the French gentleman who had been his captor. He had accepted most ungraciously the hospitality proffered him, while the host's widowed sister, a charming marquise, displayed in her attempts to entertain him the special French virtues of sociability and *courtoisie*. In the household, too, was the Englishman's daughter, who had been with her father at the time of his capture, which had occurred at sea. A love affair had developed between this girl and her host, but their desire to marry was uncompromisingly opposed by the disagreeable milord. Then it came out, accidentally, that considerable advances of money made to the Englishman's account and supposed by him to have come from a compatriot had actually been furnished by the French host, who had practiced this little deception in order to spare his captive's pride. Such generosity and delicacy of sentiment prevailed over the milord's

---

⁵ [Louis] Basset de la Marelle, *La Différence du patriotisme national chez les François et chez les Anglois. Discours lu à l'Académie des Sciences Belles-Lettres et Arts de Lyon* (Lyon, 1762), p. 36.

⁶ [Louis Bachaumont *et al.*], *Mémoires secrets pour servir à l'histoire de la république des lettres en France, depuis MDCCLXII jusqu'à nos jours; ou Journal d'un observateur . . .* (36 vols.; London, 1784-89), I, 188-94 (March 13-24, 1763), 236 (June 23, 1763), 238 (June 27, 1763), 258 (July 27, 1763).

⁷ *Ibid.*, p. 188 (March 13, 1763).

ill-humor, and his daughter's romance was permitted to have a happy ending. The French victory was rendered complete by the milord himself falling victim to the attractions of the fair marquise, who for her part had realized all along that he possessed a fundamentally noble character that simply needed humanizing.[8]

The nationalism in *L'Anglois à Bordeaux* is nowhere formally stated. It is there, but as a premise whose outlines are perhaps a little vague. In Belloy's *Le Siège de Calais,* a pretentious historical drama first performed in 1765, the nationalism, both theory and sentiment, is put in with a heavy hand. According to Belloy, his own motives in writing the play were those of a French patriot.

> Let us become accustomed [he said] to commemorating the virtues of our compatriots. By exciting the veneration of France for the great men she has produced we shall instil in the nation a self-esteem and self-respect which alone can make it again what it was formerly.... Let it not be said by those who come out of our theater: "The great men I have just seen played were Romans; I was not born in a country where I can emulate them." Let it be said sometimes at least: "I have just seen a French hero; I can be such a one, too."[9]

The patriotism celebrated in the *Siège de Calais* was almost ostentatiously shown to be really national, in no sense primarily a property of the nobility, the class traditionally entrusted with the military defense of the kingdom, but a characteristic of all true Frenchmen regardless of their estate. The heroes of the play—for the hero was actually plural—were the burghers of Calais. The traitor, a repentant traitor, to be sure, was a nobleman.

According to Belloy's version of the story, King Edward of England had demanded that the city of Calais send him six citizens to be put to death just as a warning of the danger of disobedience. The six men—the mayor, his son, and four others—who volunteered themselves were moved by love for their king and for France. The King of France then proposed that, instead of the burghers giving up their lives, he and Edward meet in single combat with the crown of France as prize. Edward agreed, but the arrangement was refused by the French army, which de-

---

[8] C.-S. Favart, *L'Anglois à Bordeaux* in *Répertoire général du théatre français* (67 vols.; Paris, 1818), XLV, 299-359.

[9] *Le Siège de Calais, tragédie dédiée au roi* (Paris, 1765), Preface, pp. vi-vii.

clared that the least of Frenchmen would have a better right to the crown of his country than an English king, no matter what the outcome of the combat. At this point the burghers of Calais were liberated by the above-mentioned repentant traitor, who had formerly deserted the French king to take service with Edward and who now desired to atone for his treason by diverting Edward's wrath from the men of Calais to himself. But when the citizens of Calais learned that they had been freed without Edward's knowledge, they went back to die. They would not be dishonored by withdrawing, as it were, the offer they had once made. In the end they were saved, not by the intercession of Queen Philippa, as the story usually goes, but by a plea of the mayor's son, who, invoking Edward's memory of his own father, begged to die first and not under his father's eyes. This finally awakened Edward's generosity and his admiration for the prisoners' conduct. In sum, the conqueror was himself morally conquered by these French patriots.

Underlying the whole story are the twin ideas of fidelity to the king and the sacredness of the national tie that binds all the subjects of one country in a common allegiance. The latter concept is quite explicitly stated in the following lines, spoken by an Englishman but intended, as the lines themselves show, to apply to Frenchmen as well, or any other nation:

> Le lien fraternel qui joint tous les Humains
> Se serre en chaque État par d'autres noeuds plus saints:
> Je sais que, mis au jour, nourri par l'Angleterre,
> Je lui tiens de plus près qu'au reste de la Terre:
> Je vois les mêmes noeuds de la France à ses Fils.
> Je hais ces coeurs glacés et morts pour leur Pays,
> Qui, voyant ses malheurs dans une Paix profonde,
> S'honorent du grand nom de Citoyens du Monde:
> Feignent, dans tout climat, d'aimer l'Humanité,
> Pour ne la point servir dans leur propre Cité.[10]

(The tie of brotherhood that joins all humanity is drawn tighter in every state by other more sacred bonds. I know that, brought into the light and nourished by England, I am bound to her more closely than to the rest of the world. I perceive the same bonds between France

---

[10] *Ibid.*, pp. 66-67, Act IV, Scene 2.

and her sons. I hate those dead and frozen hearts which, beholding their country's ill-fortune in profound composure, honor themselves with the great name of citizens of the world, and pretend to love humanity in every climate in order not to serve it in their own country.)

Here, indeed, the *patrie* cannot be conceived of apart from the nation.

According to all accounts, the success of this play was prodigious, unexceeded, said the contemporary critic La Harpe, in the previous history of the French theater.[11] The company of the Comédie Française gave a free performance for the people of Paris, who came in crowds, applauding and shouting, "Vive le roi!"[12] "The nation, whose spirit perhaps needed rekindling," wrote the Duc de Croÿ, "found in this new species [of historical drama] . . . the means of reawakening its true sentiments."[13] Revivals in later years were no less successful than the first run. Dr. John Moore, who went to a performance of the *Siège de Calais* in the 1770's, declared: "You cannot conceive what pressing and crowding there is every night to see this favorite piece."[14] There was some dissent. The Maréchal de Noailles said that he would be sorry indeed not to be "meilleur Français" than were its lines.[15] Some of the journals expressed reservations about its literary merits. But they did not say much against it and on the whole praised it for glorifying the French nation and monarchy.[16] As Baron Grimm, who was neither an ardent devotee of the monarchy nor a French nationalist, remarked:

This piece has really been a state event. . . . Those who have dared,

---

[11] J.-F. de La Harpe, *Correspondance littéraire, adressée à son A. I. Mgr le grand-duc, aujourd'hui empereur de Russie; et à M. le comte André Schowalow, chambellan de l'impératrice Catherine II, depuis 1774 jusqu'à 1791*, in *Oeuvres de La Harpe* (16 vols.; Paris, 1820-21), X, 111.

[12] Vicomte de Grouchy and Paul Cottin (eds.), *Journal inédit du duc de Croÿ 1718-1784* (4 vols.; Paris, 1906-7), II, 188.

[13] *Ibid.* Cf. Favart to the Comte de Durazzo, March 5, 1765, *Mémoires et correspondance littéraires, dramatiques et anecdotiques de C.-S. Favart*, ed. A.-P.-C. Favart (3 vols.; Paris, 1808), II, 219.

[14] John Moore, M.D., *A View of Society and Manners in France, Switzerland, and Germany: with Anecdotes Relating to Some Eminent Characters* (7th ed.; 2 vols.; London, 1789), I, 80.

[15] La Harpe, *Correspondance littéraire*, in *Oeuvres*, X, 111-12.

[16] *Journal encyclopédique*, 1765, III, 148, and IV, 115; *Mercure de France*, April, 1765, I, 47-51, and July, 1765, p. 169; *Journal des sçavans*, 1766, pp. 174-76.

I do not say to find fault with it, but to speak of it coldly and without admiration, have been regarded as bad citizens, or, what is worse, as philosophers; for the philosophers have the reputation of not being convinced of the sublimity of the piece.[17]

The timeliness of the *Siège de Calais* lay not only in the sentiments it expressed, but in the parallel suggested by its subject. Frenchmen of 1765 would not fail to compare that episode of an earlier great struggle against the English with the precise situation in which their country then found itself. In both cases France had been defeated by England, but as the English had had eventually to withdraw from France after the conquests of the fourteenth century, so England in the eighteenth century, it was confidently believed, would not long be able to remain in a position of world dominance.

Conservative nationalism abounded in confidence. Conservative publicists were full of the idea of England's imminent material decay. This was not because they agreed with the Physiocrats that a mercantilist policy was necessarily bad. On the contrary, most conservative rationalizations were in the mercantilist tradition. However, in all economic development there must be, so conservatives contended, a principle of moderation, and a kind of internal balance must be maintained between commerce, industry, and agriculture. This principle the English had disregarded. The modern Carthaginians had endeavored to extend their trade beyond the limits nature had intended for it and had overreached themselves. War, so ran the thesis, had disrupted British commerce, injured manufactures, and produced great popular distress. It had entailed a national debt of such proportions that repayment was impossible, despite a heavier burden of taxation than, as all French writers held at this time, France sustained. English agriculture was beginning to decline. Ireland, suffering from absentee landlordism and from oppressive commercial and industrial restrictions in favor of the English mercantile interest, was rife with popular disturbances. Scotland was suffering from the same maladies as Ireland, though to a somewhat slighter degree. In con-

---

[17] Maurice Tourneux (ed.), *Correspondance littéraire, philosophique et critique par Grimm, Diderot, Raynal, Meister* . . . (16 vols.; Paris, 1877-82), VI, 243 (April 1, 1765).

sequence of the prevailing misery of the population of Great Britain and Ireland, emigration was attaining such proportions, it was alleged, as to threaten a serious depopulation of the realm.

The British Empire, moreover, had become top-heavy. Governing the American colonies was a more costly enterprise than the mother country could sustain by itself, and yet the attempt of Parliament to raise a revenue in the colonies had not only been a failure but had resulted in colonial boycotts still further impairing the prosperity of home trade and industry. Sometimes it was said that the colonies of England were only a liability to her, while at other times it was said that their secession, which seemed not unlikely, would amount to an economic disaster. Whichever viewpoint was taken, however, the outlook for the English seemed bad. This unfavorable picture of England's future, to which there were few exceptions in conservative literature, began emerging before the ink was dry upon the Treaty of Paris, and ten years later all the lines were sharp and clear.[18]

France, on the contrary, was held to be a fundamentally healthy country. Her power was "natural," for her economy was balanced: her commerce was not overexpanded, and her debt remained, it was supposed, within bounds. French agriculture was said to be not inferior, by and large, to that of England. If

---

[18] [Jacob-Nicolas Moreau], *Entendons-nous, ou Le Radotage du vieux notaire, sur la Richesse de l'état* [Amsterdam, 1763], p. 2; [S.-A. Cossé, Baron de Saint-Supplix], *Le Consolateur, pour servir de réponse à la Théorie de l'impot, et autres écrits sur l'oeconomie politique* (Brussels and Paris, 1763), pp. vii, ix-xi; [Vivant de Mezague], *A General View of England . . . Argumentatively Stated; from the Year 1600, to 1762*, trans. from the French (London, 1766 [French ed. 1762]), *passim*; [Dupuy-Demportes], *Testament politique de Robert Walpole*, reviewed in *L'Année littéraire*, 1766, VIII, 154; [John Gee], *Coup d'oeil rapide sur les progrès et la décadence du commerce et des forces de l'Angleterre, ouvrage attribué à un membre du parlement*, trans. freely from the English by Joseph-Pierre Frenais (1768), pp. 1, 88-95; *Mercure de France*, 1768, pp. 95-99; *L'Année littéraire*, 1767, VIII, 282-88; *ibid.*, 1768, V, 195-206; *Journal des beaux-arts et des sciences*, 1768, III, 496-514; *Journal de Genève*, 1772, No. 2, p. 5; *ibid.*, No. 4, pp. 42, 45; *ibid.*, No. 6, p. 43; *ibid.*, No. 8, p. 42; *ibid.*, 1773, II, No. 12, p. 40, No. 17, p. 30; *ibid.*, III, No. 22, p. 44, No. 27, pp. 22-23; *ibid.*, IV, No. 32, pp. 33, 37; *ibid.*, 1775, I, No. 1, pp. 27-33; *Gazette de France*, 1773, pp. 210, 388; *Journal de politique et de littérature, contenant les principaux événemens de toutes les cours, les nouvelles de la république des lettres, etc.* [known as *Journal politique de Bruxelles*], 1775, I, 86-87; *Journal encyclopédique*, 1775, IV, 195-96; Linguet, *Du plus heureux gouvernement, ou Parallèle des constitutions politiques de l'Asie avec celles de l'Europe*, in *Oeuvres de M. Linguet* (6 vols.; London, 1774), II, 203-7, 216-17.

France had lost territory abroad, she was not beset with imperial problems, while her metropolitan resources in soil and population were many times those of her rival.[19] Only the blind pride of the English, one writer declared, kept them from recognizing the resources held by France against the caprice of fortune, whereas the English themselves would be exhausted by their struggle against a rival to whom they could do at most only slight damage.[20] In the same vein another writer asserted:

Only let a clever minister rise in France, and England will fall immediately into its original condition of mediocrity. . . . England, they say, has a good administration; but France has only to perfect hers. The soil of Britain produces a great deal; but the French monarchy has only to improve its agriculture. Great Britain has a large navy; but France has only to build one that will not be inferior to it.[21]

The feeling of confidence that inspired these and other lines often had warlike implications. "What can Britain do," scornfully demanded one commentator, "beside a power that can raise a hundred and sixty thousand seamen and two hundred and fifty thousand soldiers? Can she suppose that she will lay down the law to it?"[22] Such a thought would be an insult, not to be borne, to the national honor of Frenchmen.

The idea of honor was conspicuous in conservative nationalism. "National honor" was of course an adaptation of the concept of the honor of the nobility and reflected something of the chivalric code. National honor required that faith be kept with other nations, and, according to conservative publicists, France had kept it. The English, on the other hand, had not. They had not let any chivalric considerations stand in the way of their national

---

[19] Moreau, *Entendons-nous*, p. 2; Saint-Supplix, *Le Consolateur*, p. xix; Dupuy-Demportes, *Testament politique de Robert Walpole*, as reviewed in *L'Année littéraire*, 1766, VIII, 164; Basset de la Marelle, *La Différence du patriotisme national*, p. 72; [Ange Goudar], *L'Espion chinois; ou, L'Envoye secret de la cour de Pekin, pour examiner l'état présent de l'Europe. Traduit du chinois* (6 vols.; Cologne, 1764), V, 170; [P.-L.-C. Gin], *Les Vrais principes du gouvernement françois, démontrés par la raison et par les faits, par un François* (Geneva, 1777), pp. 77-78; *Journal de Genève*, 1772, No. 2, pp. 10-12.

[20] Basset de la Marelle, *La Différence du patriotisme national*, pp. 71-72.

[21] Goudar, *L'Espion chinois*, V, 169-70.

[22] Dupuy-Demportes, *Testament politique de Robert Walpole*, quoted in *L'Année littéraire*, 1766, VIII, 164.

economic advantage.[23] Fortunately, honor did not imply meekness, but, on the contrary, it demanded the defense of one's own rights and those of others against the aggressor. In other words, France as a great power had a mission to defend the rights of nations against the "injustice" of another nation.

As the material strength of France was proudly compared with that of England, so was her civilization. The *Dictionnaire social et patriotique*, which revealed in its author a certain breadth of intellectual interests, averred that for "reason and good sense" the French compared very well indeed with the English. For Steele, he said, there was La Rochefoucauld; for Bolingbroke, there was Bayle; for Tillotson, Bossuet; for Pope, Voltaire. And whom had the English to compare with Montesquieu?[24] Most conservatives, who generally deprecated the "philosophic" tendencies of the age and usually excluded all the "philosophers" save Montesquieu from their catalogue of immortals, were thinking chiefly of their seventeenth-century heritage when they compared English and French civilization. "People say," wrote a contributor to the *Mercure de France*, "that we should give our orations and public writings a tincture of that energy which infuses English public speaking. Sublime and vigorous Bossuet! Elegant Fléchier! And you, amiable Fénelon, the friend of men! *You* but cold and languishing orators!"[25]

To be sure, conservatives in those days as they do now invoked patriotism in order to prevent change. But the fact that an idea or a sentiment has been put to certain extraneous uses is really a tribute to its potency rather than an argument for its nonexistence. Nor are those who so use the sentiment necessarily insincere. To conservatives, the cosmopolitanism of the Anglophiles was an offense like their liberalism. Thus a writer hostile to Anglomania complained:

If it is desired to cite a heroic action, foreign annals are thumbed. If it is desired to speak of a country fertile in resources, this is looked for

[23] Basset de la Marelle, *La Différence du patriotisme national*, pp. 6-7, 62; cf. [Pierre Lefèvre de Beauvray], *Dictionnaire social et patriotique, ou Précis raisonné de connoissances relatives à l'économie morale, civile et politique* (Amsterdam, 1770), p. 22. These notions about honor, while frequently implicit rather than explicit, are ubiquitous.

[24] Lefèvre de Beauvray, *Dictionnaire social et patriotique*, p. 26.

[25] *Mercure de France*, Aug., 1776, p. 6.

among our neighbors. If it is desired to praise good citizens, our enemies are extolled. Such is the tone of the century, and the impartial man who pretends to defend the cause of his country is regarded as a singular being who has seen nothing, as a man without experience.[26]

Similarly, the *Dictionnaire social et patriotique* in the article "Anglomania" denounced people "who, to excuse themselves for not being citizens, loudly proclaim that they are cosmopolitan philosophers . . . and who cry continually that their nation is decadent."[27] A journalist, replying to a query as to why so many young men should want to imitate the manners of Englishmen, observed shortly: "Doubtless it is because they have ceased to be Frenchmen."[28] The authors of these remarks were in general defenders of the *status quo,* but they were French nationalists, too.

The strongest nationalists among the advocates of reform before the War of American Independence were the Physiocrats. The peculiar coloration of their nationalist theory came from their agrarian predilections. In their eyes only an agrarian society could be truly national,[29] for in order to be conscious of his allegiance a citizen must have a stake in the soil. "Monied fortunes," asserted Quesnay, "are clandestine riches which know neither king nor country."[30] This was another reason why the French ought not to imitate the English, whose commercial and financial society could not have any loyalties except to what Quesnay, again, disparagingly called "the universal republic of traders."[31]

The Physiocrats were intensely proud of their own land and people. They preferred French civilization to any other, even in their capacity as reformers. Their "legal despotism" was a kind of idealization of the historic French monarchy. They vigorously

---

[26] *Ibid.*, p. 7.
[27] Lefèvre de Beauvray, *Dictionnaire social et patriotique*, p. 24. Cf. *Journal des beaux-arts et des sciences*, 1769, IV, 344-45.
[28] [Métra, J. Imbert, *et al.*], *Correspondance secrète, politique et littéraire, ou Mémoires pour servir à l'histoire des cours, des sociétés et de la littérature en France, depuis la mort de Louis XV* (18 vols.; London, 1787-89), I, 55 (Aug. 25, 1774).
[29] [François Quesnay], *Dialogues sur le commerce*, in Dupont [de Nemours] (ed.), *Physiocratie, ou Constitution naturelle du gouvernement le plus avantageux au genre humain* (Leyden and Paris, 1768), pp. 280, 283.
[30] *Maximes générales du gouvernement économique d'un royaume agricole, ibid.*, p. 121.
[31] *Dialogues sur le commerce, ibid.*, pp. 280, 283.

defended the French national character and intelligence against the imputation of inferiority to the national character and intelligence of the English. For example, when someone published the view that freedom of trade in grain could not be expected to work so well in France as it had worked in England because Frenchmen were less enlightened and less public-spirited than Englishmen, and French officials less impartial and more irregular in the administration of the laws,[32] Dupont de Nemours, then a rising journalist, protested indignantly.

> Since the author makes such a point of national character in this question [he wrote], and since after gratuitously imputing to the French a general opposition to their own best interests, he concludes that it is better to leave them in poverty than to make them wealthy in spite of themselves, I believe that I in turn am justified in asserting that the nation, when instructed, will have as much influence in maintaining good principles as in supporting the principle of its own destruction. I add that of all the peoples of Europe, no other is attached with so much constancy to the maxims it embraces: read our laws, study our forms; there you will see necessary changes, but slow and infrequent ones; the basic structure is always preserved. That is the result of the great confidence the people have in the government, and the respect of the government for the laws. It is for this reason that we ask not a temporary permission but a permanent law [allowing the free export of grain]. The guardians of this law will be the same as those who watch over our few fundamental laws and the essential supplementary laws. . . . It is clear then that we have as many means of being wise and happy as the English.[33]

In much the same tone Turgot took issue with Richard Price over certain remarks contained in the first edition of the latter's *Observations on the Nature of Civil Liberty*, where it was implied that French opinion had been deeply shocked by Turgot's reform edicts. "I think," said Turgot, "that you have done justice neither to me nor to my nation, where there is much more wisdom than is generally believed in your country, and where it is perhaps even

---

[32] *Gazette du commerce*, March 3, 1764. Referred to in Dupont de Nemours, *De l'exportation et de l'importation des grains (1764)*, ed. Edgard Depitre (Paris, 1911), pp. 59-60.

[33] *Gazette du commerce*, March 10, 1764. Quoted in Dupont de Nemours, *De l'exportation et de l'importation des grains*, ed. Depitre, pp. 68-69.

easier than with you to bring the public around to reasonable ideas."[34]

The Physiocrats thought not only that the French were quite capable of working out their own salvation, toward which the English could offer little if anything, but that it was France which was destined to be the chief propagator of the philosophic enlightenment in Europe. The following apostrophe by Le Trosne illustrates their concept of a national civilizing mission:

> O France! O my country! This is the role which it is your part to play in Europe.... From you the light has gone forth which reveals to men their rights and duties, their true interests, the essential principles of justice, the laws and structure of the social order which govern the relations of nations with each other as well as those of citizens.[35]

The ideal international order to which Le Trosne referred in this quotation, and which like the Physiocrats' ideal domestic economy was to be founded upon free trade, was not a concept that contravened their nationalism. For their belief in international free trade really gave the measure of their faith in the capacity of France to profit from the conditions of world economic competition. The assumptions of the Physiocrats in this respect were quite analogous to those of English economic liberals in the nineteenth century: in either case free trade, though it would in theory increase the prosperity of all nations, would be especially advantageous to one nation. The chief difference between these French liberals of the eighteenth century and the English liberals of the nineteenth lay in the material foundations for their optimism. Whereas the English were to base their policy upon England's proved industrial superiority, the Physiocrats attached theirs to an as yet unrealized but alleged potential superiority of France in agriculture and in natural resources in general. The Physiocrats confidently measured their country against England. "The territorial extent of France," said Le Trosne, "is more than double that of England, and the population three times greater. Husbandry is good enough in England itself; it is quite inferior in

[34] Turgot to Price, March 22 [1778], in Gustave Schelle (ed.), *Oeuvres de Turgot et documents le concernant avec biographie et notes* (5 vols.; Paris, 1913-23), V, 533.
[35] *De l'ordre social* ... (Paris, 1777), p. 430.

Scotland and in Ireland; and France has provinces as rich as the richest in England."[36] If French agricultural policy had been as enlightened as English policy had been throughout the past three quarters of a century, said the *Éphémérides du citoyen* in the year 1767, French agriculture would now be the more flourishing of the two.[37] For the pre-eminence of the English in agriculture was "not in the nature of things."[38] The Physiocrats, of course, took no stock in England's industrial development. On the contrary, when it was pointed out to them that British commerce in manufactured goods was ten times greater than that in the products of the land, they saw in this fact only a harbinger of decadence.[39] At a later period, when the concern of some Physiocratic theorists with the condition of agriculture had become less exclusive, their confidence in the capacity of France to compete successfully with her rival England was transferred from the sphere of agriculture to that of industry. On the eve of the Revolution, in the midst of an industrial crisis that was being generally attributed to the low-tariff Anglo-French treaty of 1786, Dupont de Nemours asserted that free competition would not destroy French industry but would merely toughen it.[40]

In the confident predictions of the Physiocrats about the future material greatness of their country there no doubt lurked some degree of a *revanche* sentiment. But, unlike the analogous feeling of conservative nationalists, it lacked bellicosity, for the Physiocrats frowned upon war as being both contrary to humane principles and expensive. There were other differences between the nationalism of the Physiocrats and that of the conservatives. The Physiocrats, unlike the conservatives, did not view the monarch as a symbol of the nation. In their thought the role of the legal despot was strictly functional and had little to do with their nationalism except indirectly, in their preference for the absolutist

---

[36] *De l'administration provinciale, et de la réforme de l'impôt* (2 vols.; Basel and Paris, 1788 [first published in 1779]), I, 473.
[37] *Éphémérides du citoyen*, 1767, XII, 96-97.
[38] *Ibid.*, VIII, 130.
[39] Georges Weulersse, *Le Mouvement physiocratique en France de 1756 à 1770* (2 vols.; Paris, 1910), II, 708.
[40] *Lettre à la chambre du commerce de Normandie; sur le mémoire qu'elle a publié relativement au traité de commerce avec l'Angleterre* (Rouen and Paris, 1788), pp. 48-50 *et passim*.

tradition of their own country. The Physiocrats, again, were reformers whose national ideal demanded the achievement of a greater degree of unity, both cultural and economic, than France at the time possessed, whereas conservatives thought of the unity of France as already sufficient. The Physiocrats, furthermore, were *philosophes* who took pride in the leadership of French rationalism in Europe, whereas conservatives tended to extol only the seventeenth-century achievements of French letters and to think "philosophy" un-French. The Physiocrats' concept of a national mission was related to their rationalism, while that of the conservatives was related to the notion of honor. Nevertheless, despite these differences, both types of nationalist thinking were aggressive and self-conscious, and both were largely developed in hostility to the imperialism of the English and the Anglophile cosmopolitanism of numerous contemporary Frenchmen.

It would be difficult to classify as nationalists in the same sense as the Physiocrats and the conservatives the French liberals who have been called the precursors of the school of Rousseau, or the popular school. For they were still too close in feeling to the cosmopolitanism of that Anglophile tradition from which they had deviated. Yet, paradoxically, their role was of the greatest significance in the history of French nationalism, for the most notable of all contemporary developments in the *theory* of nationalism, as distinguished from the sentiment, were the concepts of the general will and the sovereignty of that will. These concepts would be united with nationalist sentiment in due time.[41] Moreover, the founders of the school of Rousseau were not completely deficient in that pride of nationality that desires one's own people to seem more glorious than others. Diderot, for one, was of the opinion that the "adventurous genius of the French," who in regard to "reason and philosophy" had owed so much to the English, had now caused them to overtake their one-time mentors.[42]

Even some publicists who were in most respects Anglophile were beginning to think that the intellectual products of French liberalism compared very favorably with what the English had produced, if indeed the English had not been outdistanced. One

---
[41] This development is discussed in the final chapter, pp. 119-20.
[42] From the memoirs of Sir Samuel Romilly, quoted in R. Loyalty Cru, *Diderot as a Disciple of English Thought* (New York, 1913), pp. 112-13.

such writer, extolling the progress of French civilization during the reign of Louis XV, pointed to "all those books of a hardy metaphysics" which he said had "taken from England the claim of having produced writers more audacious than those of France."[43] The Abbé Morellet, who was a partisan of the English in general and the Whigs in particular, thought that in economic theory the French had surpassed the English.[44] Voltaire himself allowed: "We are in many things the disciples of the English; we shall end by being the equals of our masters."[45] Yet such remarks are no more than straws in the wind. Certainly neither Morellet nor Voltaire was, in fundamental outlook, a nationalist.[46]

[43] [Gudin de la Brunellerie], *Aux manes de Louis XV, et des grands hommes qui ont vécu sous son règne, ou Essai sur les progrès des arts et de l'esprit humain sous le régne de Louis XV* (Deux-Ponts, 1776), p. 288.

[44] Morellet to Lord Shelburne, March 12, 1776, in Lord Edmond Fitzmaurice (ed.), *Lettres de l'abbé Morellet de l'Académie française à Lord Shelburne depuis marquis de Lansdowne, 1772-1803* (Paris, 1898), p. 102.

[45] Voltaire to Mme d'Épinay, July 6, 1766, in *Oeuvres complètes de Voltaire* (new ed.; 52 vols.; Paris, 1877-85), XLIV, 329.

[46] Despite the contrary contention of his biographer Condorcet, Voltaire seems to have remained to the end of his life in most respects a confirmed Anglophile. Condorcet supported his contention merely by adducing the fact that Voltaire had defended the cause of "taste and reason" against the current enthusiasm in France for Shakespeare. See his *Vie de Voltaire*, in A. Condorcet O'Connor and M. F. Arago (eds.), *Oeuvres de Condorcet* (12 vols.; Paris, 1847-49), IV, 31. This hardly seems significant in view of the very considerable evidence that Voltaire remained in other respects a strong admirer of the English. Condorcet's memory of Voltaire may have been influenced by the fact that when he wrote the *Vie de Voltaire*, about 1787, he was himself deeply interested in combating the Anglophiles on political grounds.

CHAPTER FIVE

THE JUSTIFICATION OF THE WAR OF AMERICAN INDEPENDENCE

THE WAR OF AMERICAN Independence was an event of no little significance in the history of the controversy between Anglophobes and Anglophiles in France. It was, of course, a consequence of the American Revolution, in which Frenchmen thus became participants. In order to understand how the latter regarded their country's intervention in Anglo-American affairs, it is necessary first to inquire what they thought about the nature and the justice of the Americans' revolt.

From one point of view, that revolt appeared to be a late phase of the struggle between liberty and authority that to Frenchmen had been the theme of English political history for centuries. The antagonists still were, as they always had been, the nation and the king. The colonists were a part of the English nation. It was assumed that there was no difference in the constitutional status of Englishmen and Americans, that the rights and liberties that pertained to the inhabitants of the realm pertained also to those of the dominions beyond the seas, that in England and America there was the same fundamental law. The fact that Parliament, which had once led the nation against the king, was now conspicuously hostile to the colonists was explained as a consequence of "influence." The loud contention of the parliamentary opposition that the colonial policy of the ministry was related to the maneuvers of the crown against liberty in England itself no doubt contributed to this interpretation, which appeared to be confirmed by the American Declaration of Independence, a bill of grievances against the crown alone, and by the provisions of the first American constitutions, which carefully circumscribed the authority of the executive while enlarging that of the legislature.

It seemed that the liberties of Englishmen were being more effectively defended in the colonies than they were at the same time in the mother country. Some Frenchmen, such as the Abbé de Mably, thought of the ability of the crown to wage war against the colonists as being in itself an indication of the general decay of political virtue among Englishmen at home,[1] resulting in a softening of their will to resist tyranny. The idea was current in France, although by no means universally entertained,[2] that the defeat of the colonies would be followed by the triumph of despotism in England.[3]

The ultimate justification for the American Revolution was, to Frenchmen, that right of resistance to oppression which they generally held to be a constitutional right of Englishmen. But what did oppression in this case mean? It meant, first, that the British were disregarding utterly the right of the colonists to self-taxation, another constitutional right,[4] which Frenchmen deduced from Parliament's control over taxation in England and from the premise that the constitutional law that applied in the realm applied also in the colonies. Secondly, it meant that British policy regarding colonial trade was oppressive. Exponents of laissez-faire economics held that there was a natural right of free trade, deduced

---

[1] *Notre gloire ou nos rêves* [posthumous; written about 1779], in *Collection complète des oeuvres de l'abbé de Mably* (15 vols.; Paris, 1794-95), XIII, 377-78; *Observations sur le gouvernement et les lois des États-Unis d'Amérique* [first published in 1784], *ibid.*, VIII, 350, 422. Cf. the anonymous pamphlet *Exposé des droits des colonies britanniques, pour justifier le projet de leur indépendance* (Amsterdam, 1776), pp. 1-10.

[2] Turgot for one regarded it as unlikely. See his *Réflexions rédigées à l'occasion d'un mémoire remis par de Vergennes au Roi sur la manière dont la France et l'Espagne doivent envisager les suites de la querelle entre la Grande-Bretagne et ses colonies, 6 avril* [1776], in Gustave Schelle (ed.), *Oeuvres de Turgot et documents le concernant avec biographie et notes* (5 vols.; Paris, 1913-23), V, 386-87.

[3] Anon., *Exposé des droits des colonies britanniques*, p. 17; *Affaires de l'Angleterre et de l'Amérique*, III, No. 11 [1776], p. 7; *Mercure de France*, Jan. 6, 1781, p. 23; [Comte de Mirabeau], *Des lettres de cachet et des prisons d'état. Ouvrage posthume* [sic] *composé en 1778* (2 vols.; Hamburg, 1782), I, 211-22; Abbé Morellet to Lord Shelburne, April 22, 1782, in Lord Edmond Fitzmaurice (ed.), *Lettres de l'abbé Morellet de l'Académie française à Lord Shelburne depuis marquis de Lansdowne, 1772-1803* (Paris, 1898), p. 191.

[4] This idea underlies generally the comments in the French sources on the American Revolution.

by them from the natural right of property, which Britain's monopolistic colonial policy completely contradicted.[5] However, one did not have to believe in a natural right of free trade in order to find economic justice in the colonial rebellion. One could simply hold that Britain's colonial policy was, if not precisely wrong in principle, oppressive in application. This seems to have been the sense of many rather vague references to the tyranny of England over her colonies.

When viewed as an instance of resistance to a monopolistic commercial policy, the American Revolution frequently underwent a subtle change of aspect. From being essentially a civil war it became, at this point, almost an international war, another in the long series that English avarice, or "jealousy of trade," had engendered. In this case the villain in the piece was not just the king, or the ministry, or the court party, but the entire English nation. Frenchmen did not usually espouse one or the other view of the American Revolution exclusively but adopted both, passing back and forth between them easily.

It should perhaps be pointed out that the case of the Americans was not regarded as an isolated phenomenon in the British Empire. For some time prior to the American Revolution French critics of the English had been citing the existence of misgovernment and oppression, both economic and religious, in Ireland;[6] and after the rebellion in America began, Irish affairs commanded still more attention. Frenchmen knew that Irish reformers were demanding free trade, the removal of religious disabilities, and legislative independence, and that these demands were being supported, from 1778, by an armed volunteer organization among the Irish.[7]

---

[5] Marquis de Chastellux, *De la félicité publique, ou Considérations sur le sort des hommes dans les différentes époques de l'histoire* (new ed. [first published in 1772]; 2 vols.; Paris, 1822), II, 203-5; Morellet to Lord Shelburne, Nov. 26, 1774, *Lettres de l'abbé Morellet . . . à Lord Shelburne*, p. 51; Morellet to the same, March 12, 1776, *ibid.*, p. 103; [J.-P. Brissot de Warville], *L'Indépendance des Anglo-Américains démontrée utile a la Grande-Bretagne. Lettres extraits du Journal d'agriculture, avril et may 1782* (n.p., n.d.), pp. 19-21; *L'Année littéraire*, 1781, V, 291-92; [Baron de Sainte-Croix], *Observations sur le traité de paix conclu à Paris le 10 février 1763 . . . relativement aux intérêts de ces puissances dans la guerre présente* (Amsterdam, 1780), pp. 269-70.

[6] See above, p. 59.

[7] Morellet to Shelburne, June 1, 1779, in *Lettres de l'abbé Morellet . . . à Lord Shelburne*, p. 153; *Annales de Linguet*, VII (1779), 115-17; *Gazette de France*, 1779, p. 95; *ibid.*, 1780, p. 49; *Journal de Genève*, 1779, II, 339; *ibid.*,

Pro-American propagandists in France used the parallel between Ireland and America to strengthen Anglophobe feeling and to help spread the idea that England was really in a very weak position.[8] In India, too, French publicists called attention to oppression and revolt which they thought traceable fundamentally to the characteristic rapacity of the English.[9] But Ireland and India were much overshadowed in interest by America.

In 1778 the French government joined forces with the revolted colonies, and all the indications are that the ensuing War of American Independence was popular in France. Why? Bernard Faÿ, who has written what is to date the most comprehensive and also probably the most influential study of French opinion regarding the American Revolution, holds that the reason is to be found in the existence of a revolutionary spirit—presumably, a spirit of liberal ideals—then sweeping through French society.[10] The classic legend of the youthful Marquis de Lafayette's joining the Americans as a knight-errant of liberty fitted nicely into this thesis. But that legend has since been destroyed: the truth is simply that Lafayette was avid for a military career and that he fervently hated the English.[11] To the present writer it appears that most Frenchmen were reacting to the American war from a similar emotional bias, that their enthusiasm for intervention in American affairs was less an expression of predilection for the cause of civil and political liberty than it was an indication of nationalist sentiments—that, as the Abbé Morellet put it at the time, many of the partisans of America at Paris were not so much friends of Ameri-

---

IV, 259; *Journal politique de Bruxelles*, Jan. 1, 1780, p. 10. The last-named publication had become the political section of the *Mercure de France* in June, 1778. It was, at least as early as June, 1779, under the same editorship, that of Dubois-Fontanelle, as the *Journal de Genève*, although the texts of the two journals were not identical.

[8] *Affaires de l'Angleterre et de l'Amérique*, X, Part I, pp. xxx, clxii-clxxi [1778]; *ibid.*, XIII, clxxxv-clxxxix [1779]; *ibid.*, XIV, cx-cxi, ccxxxii-ccxxxiii [1779].

[9] [Comte de Mirabeau], *Essai sur le despotisme* (2d ed.; London, 1776 [1st ed. 1775]), p. 19; *Annales de Linguet*, I (1777), 277-78; *Gazette de France*, May 11, 1781, p. 170.

[10] Bernard Faÿ, *The Revolutionary Spirit in France and America. A Study of Moral and Intellectual Relations between France and America at the End of the Eighteenth Century*, trans. Ramon Guthrie (New York [1927]), pp. 3-104.

[11] Louis Gottschalk, *Lafayette Comes to America* (Chicago [1935]), p. viii *et passim*.

can liberty as they were enemies of Great Britain.¹² Morellet, writing to an English friend, Lord Shelburne, may even have been politely understating his observation.

There was certainly, among all save the most Anglophile Frenchmen, a strong feeling that it would be salutary if the "haughty islanders" were humbled. In regarding the American Revolution as a trade war the French had identified the cause of the Americans with their own quarrel against England. It was their belief that the British Acts of Trade and Navigation (which they generally referred to as "the Navigation Act") were injurious to the rights not only of the Americans but of other nations, including themselves, and that the rules of international maritime law upheld by the British navy constituted a list of palpable injustices against which all other states should protest. France appeared to them to be a nonimperialistic power with a mission to defend the rights of men and peoples against aggression. This concept of a mission was suffused with the idea of liberty. In this case, however, liberty meant chiefly, not civil or political liberty, but what was called "the freedom of the seas." In the twentieth century that phrase signifies merely certain rules of international maritime law designed to favor neutrals against belligerents. In eighteenth-century France it meant this and more, namely, the destruction of the whole maritime commercial superiority of the English nation.

M. Faÿ indeed notices at the beginning of his discussion of the subject of French opinion of the American Revolution that Frenchmen were smarting under the humiliation of the defeat of 1763, but he later seems to lose sight of such nationalist anti-English feeling and writes only of "revolutionary" feeling.¹³ Apparently he has failed to distinguish between the uses of the term "liberty" in the sources—between the use which meant civil and political liberty and that which meant the freedom of the seas. No doubt this confusion of the issues is the cause, at least in part, of his overrating of liberalism as a motive for French intervention in the American Revolution and his minimizing of the weight and

---

[12] Morellet to Shelburne, Jan. 5, 1777, in *Lettres de l'abbé Morellet . . . à Lord Shelburne*, p. 110.
[13] Faÿ, *The Revolutionary Spirit in France and America*, pp. 3-104.

misinterpretation of the significance of conservative opinion at that juncture. If the distinction in the uses of the term "liberty" is observed, it will be seen that among the supporters of the War of American Independence the conservatives were by no means negligible.

The bulk of articulate conservative opinion seems to have favored intervention,[14] and few advocates of the freedom of the seas were more ardent than conservative interventionists.[15] There were, of course, dissenters, like the editor of the *Journal historique et littéraire*, who declared that if this revolution were condoned, all lawful government would be endangered. He was not pro-British, though. "It is said," he announced, "that people want to humiliate England. Good! If those haughty islanders abuse their power with regard to an independent nation, I can approve of that nation's vengeance . . . but, without disavowing the morality I profess, I cannot desire that rebels should exist or be successful."[16] Propaganda obviously inspired by British sources made its appeal to scruples like these, while it implied that, logically,

[14] Anglophile conservatives like Madame Du Deffand, the friend of Horace Walpole, seem to have been very few in number. See Mme Du Deffand to Horace Walpole, Dec. 29, 1776, in W. S. Lewis and Warren Hunting Smith (eds.), *Horace Walpole's Correspondence with Madame Du Deffand and Wiart* (6 vols.; New Haven, 1939), VI, 385; same to same, March 12, 1777, *ibid.*, p. 417; same to same, Nov. 12, 1777, *ibid.*, p. 492.

[15] M. de Lescure (ed.), *Correspondance secrète, inédite, sur Louis XVI, Marie-Antoinette, la cour et la ville, de 1777 à 1792* (2 vols.; Paris, 1866), I, 60, 74-75, 119, 227, 275 [1777-78]; Vicomte de Grouchy and Paul Cottin (eds.), *Journal inédit du duc de Croÿ 1718-1784* (4 vols.; Paris, 1906-7), IV, 78-79; [P.-A. Caron de Beaumarchais? or C. Guilloton-Beaulieu?], *Influence du despotisme de l'Angleterre sur les deux mondes* (Boston [1780]), *passim;* Madame de Sabran to the Chevalier de Boufflers, April 25 [1778], in E. de Magnieu and Henri Prat (eds.), *Correspondance inédite de la comtesse de Sabran et du chevalier de Boufflers 1778-1788* (Paris, 1875), p. 4; Gilbert, *Ode sur la guerre présente*, quoted in [Métra, J. Imbert, et al.],*Correspondance secrète, politique et littéraire, ou Mémoires pour servir à l'histoire des cours, des sociétés et de la littérature en France, depuis la mort de Louis XV* (18 vols.; London, 1787-89), VII, 134-38 (Nov. 16, 1778); Baron de Sainte Croix, *Observations sur le traité de paix*, pp. 85, 251, and *Histoire des progrès de la puissance navale de l'Angleterre suivie d'observations sur l'acte de navigation, et des pièces justificatives* (2 vols.; Yverdon, 1782), II, 174; *Annales de Linguet*, I (1777), 276-78; *Journal de Genève*, 1775, I, 28-33; *ibid.*, 1776, I, 87-88; *ibid.*, 1779, I, 76-77, 81; *Journal encyclopédique*, 1775, III, 28-29; *Journal politique de Bruxelles*, Jan. 5, 1779, pp. 73-74, 80-81; *ibid.*, Jan. 5, 1782, pp. 2, 10; *Mercure de France*, Oct. 28, 1780, pp. 181-82; *Gazette de France*, 1781, p. 16.

[16] *Journal historique et littéraire*, 1777, II, 418. See also pp. 407-19, *passim*.

French conservatives ought to support the policy of King George III because it represented those forces in English government that made for social and political stability.[17] This argument was answered directly by a pamphleteer who struck the keynote of the typical conservative view:

> I do not confound the constitutions of different states. I distinguish that of the English [from others], and I think with everyone else that the Americans seek only to profit from, or rather to maintain themselves in, the rights it gives them. What I call virtue with them, I should call crime, revolt, in other colonies, if their sovereigns asked only what they have the right to demand according to the constitution of the state. In Spain, in France, and in some other European states the right of taxation belongs to the government; the people have no choice but to obey.[18]

Conservative interventionists *were* concerned lest seditious ideas be encouraged by the participation of France in the American Revolution. Hence they continued to denounce the English constitution (which was also in their eyes the constitution of the colonies), ringing all the familiar changes upon the themes of license, corruption, and chronic instability, of which the colonial revolt itself seemed to be the crowning example, while they contrasted with this sorry condition of things the happy moderation of the French monarchy.[19] But because they wanted to fight

---

[17] [Isaac de Pinto], *Lettre de Mr.***** à Mr. S. B., docteur en mèdicine à Kingston, au sujet des troubles qui agitent actuellement toute l'Amérique septentrionale* (The Hague, 1776), pp. 13-17, 29; *Seconde lettre de M. de Pinto, à l'occasion des troubles des colonies, contenant des réflexions politiques sur les suites de ces troubles, et sur l'état actuel de l'Angleterre* (The Hague, 1776), pp. 7-11.

[18] Anon., *Observations d'un homme impartial sur la Lettre de Mr.***** à Mr. S. B., docteur en médecine à Kingston* . . . (London, 1776), pp. 58-59.

[19] Barbeu-Dubourg, *Calendrier de Philadelphie*, quoted in Métra, *Correspondance secrète*, VI, 19-20 (Feb. 11, 1778); Anon., *Lettre d'un jeune homme à son ami, sur les Français et les Anglais, relativement à la frivolité reprochée aux uns, et la philosophie attribuée aux autres; ou Essai d'un parallèle à faire entre ces deux nations* (Amsterdam, 1779), pp. 28-35, 49, 53, 55; Ange Goudar, *L'Espion françois à Londres, ou Observations critiques sur l'Angleterre et sur les Anglois* (2 vols.; London, 1780), I, 59-60, 134; ibid., II, 9, 183, 201-2; "De l'anglomanie," *Mercure de France*, Nov. 5, 1778, pp. 22-30, reprinted from J.-B.-R. Robinet (ed.), *Dictionnaire universel des sciences morale, économique, politique et diplomatique; ou Bibliothèque de l'homme-d'état et du citoyen* (30 vols.; London, 1777-83), V, 250-54; *Mercure de France*, Nov. 25, 1778, p. 279; *Journal encyclopédique*, 1775, IV, 191-98; ibid., 1779, IV, 456,

England, they persuaded themselves and argued with others that there could be no real inconsistency in their position, and no bad faith on the part of France toward England, if they supported the Americans in the maintenance of rights which were theirs according to the theory of the English constitution itself—rights which, as the *Journal de Genève* pointed out, included that of resistance to oppression.[20] Conservatives were saying the same thing in 1783 when the war had been won and the principles of 1688 (so they thought of the matter) vindicated. One must recognize, said the *Année littéraire*, that there were governments where the doctrine of the sovereignty of the people was fundamental, else one must resolve never to read a page of English history; but one could still do this without prejudice to one's own religious and political convictions.[21]

Apparently, in some cases the very antipathy of conservatives for republican principles made them, not hesitant to aid the Americans, but anxious to do so in order to discredit republican Britain as well as to bring low the imperial rival of France. This was the attitude reflected in the political writing of Beaumarchais, dramatist and Franco-American secret agent, who referred scornfully to "mixed and turbulent governments like the English royal-aristo-democracy."[22] The conservatism of Beaumarchais, the satirist of the nobility, like that of the journalist Linguet, was not social but political.

Sometimes pro-British propagandists undertook to dissuade the French from making an American alliance on the ground that America, once independent, would in time grow powerful enough to dominate the Western Hemisphere and effectually exclude European states therefrom. In attempting to retain her American empire Britain was, they said, acting in the real interest of all

---

463; *Journal de Genève*, 1778, I, 11; *ibid.*, 1781, I, 6-7; *Journal politique de Bruxelles*, Jan. 5, 1779, pp. 84-85; *Annales de Linguet*, V-VII (1779), *passim*; *L'Année littéraire*, 1780, VII, 247-53; *Gazette de France*, June 20, 1780, p. 233. Cf. Queen Marie-Antoinette to the Empress Maria-Theresa, July 13, 1780, quoted in Amédée Britsch, "L'Anglomanie de Philippe Égalité, d'après sa correspondance autographe (1778-1785)," *Le Correspondant*, CCCIII (April 25, 1926), 287-88.
[20] *Journal de Genève*, 1781, I, 8.
[21] *L'Année littéraire*, 1783, VII, 118.
[22] *Observations sur le mémoire justificatif de la cour de Londres* (London and Philadelphia, 1779), p. 15.

European states.[23] This argument did not fall upon entirely barren soil. It appeared in the conservative *Journal historique et littéraire*.[24] It stirred uneasily in the back of the Duc de Croÿ's mind as he recorded in his journal his predominant feeling of satisfaction with the recently concluded Franco-American alliance.[25] It occurred also to the Abbé Galiani,[26] the Parisian-Neapolitan who was the most noteworthy contemporary antagonist of the laissez-faire economists. But it was of too little immediate concern to count for much against the great desideratum to be achieved through the independence of America—the freedom of the seas.

The optimism of conservative opinion at the beginning of the war is reflected in the following quotation taken from a survey of the events of the year 1778 in the *Journal de Genève:*

> England in her days of splendor did not believe that her invasions and conquests must be limited; an immense trade contributed both to her natural pride and to the audacity born of her riches. . . . [Then] finally worn out by her conquests, by her victories if you will, England thought to find in her colonies indemnities and inexhaustible resources, a blind obedience that no vexation or the yoke of the heaviest despotism could alter. We have seen the falsity, the illusion, of this system: her tyranny abhorred, attacked, destroyed!

As for France, the *Journal de Genève* continued:

> . . . she resumes her empire, her former preponderance, or at least returns to the place she should never have forfeited among the first powers of Europe. Her navy . . . rises again. . . . Order and economy today watch over all parts of the government.[27]

There is no need to suppose that such utterances as this were purely official in their inspiration, for the same kind of sentiments had been published long before the government decided to abet the

---

[23] *Seconde lettre de M. de Pinto*, pp. 16-29. Cf. [James Macpherson], *Les Droits de la Grande Bretagne, établis contre les prétentions des Americains. Pour servir de réponse à la déclaration du congrès général*, trans. M. Fréville (The Hague, 1776), p. 62.

[24] *Journal historique et littéraire*, 1777, II, 413-15.

[25] *Journal inédit du duc de Croÿ*, IV, 79.

[26] The Abbé Galiani to Madame d'Épinay, July 25, 1778, in Eugène Asse (ed.), *Lettres de l'abbé Galiani à Madame d'Épinay, Voltaire, Diderot, Grimm, le baron d'Holbach, Morellet, Suard, d'Alembert, Marmontel, la vicomtesse de Belsunce, etc.* (2 vols.; Paris, 1881), I, 322.

[27] *Journal de Genève*, 1779, I, 76-77, 81.

Americans' revolt. Moreover, this and other similar expressions of opinion have the tone of spontaneity, while all kinds of sources bear witness to the prevalence of such feelings of pride and rejoicing among conservatives.

But what of liberal opinion? How did the liberals regard the proposed intervention of France in the affairs of the Americans? They might not unnaturally be expected to have favored it almost to a man, yet this was not the case. Among the opponents of intervention were Anglophiles who, continuing to extol England as the palladium of civil and political liberty and refusing to believe that her government and economy were about to collapse, declined to see even in her imperialism a sufficient reason for fighting her and showed no sympathy at all for the Americans.[28] Although most Anglophiles did sympathize with the Americans, they did so only to a degree. They were partisans of the Americans in the sense in which they were partisans of the Whigs in England. They frequently had reservations about both the desirability of American independence and French intervention to effect it. For example, the Abbé Morellet, after writing to Lord Shelburne at the beginning of the year 1777 that much of the pro-American sentiment in Paris was really anti-British sentiment, added: "I am very happy to tell you that not every one is so anti-British, that I wish you a great prosperity at the same time that I desire the Americans to be free, and that we [meaning, presumably, the 'philosophers'] are much of this opinion."[29] Morellet did not at first favor independence for the Americans, because he thought that England, shorn of her colonies, would lose weight in European opinion, wherein, for the sake of her free institutions, she ought to be able to command respect.[30] Later, after he had decided that the independence of the colonies was the only feasible solution of the Anglo-American problem, Morellet deplored the

---

[28] [James Rutledge or Rutlidge], *Essais politiques sur l'état actuel de quelques puissances* (London, 1777), *passim* (on Rutledge, see chap. ii, n. 8); [Abbé G.-F. Coyer], *Nouvelles observations sur l'Angleterre par un voyageur* (Paris, 1779), p. 53 *et passim*; [Louis-Sébastien Mercier], *Tableau de Paris* (new ed.; 4 vols.; Amsterdam, 1782-83 [first ed. 1781]), I, 34, 286-87; *ibid.*, II, 62, 193-94, 206; *ibid.*, III, 179-80, 223.

[29] Morellet to Shelburne, Jan. 5, 1777, *Lettres de l'abbé Morellet . . . à Lord Shelburne*, p. 110.

[30] Morellet to Shelburne, Sept. 4, 1775, *ibid.*, p. 83.

fighting of an Anglo-French war to bring it about. He wrote of the "villainous national hatreds" such a war would arouse.³¹ The Anglophile Voltaire, who was inclined to pacifism, said that he was "disappointed . . . that the inhabitants of Pennsylvania [i.e., the Quakers] should today be denying their [Quaker] principles by raising troops against their mother country."³² Besides, Voltaire did not think that France was in a position to win a maritime war against her rival.³³

When Anglophiles became interventionists, they were motivated, not by their liberalism, but by their desire to establish the freedom of the seas. How mixed their feelings on the subject of the war might be is well illustrated in the words of Michel Servan, a lawyer and publicist who had continually praised English jurisprudence. "Abandon the empire of the seas," he exclaimed, apostrophizing England, "if to achieve it means to redden them with men's blood, and content yourself with the honor of your laws, which conserve it. Proud nation! If you wish to humiliate us, say only, 'My laws have saved innocent men whom yours would have assassinated.' "³⁴ The sentiments of Anglophiles to whom the freedom of the seas could be the only justification of the war against England are likewise evident in the following example of contemporary political versification:

> Le monde d'elle seule [France] attend sa délivrance,
> Peuple digne en effet de vaincre les Anglois,
> Livrez-vous tout entier à ces nobles projets,
> Rendez l'Océan libre aux peuples de la terre,
> Et si vous triomphez, respectez l'Angleterre;
> La liberté, les loix, les vertus, les talents,
> N'y sont point opprimés sous d'absurdes tyrans:
> Modèle des États, l'Europe la contemple,
> L'Univers a besoin de l'avoir en exemple.

---

³¹ Morellet to Shelburne, June 1, 1779, *ibid.*, p. 152; July 14, 1779, *ibid.*, p. 158.
³² Voltaire to M. d'Oigny du Ponceau, Oct. 12 [1775], in *Oeuvres complètes de Voltaire* (new ed.; 52 vols.; Paris, 1877-85), XLIX, 406.
³³ Voltaire to Frederick II, April [1777], *ibid.*, L, 221.
³⁴ *Réflexions sur quelques points de nos lois, à l'occasion d'un événement important* [first published in 1781], in X. de Portets (ed.), *Oeuvres choisies de Servan* (new ed.; 5 vols.; Paris, 1822), II, 169.

Louons-la; mais forçons ses citoyens si fiers,
De perdre l'Amérique et le sceptre des mers.[35]

(The world awaits its deliverance from her [France] alone. People worthy indeed of conquering the English, devote yourself with a whole heart to these noble purposes; make the ocean free to the peoples of the earth, and if you are victorious, spare England. Liberty, law, virtue, talent are not there oppressed under absurd tyrants. Model of states, Europe contemplates her; the universe has need of her for an example. Let us praise her; but let us compel her proud citizens to give up America and the rule of the seas.)

As for the *frondeur* nobility at this juncture, their liberalism was, according to the Comte de Ségur, its principal contemporary historian, very vague, very much subordinated to the desire of winning military glory and of fighting the English,[36] with whom the nobility, as the traditional military class, had a score to settle. The *frondeur* viewpoint regarding the War of American Independence is reflected in some other contemporary political verses:

> Bravo, Messieurs les Insurgens,
> Vainqueurs dans une juste guerre,
> Vous donnez par vos sentimens
> Un peuple de plus à la terre;
> Fermes, courageux, patiens,
> Doués d'une franchise altière,
> Libres sur-tout! . . . Voilà mes gens.
> Aprés des exploits éclatans,
> Il faudroit un jour, pour bien faire,
> Envoyer danser vos enfans
> Sur les débris de l'Angleterre.
> Apprenez bien aux nations,
> Qu'il en est une qui méprise
> Les despotes pales et blonds,
> Respirant le feu des charbons
> Et les brouillards de la Tamise.
> Viendra le temps qu'avec éclat,
> Vous renverserez les tribunes

---

[35] Gudin de la Brunellerie, "Épître à mon ami Mr. de Beaumarchais," *Courier de l'Europe*, IV, No. 33 (Oct. 23, 1778), p. 266.

[36] *Mémoires ou Souvenirs et anecdotes* (3d ed.; 3 vols.; Paris, 1827), I, 77-79, 104, 106, 131.

De ces marchands, hommes d'état,
Petits Consuls dans les Communes.[37]

(Bravo, insurrectionists, victors in a just war! Your [noble] sentiments have given the earth yet another people. Firm, courageous, long-suffering, endowed with a proud frankness, bold above all! ... You are the men for me. Some day, to fulfil your brilliant deeds, you must send your children to dance on the ruins of England. Show the nations that there is one of them which despises the pale, fair-haired despots who breathe coal-smoke and the fogs of the Thames. The time will come when with a loud crash you will tear down the tribunes of these merchants, these statesmen, these insignificant commercial magistrates in the Commons.)

A much-diluted political liberalism, an aristocratic contempt for a "nation of tradesmen," and the sentiment of revenge which the thought of the military and naval successes of that nation inspired—these are the feelings revealed in the lines just quoted.

The liberals who did not regard England as the source of their political inspiration were likewise divided in their attitude toward the war. Mably and Turgot were among those who held that France ought not to intervene in the affairs of the Americans. They believed in the justice of the American cause on every count, but they were of the opinion, which was in fact quite widely held,[38] that America was destined to become independent later if not sooner, and regardless of the policy France adopted. This belief was associated in Turgot's mind with a theory of progress envisioning a total world revolution in commercial policy.[39] Mably's calculations were based upon the more usual notion of the top-heaviness of the British Empire and the progressive decay of English political virtue and power.[40] In either case, however, why

---

[37] "Aux Insurgens: salut," Métra, *Correspondance secrète*, VI, 7 (Feb. 7, 1778).

[38] *Seconde lettre de M. de Pinto*, p. 16; Anon., *Exposé des droits des colonies britanniques*, Letter I, p. 18; *Journal politique de Bruxelles*, 1777, I, 6; *ibid.*, Jan. 5, 1779, p. 73; *L'Année littéraire*, 1780, VII, 262-63. See also nn. 39 and 40, following.

[39] *Réflexions rédigées à l'occasion d'un mémoire . . . de Vergennes*, in *Oeuvres de Turgot*, V, 385-86, 390-91.

[40] *De l'étude de l'histoire, à monseigneur le prince de Parme* [first published about 1775], in *Oeuvres*, XII, 238-40; *De l'étude de la politique* [posthumous; written about 1775-77], *ibid.*, XIII, 130-31; *Notre gloire ou nos rêves*, *ibid.*, p. 377.

should France waste her strength and her livelihood in a war with England to bring about what was going to happen anyway? Turgot also argued that even if England did temporarily reconquer her colonies France would profit, since her rival would thereafter be so engrossed with the problem of maintaining her authority in America that she could not spare any attention for Europe, where there would be a long period of peace.[41] Mably belonged to the school which thought that France's proper sphere of action was not the sea, where a war for the independence of America would be fought, but the continent of Europe: France was properly a continental power.[42] Thus the attitude of Mably and Turgot toward the American Revolution was influenced primarily by their conception of the national advantage; but they interpreted national advantage to mean neutrality rather than, as most people saw it, intervention. Their liberalism did not conflict with this view but actually supported it after a fashion. That is, being reformers, they were not so sanguine as the conservatives about the immediate condition of the country, which a war would certainly not improve.

The Anglophobe liberals who did favor intervention favored it in part because of their liberalism. They thought that France, by helping the Americans to recover the civil and political liberties which as Englishmen they were supposed rightly to have possessed, would advance the cause of liberty in general. The future Girondin Brissot, who made his journalistic debut at the time of the American Revolution,[43] belonged to this group. Although a great admirer of the civil liberty that he discovered in England,[44] Brissot thought that political liberty was in decay there;[45] and since he set a great value upon political liberty, he was enthusiastically pro-American. The Comte de Mirabeau, son of the Physiocratic marquis of that name, evinced a similar attitude. The views of this future champion of the royal prerogative in the Constituent

---

[41] Turgot, *Réflexions rédigées à l'occasion d'un mémoire . . . de Vergennes*, in *Oeuvres de Turgot*, V, 390, 404-15; Turgot to Dupont, Sept. 27 [1776], *ibid.*, p. 505.

[42] Mably, *Notre gloire ou nos rêves*, in *Oeuvres*, XIII, 377.

[43] As a pamphleteer and as one of the editors of the *Courier de l'Europe*.

[44] J.-P. Brissot de Warville, *Théorie des loix criminelles* (2 vols.; Berlin, 1781), I and II, *passim*; II, 222.

[45] [Brissot], *Testament politique de l'Angleterre* (1780), p. 36; *L'Indépendance des Anglo-Américains*, pp. 28-29.

Assembly were at the time of the American Revolution very "republican," and closer to the liberalism of Mably and of Holbach than to the aristocratic constitutionalism of the *frondeur* nobility, among whom, if he had been more respectable, Mirabeau might perhaps have been numbered. The English, Mirabeau asserted, did not have political liberty to the extent that they had civil liberty, and in the last analysis the two must stand or fall together. He thought that the "sublime resistance" of the Americans might even be the salvation of the English, by showing them that the fine theory of their government was badly applied and that they were in imminent danger of royal despotism. Mirabeau, who was writing from prison, declared that if he had been free he would have been fighting with the Americans.[46]

And yet the interventionist enthusiasm of Brissot and of Mirabeau was based by no means exclusively upon their liberalism. It had another basis in their nationalist hostility toward the English. Mirabeau denounced the latter as implacable tyrants in their relations with peoples outside the realm of England.[47] Brissot published a pamphlet entitled *England's Last Will and Testament (Testament politique de l'Angleterre)* in which he prophesied that France, having embraced the cause of the persecuted colonists, would fall heir to the grandeur of her rival, who was in the last agonies.[48] The tone of another pamphlet, in which Brissot undertook to justify the American rebellion on the ground of an alleged right of freedom of trade, was also very hostile toward the English.[49]

The *Affaires de l'Angleterre et de l'Amérique*, a journal that numbered Benjamin Franklin among its editors,[50] is an interesting example of consciously directed interventionist propaganda. The *Affaires* published in whole or in part such documents as Richard Price's *Observations on the Nature of Civil Liberty*, Thomas Paine's *Common Sense*, the Declaration of Independence, and some of the new American constitutions. M. Faÿ finds that the

[46] *Des lettres de cachet*, I, 211-12, 260; II, 164, 206-9.
[47] Mirabeau, *Essai sur le despotisme*, p. 19.
[48] *Testament politique de l'Angleterre*, pp. 39, 78.
[49] *L'Indépendance des Anglo-Américains*, pp. 18-21 *et passim*.
[50] Eugène Hatin, *Bibliographie historique et critique de la presse périodique française* . . . (Paris, 1866), p. 74.

chief purpose of the editors in doing this was to exploit liberal opinion.⁵¹ He is perhaps correct. However, his presupposition that an appeal to public opinion to support intervention could have been made only to the liberals apparently prevents him from discerning the broader basis of the journal's strategy. While presenting material to excite the liberals, the *Affaires* kept the conservatives in mind, too. (M. Faÿ notes this fact but discounts it.) The tracts by Price and Paine and the Declaration of Independence contained hostile attacks on English government and policy—for instance, Paine's indictment of the government for tyranny, corruption, and disorder⁵²—which in France would go down equally well with liberals and conservatives. Moreover, in presenting these tracts the journal was considerate of conservative prejudices. *Common Sense,* which repudiated the principle of monarchy completely, was accompanied by editorial remarks to the effect that only the principle of hereditary monarchy had enabled England to survive its numerous civil wars.⁵³ The Declaration of Independence was toned down with the following comment: "It is without contradiction the greatest event of the campaign, of the war itself, and perhaps of this century. . . . Happily, such writings and subversions of empire are very infrequent!"⁵⁴ In connection with the American constitutions (the state constitutions, of course), the *Affaires* said that they, like the English constitution, although more perfect in their kind, involved certain basic concepts opposed to the accepted political principles of most civilized peoples, and that the Americans certainly had no idea of insisting on the universal validity of their own principles.⁵⁵

The *Affaires* made its chief positive appeal, however, not on the ground of political ideology but of national feeling, where liberals and conservatives could agree without reservation. It presented persistently the thesis that England was in a sad state as a result of corruption and misgovernment and could not hope to win the war. It documented this contention by reference to the opposition's charges of administrative inefficiency, to the necessity

---

⁵¹ Faÿ, *The Revolutionary Spirit in France and America*, pp. 90-91.
⁵² *Affaires de l'Angleterre et de l'Amérique*, I, No. 4 (June 15, 1776), 35-40.
⁵³ *Ibid.*, p. 40.
⁵⁴ *Ibid.*, II, No. 7 (Aug. 16, 1776), 88.
⁵⁵ *Ibid.*, IV, No. 17 (Feb. 24, 1777), lvi-lvii.

in which the government found itself of hiring foreign mercenaries to do the fighting and of procuring seamen through the barbarous method of impressment, and by reference also to the burden of taxation and the enormous national debt.[56] Then, from the middle of the year 1777, the *Affaires* played up the threat of an Anglo-American reconciliation, which would destroy the alleged unparalleled opportunity for France to end the menace of British sea power. The conjuncture of circumstances at that time was, said the paper, "the most favorable ever given to any nation to increase its own wealth and power while humiliating and weakening the most formidable, the most insolent, and the most inveterate enemy," a moment "such as the most zealous French patriot could hardly have hoped to see come to birth in this century." Characterizing the English as an aggressor people, the *Affaires* asserted that if France did not prevent an Anglo-American reconciliation, she would only find herself at war with England without the advantage of the American alliance. It was not merely the court party in England that wanted war with France, but the entire nation.[57] Finally, the *Affaires* did not neglect to say that the French navy had become very powerful since the end of the Seven Years' War.[58]

Another interventionist publication, appealing similarly to all sorts of sentiments, said that, while Englishmen might perhaps be happier under their government than Frenchmen under theirs, the French had the advantage of their government's being the more powerful because better able effectively to dispose of its forces. For this reason, and because of the fertility of its soil, its large population, and its good system of communications, the international position of France was more favorable than that of England. This tract dwelt at length upon the rivalry of France

---

[56] *Ibid.*, I, No. 1 (May 4, 1776), 3-16, 21-25, 33, 81-103; *ibid.*, No. 2 (May 17, 1776), 65-73; *ibid.*, No. 5, pp. 14, 17; *ibid.*, V, No. 24 (June 28, 1777), clxiv-ccxvii; *ibid.*, VI, No. 28, p. cxx; *ibid.*, IX, Part I [No. 36] (Feb. 21, 1778), pp. i-liv; *ibid.*, No. 37 (March 9-20, 1778), pp. cviii-cxxiii, cxxvi; *ibid.*, XV [No. 76] (Aug. 3, 1779), xxvii.

[57] *Ibid.*, I, No. 1, 17-18; *ibid.*, V, No. 24 (June 28, 1777), ccxxiii-ccxxxviii; *ibid.*, VI, No. 26 (Aug. 14, 1777), i-viii; *ibid.*, VII, No. 32 (Nov. 17, 1777), liii; *ibid.*, IX, Part I [No. 36] (Feb. 21, 1778), xv; *ibid.*, XI [No. 50] (July 12, 1778), lxxxix-xcii; *ibid.*, XV [No. 79] (Sept. 8, 1799), cxlix-ccx.

[58] *Ibid.*, XI [No. 50] (July 12, 1778), xcii.

and England and created a vision of the time when France would be the mightier of the two.[59]

When the interventionist movement is looked at from the angle of its relation to the structure of French society, it is seen to have been—this is abundantly evident—of a general or national rather than a class character. To be sure, the nobility, because of their military tradition and position, were the most conspicuous element in it. "If men of every class among us have taken fire for the American cause," wrote the author of the Métra correspondence, "its most numerous and ardent partisans are among our military men and our seigneurs."[60] But in an entry of a few months later, the same source played up the Anglophobe sentiments of the bourgeoisie, relating an anecdote about "a brave and gallant man, albeit a picture-dealer," who had upheld the honor of his nation against the insults which an Englishman had broadcast in a Parisian café. The picture-dealer had challenged the Englishman to a duel, and, on being informed by the latter that he could not cross swords with one who was not a gentleman, had replied with spirit that "in this country, for such an affair especially, nobility of sentiment is as highly thought of as that of parchment."[61]

Servan, too, testified that nationalist sentiment was strong among commoners. When looking back on the War of American Independence from the vantage ground of 1789 he exclaimed:

> The war we have recently suffered, that abyss of so much money, the greatest cause of our financial disorder and of the evils with which France is now assailed, that war in which we so nobly shared with our allies, leaving them liberty and keeping poverty for ourselves—in short, gentlemen of the Third Estate, who wanted that war, who asked for it? You yourselves, who, in your homes, in your public places, in your cafés and even in your taverns, saw in imagination the whole English navy swallowed up, and drank in long draughts, in advance, the pleasure of vengeance.[62]

According to the journalist Louis-Sébastien Mercier, who

---

[59] Anon., *Coup d'oeil sur la Grande-Bretagne* (London, 1776), pp. 30-37.
[60] Métra, *Correspondance secrète*, V, 350-51 (Dec. 25, 1777).
[61] *Ibid.*, VI, 26-27 (Feb. 16, 1778).
[62] [J.-M.-A. Servan], *Avis salutaire au tiers état; sur ce qu'il fut, ce qu'il est, et ce qu'il peut être. Par un jurisconsulte allobroge* (1789), pp. 30-31.

vividly described the society of Paris at the time of the war, the beau monde and the bourgeoisie were virtually at one in their ideas about the ease with which the English could be defeated, and in their general enthusiasm for the war. Fine ladies talked glibly about the freedom of the seas, he said, while all the cope-makers of the Tuileries and the Luxembourg spoke of nothing but the hoped-for invasion of England.[63]

> In the cafés [said Mercier] one hears people who, the *Gazette de France* in hand, affirm upon the slightest advantage gained that the English people is reduced to extremities. . . . It is a corner grocer who meditates on sugar and coffee who makes these fine prophecies; he will tell them in the evening to his wife, who hates the English because they are heretics.[64]

Thus it appears that the waging of the War of American Independence was primarily the expression of a national sentiment evident among all articulate elements in French opinion save the strongest Anglophile liberals, who were also in general the most notable cosmopolitans. Conceived as a crusade for the freedom of the seas, its ultimate object was the glory of France, for the decline of the imperial tyrant, England, implied the elevation of her rival. The power of France was to be both the instrument and the end of the crusade.

It would seem that M. Faÿ, in overrating the importance of liberalism—his "revolutionary spirit"—as a motive for French intervention in the American Revolution, has not only failed to distinguish between that concept of liberty which appertained to government and that which meant the freedom of the seas, but has also somewhat confused cause and consequence in the relationship between the American Revolution and French liberalism. As contemporaries themselves pointed out[65] (and as some of them

---

[63] Mercier, *Tableau de Paris*, I, 34; III, 182. Cf. [Lally-Tollendal?], *Mémoires de Weber, concernant Marie-Antoinette* . . . , ed. MM. Berville and Barrière ("Collection des mémoires relatifs à la Révolution française," XI-XII; 2 vols.; Paris, 1882), I, 124.

[64] Mercier, *Tableau de Paris*, III, 179.

[65] Lally-Tollendal?, *Mémoires de Weber, concernant Marie-Antoinette*, I, 128-32, 170-72; Dominique-Joseph Garat, *Mémoires historiques sur la vie de M. Suard, sur ses écrits, et sur le XVIIIe siècle* . . . (2 vols.; Paris, 1820), II, 319; Comte de Ségur, *Mémoires ou Souvenirs et anecdotes*, I, 291, and II, 30-31; Prince de Montbarey, *Mémoires autographes* (3 vols.; Paris, 1826-27), III,

indeed had feared), the War of American Independence had the effect of greatly stimulating the growth of liberal ideas among Frenchmen. That is to say, liberal ideas became more general in the following decade than they had been before, and the leadership in liberal opinion passed leftward from the Anglophiles to the Anglophobes. In this period the new, independent America, bound no longer to the iniquities of the old world, and presenting to the admiring eyes of Europeans a social system of antique simplicity, shone with a utopian refulgence.[66] The trains of thought induced in liberals by the American ideal will be discussed at some length in the next chapter. M. Faÿ has apparently read back into the 1770's both that effervescence of revolutionary sentiment that belongs rather to the 1780's and the utopian image of America. Although the latter was in the process of formation from the time of the Declaration of Independence and the publication of the first state constitutions, it had not, when France went to war on behalf of the Americans, taken precedence over the more nearly if not entirely historical concept of America—a land whose laws were English laws and whose destinies had been determined largely by the imperial ambitions of Englishmen.

---

135 ff.; Marquis de Clermont-Gallerande, *Mémoires particuliers pour servir à l'histoire de la révolution qui s'est opérée en France en 1789* (3 vols.; Paris, 1826), I, 10; Comte Valentin Esterhazy, *Mémoires*, ed. Ernest Daudet (Paris, 1905), p. 186; Marquis de Bouillé, *Mémoires du marquis de Bouillé* . . . , ed. MM. Berville and Barrière ("Collection des mémoires relatifs à la Révolution française," XLV; 2nd ed.; Paris, 1822), p. 20; [Jacques Lescène Desmaisons], *Histoire politique de la révolution en France, ou Correspondance entre Lord D*** et Lord T**** (2 vols.; London, 1789), I, 6-7. Cf. Louis Gottschalk, *Lafayette and the Close of the American Revolution* (Chicago [1942]), pp. 420-21.

[66] Robert R. Palmer has discussed America as a symbol on the eve of the Revolution, pointing out its utopian character, in "The French Idea of American Independence on the Eve of the French Revolution" (Unpublished Ph.D. dissertation, Cornell University, 1934).

CHAPTER SIX

ANGLOPHOBIA AND THE FRENCH REVOLUTION

FOLLOWING THE WAR of American Independence there occurred in France, as contemporaries remarked,[1] a revival of Anglomania. This phenomenon distressed conservatives of an absolutist stripe, who, although apparently fewer or less vocal than formerly, had by no means ceased to be articulate. As before, such people continued to regard all liberals as Anglophiles and to see in Anglomania, including the ideal of a limited monarchy, a subversive and essentially republican doctrine. If there was any change at all in their viewpoint, it was in the direction of reaction. To this period belongs one of the most extreme of all conservative statements of belief, a work entitled *Coup d'oeil sur le gouverne-*

[1] [L.-A. de Caraccioli], *Les Entretiens du palais-royal* (2 vols.; Utrecht and Paris, 1787), I, 6-7; Vicomte de Grouchy and Paul Cottin (eds.), *Journal inédit du duc de Croÿ 1718-1784* (4 vols.; Paris, 1906-7), IV, 303; [J.-M.-A. Servan], *Apologie de la Bastille. Pour servir de réponse aux Mémoires de M. Linguet sur la Bastille. . . . Par un homme en pleine campagne* (Kehl and Lausanne, 1784), pp. 53-55; [Jacques Lescène Desmaisons], *Histoire politique de la révolution en France, ou Correspondance entre Lord D*** et Lord T**** (2 vols.; London, 1789), I, 6-10; Marquis de Condorcet, *Lettres d'un bourgeois de New-Haven* [usually written "New-Heaven"] *à un citoyen de Virginie, sur l'inutilité de partager le pouvoir législatif entre plusieurs corps* (1787), in A. Condorcet O'Connor and M. F. Arago (eds.), *Oeuvres de Condorcet* (12 vols.; Paris, 1847-49), IX, 75; [P.-S. Dupont de Nemours], *Lettre à la chambre du commerce de Normandie; sur le mémoire qu'elle a publié relativement au traité de commerce avec l'Angleterre* (Rouen and Paris, 1788), p. 248; Jean-Paul Marat to the President of the Estates-General, Aug. 23, 1789, in Charles Vellay (ed.), *La Correspondance de Marat* (Paris, 1908), p. 100; Comte de Ségur, *Mémoires ou Souvenirs et anecdotes* (3d ed.; 3 vols.; Paris, 1827), II, 30-31; Chateaubriand, *Mémoires d'outre-tombe*, quoted in Alphonse Aulard, *The French Revolution, a Political History*, trans. Bernard Miall (4 vols.; New York, 1910), I, 113 n.; Dominique-Joseph Garat, *Mémoires historiques sur la vie de M. Suard, sur ses écrits, et sur le XVIIIe siècle* (2 vols.; Paris, 1820), II, 319; *L'Année littéraire*, 1787, II, 83.

ment anglois, by the Abbé Dubois de Launay, who declared that old laws, although imperfect, were preferable to newer and wiser ones, and that the greatest vice of the English was love of novelty.² The *Année littéraire*, while unable to be quite so reactionary as this, nevertheless found Dubois de Launay's book on the whole sound and useful. Said this journal:

> It is truly patriotic to contribute, by the comparison [of governments], reasons additional to those all of us have for blessing the government under which we live. It is important for the tranquillity of the state that its subjects should obey it with love and joy, as they will never do if their prejudiced imagination continually envisages a neighboring people as being happier and better governed.... Anglomania having repaired its losses, as the author says, since the close of the war [the War of American Independence], it is important to see that ignorance does not add credit to the invidious comparisons between our regime and that of our neighbors which one hears daily.³

There were also less immoderate expressions of hostility to the example of the English. Enlightened conservatives might admit now, as they had done previously, that England had in certain respects a good administration.⁴ However, they would not admit that the English constitution was anything but incompatible with that *summum bonum*, the public tranquillity.⁵

One of the first targets of conservative snipers during the decade of the 1780's was the banker Necker, who in 1781, as director-general of the finances, published the first treasury statement in French history, the famous *Compte rendu au roi*. Rightly or wrongly, Necker inspired more confidence among sympathizers of reform than any other man then in public life, and conversely he was hated by many conservatives from either personal (as in the

---

² Abbé Dubois de Launay, *Coup d'oeil sur le gouvernement anglois* (1786), pp. 36-37.
³ *L'Année littéraire*, 1787, II, 73, 83.
⁴ [François-René] Turpin, *Histoire des révolutions d'Angleterre, pour servir de suite à celles du père d'Orléans* (new ed.; 2 vols.; Paris, 1793 [1st ed., 1786]), I, xl.
⁵ *Ibid.*, xxxiii-xxxix; Caraccioli, *Les Entretiens du palais-royal*, I, 9-10, 27-28; [Dusaulx], *Observations sur l'histoire de la Bastille, publiée par M. Linguet, avec des remarques sur le caractere de l'auteur, suivies de quelques notes sur sa maniere d'écrire l'histoire politique, civile et littéraire* (London, 1783), pp. 115-17 *et passim*; [Gabriel Sénac de Meilhan], *Considérations sur l'esprit et les moeurs* (London, 1787), pp. 102-3, 159.

case of courtiers who lived on government pensions) or general motives. Necker's enemies had accused him of deferring to the interest of English banking connections during his incumbency as director-general and while the American war was in progress. Although a recent biographer thinks there may have been something in it, the charge could not be substantiated.[6] Nevertheless, Necker was open to attack on the score of being Anglophile in another sense, in regard to his ideas about government. Even before the American Revolution he had praised the representative institutions of the English.[7] Now he was taken to task for his assertion in the *Compte rendu* that public knowledge of the government's financial position was one of the chief reasons for the strength of the credit of the English government.[8] Necker's purpose in publishing the *Compte rendu* was, of course, to strengthen the credit of the French government, and incidentally to justify his own administration. In both he succeeded, at least temporarily, for the statement gave the impression of a surplus where there was in reality a deficit. Necker's enemies declared, however, that the principle of the reference of these matters to the public was subversive of the monarchy itself, that Necker, by his parallels with England, was seeking to inspire a preference for English forms of government, and that in any case the *Compte rendu* and other such statements could not have the same effect in France as a financial report presented by the English ministry to Parliament. For, by the nature of the government in France, the nation was not in a position to control the treasury, and, if permitted to scrutinize the government's accounts, would be disturbed by fears and suspicions which, not being put at rest, would jeopardize the public tranquillity.[9]

[6] E. Lavaquery, *Necker fourrier de la Révolution 1732-1804* (Paris [1933]), pp. 181-84.

[7] *Éloge de Jean-Baptiste Colbert; discours qui a remporté le prix de l'Académie françoise en 1773*, in Baron de Staël (ed.), *Oeuvres complètes de M. Necker* (15 vols.; Paris, 1820-21), XV, 83-84, 119; *Sur la législation et le commerce des grains* (Paris, 1775), *ibid.*, I, 131-34.

[8] *Compte rendu au roi*, *ibid.*, II, 3.

[9] [De Coppons], *Observations sur le Compte rendu au roi par M. Necker, directeur général des finances, au mois de janvier 1781*, in *Critique de la théorie et pratique de M. Necker, dans l'administration des finances de la France* (2 vols.; 1785), I, 32-33; Bourboulon [pseud.?], *Réponse du sieur Bourboulon, officier employé dans les finances de Mgr. le comte d'Artois, au Compte rendu au roi, par*

In his treatise on government finance, *De l'administration des finances de la France*, published a few years after the *Compte rendu*, Necker repeated not only the views of the last-named work on the relation between politics and credit,[10] but also the idea, which he had published in the preceding decade, that the well-being of the English people was, like the credit of the government, attributable to their representative institutions.[11] His critics countered with the question, What was the advantage of a national assembly in view of the fact (as it was generally taken to be) that the per capita debt in England was so much greater than it was in France,[12] and why was the poor tax so enormous in England if the people were as happy as he said they were?[13]

Most conservative publicists, moreover, strongly disapproved of Necker's policy of extensive borrowing. Here they again accused him of taking England for his model and of seeking thereby to foster attitudes hostile to the monarchy, besides encouraging the propagation of an undesirable race of stockjobbers. According to these publicists, too, the capitalists who held the state's obligations were threatening both to dictate national policy and, in alliance with English capitalists, to pursue measures harmful to the welfare of their own country.[14]

About the same time as this attack upon Necker, during the first half of the decade, ultraconservative apologists took up their pens against reformers of judicial procedure who looked to England for their model and who had just secured the partial abolition of the use of torture. One Boucher d'Argis, a magistrate at the court of the Châtelet in Paris, conceded that the rigor and complexity of the criminal law needed to be modified but took a strong

---

M. Necker, *directeur général des finances* (London, 1781), p. 15; Vergennes, quoted in Marcel Marion, *Histoire financière de la France depuis 1715* (6 vols.; Paris, 1914-31), I, 330 n.

[10] *De l'administration des finances de la France* (1784), *Oeuvres*, V, 448.

[11] *Ibid.*, IV, 165-70.

[12] [De Coppons], *Réponse au livre de M. Necker, sur l'administration des finances de la France*, in *Critique de la théorie et pratique de M. Necker*, II, 127-28.

[13] [Comte de Dubuat-Nançay], *Remarques d'un Français, ou Examen impartial du livre de M. Necker sur l'administration des finances de la France, pour servir de correctif et de supplément à son ouvrage* (Geneva, 1785), p. 153.

[14] *Ibid.*, pp. 168-76; De Coppons, *Observations sur le Compte rendu au roi*, in *Critique de la théorie et pratique de M. Necker*, I, 30-31; Anon., *Les Francs* (1785), pp. 1, 31-32.

stand against public trials. Public criminal trials, he said, would only injure the reputation of the defendant, lead to the intimidation of the judges, and permit the escape of accomplices.[15] The jurist was provoked to the point of writing the following burst of Anglophobe rhetoric:

> Must we always elevate a rival nation above our own country and, because an abuse has there been consecrated by long usage, set it up as a work of wisdom? Has reason located her empire only on the banks of the Thames? It seems that Anglomania today is extended over all things alike; this taste for a foreign fashion has advanced by degrees from dress to customs *(moeurs)* and from customs to laws. . . . Let us leave in England her principles and customs. The multitude of crimes that are committed there with such frequent impunity ought to prevent us from praising or adopting her practices.[16]

In reviewing this work the *Mercure de France,* which at this time tended to be both "philosophic" in intellectual matters and quite conservative in politics, took exception to the author's stand regarding publicity of trials, but otherwise thought that his book could be read with interest and profit.[17]

In the latter half of the decade there occurred a war of pamphlets between absolutist conservatives and the partisans of the parlements reminiscent of the contest between the same adversaries at the end of the reign of Louis XV and the beginning of that of Louis XVI. Indeed, some of the literature published in connection with the earlier controvery was dusted off and reissued during the later one.[18] The events that were the basis of the controversy were, in brief, as follows: During August, 1787, the Parlement of Paris successfully resisted certain edicts that would have destroyed the financial immunity of the privileged classes, affirming that such taxes could only be levied by the Estates-General of the kingdom. The government, to meet its immediate needs in the face of threatening bankruptcy, determined to float a large

---

[15] [A.-J.] Boucher d'Argis, *Observations sur les loix criminelles de France* (Amsterdam and Paris, 1781), pp. 63-68.

[16] *Ibid.,* pp. 56-62, 69.

[17] *Mercure de France,* May 11, 1782, pp. 78-88.

[18] [Saige], *Catéchisme du citoyen, ou Elémens du droit public françois, par demandes et réponses; suivi de Fragmens politiques par le même auteur* ("En France," 1788). First published in 1775; see above, chap. i, p. 14 n. 13.

loan. To circumvent the resistance it expected from the Parlement, it resorted to a summary procedure of registration which amounted to a *lit de justice,* the king being present and registration ordered without a vote being taken. The conflict, in which the Parlement of Paris was supported by the other sovereign courts as well as all other opponents of absolute monarchy, only increased in bitterness. Following an attempt of the parlements to sabotage the collection of taxes, the ministry, in a *lit de justice* of May 8, 1788, instituted a reorganization of the judicial system resembling the Maupeou reform of 1771: the parlements were deprived of their right of registration, which was conferred instead upon a plenary court of royal appointees, and lost a good part of their strictly judicial business, too. The ensuing agitation throughout the country caused the suspension of justice. All dissatisfied parties for the moment combined with the parlementarians. Revolts occurred in several provinces, some in defense of local privilege, others in advocacy of general and fundamental reforms. The government, whose financial position had become yet more desperate, retreated. After announcing (August 8, 1788) that the Estates-General would meet during the following May, it recalled Necker to the ministry and on his advice restored their former functions to the parlements, which resumed them with all their former pretensions.[19]

The pamphlets that defended the government in this controversy accused the parlements of Anglomania, less because the latter had demanded the convocation of the Estates-General than because they obviously desired to play a prominent political role themselves. They were again, as in 1770 and 1771, said to be trying to imitate the English Parliament. The generality of progovernment pamphlets set forth the familiar conservative arguments: the English form of government would bring political instability,

---

[19] A. Esmein, *Cours élémentaire d'histoire du droit français à l'usage des étudiants de première année,* ed. R. Génestal (15th ed.; Paris, 1925), pp. 525-27; E. Glasson, *Le Parlement de Paris. Son rôle politique depuis le règne de Charles VII jusqu'à la Révolution* (2 vols.; Paris, 1901), II, 470-85; H. Carré, P. Sagnac, and E. Lavisse, *La Règne de Louis XVI (1774-1789),* in *Histoire de France depuis les origines jusqu'à la Révolution,* ed. Ernest Lavisse (9 vols.; Paris, 1900-[1911]), IX, Part I, 336-64; Albert Mathiez, *The French Revolution,* trans. Catherine Alison Phillips (New York, 1928), pp. 24-33.

and in any case it was not appropriate to France.[20] The absolute monarchy, in other words, was the best defense of the *status quo*, and if the privileged orders deserted it, they would be sorry in the end. A minor note was sounded, however, in a progovernment pamphlet by Linguet, addressed, not to those who believed privilege natural to a monarchy, but to the opponents of privilege. According to Linguet, Anglomania was to be deprecated because it put a false valuation on the acts of the parlements, which, though ostensibly speaking for the nation, were *corps intermédiaires* in the sense used by Montesquieu. In England there were no *corps intermédiaires* of any kind.[21] During a sojourn in the Bastille, Linguet had changed his mind[22] about the composition of English society and government and no longer asserted, as he once had,[23] that they were controlled by a tyrannical aristocracy.

With the restoration of the parlements to the position they had occupied before the *lit de justice* of May 8, general interest shifted from the affairs of the magistracy to the impending meeting of the Estates-General. Indeed, the appearance of the Estates-General deprived the parlements of most of their political importance. But even when the ultraconservatives foresaw this result, they took small comfort in the prospect, for, as a commentator close to the royal court prophesied, one needed only to read English history to see how far the Estates-General would carry their attack on the crown's authority.[24] With such forebodings Moreau, the official historiographer of France and long a mouthpiece of clerical conservatism, protested to the keeper of the seals, Lamoignon, in the name of "that ancient constitution which people wanted

---

[20] [Ange Goudar], *L'Autorité des rois de France est indépendante de tout corps politique; elle étoit établie avant que les parlemens fussent créés* (Amsterdam, 1788), pp. 67-68 *et passim*; Anon., *Je m'en rapporte à toute le monde, ou Réflexions impartiales sur les affaires actuelles* (London, 1788), pp. 71-74, 93-94.

[21] *La France plus qu'angloise, ou, Comparaison entre la procédure entamée à Paris le 25 septembre 1788 contre les ministres du roi de France, et le procès intenté à Londres en 1640, au comte de Strafford, principal ministre de Charles premier, roi d'Angleterre. Avec des réflexions sur le danger imminent dont les entreprises de la robe menaçent la nation, et les particuliers* (2d ed.; Brussels, 1788), pp. 114-22, 140, *et passim*.

[22] *Annales de Linguet*, XI (1784), 68-187.

[23] See above, p. 23.

[24] M. de Lescure (ed.), *Correspondance secrète, inédite, sur Louis XVI, Marie-Antoinette, la cour et la ville, de 1777 à 1792* (2 vols.; Paris, 1866), II, 248 (April 20, 1788). Cf. *ibid.*, pp. 318 (Jan. 3, 1789), 335 (March 6, 1789).

to destroy because it was not the great charter of England,"[25] that the government's strategy was ruining the monarchy. Clearly, to Moreau the example of England was both a warning and the source of the mischief that was abroad in the land.

But once the decision to summon the Estates had been taken, all that the ultraconservatives could do was to throw their weight behind the preservation of the traditional organization of that body, according to which voting went by order with unanimity of the three orders required to secure the enactment of a measure. In December, 1788, the government conceded the demand of the Third Estate for a representation equal to that of the First and Second Estates together, but did not pronounce upon the Third Estate's corollary demand for vote by head. Since it was expected that the representatives of each of the first two estates would contain a liberal minority, vote by head would give the program of the Third Estate a numerical preponderance. This issue was fought out in the press for months before the Estates-General convened. Extreme conservative publicists attributed the Third Estate's demand for preponderance to the influence of Anglophile ideas.[26] To them, Anglomania remained, even in 1789, republican and egalitarian, and all liberals were Anglophiles.

This view, though incorrect, was not entirely without foundation. There is no doubt that Anglophile liberalism had survived the American war. It seems sometimes as though it might have absorbed the central dogma of the popular school—the dogma of the sovereignty of the general will, or the nation. For example, Brissot, who during the American Revolution had said that the English had all but lost political liberty,[27] now changed his tune. True, he praised the constitution of Pennsylvania above that of England because it provided for a greater measure of popular

[25] Jacob-Nicolas Moreau, *Mes souvenirs*, ed. Camille Hermelin (2 vols.; Paris, 1898-1901), II, 360-64.

[26] [Abbé Charles de Gourcy], *Des droits et des devoirs du citoyen dans les circonstances présentes, avec un jugement impartial sur l'ouvrage de M. l'abbé de Mably. Par un citoyen ami des trois ordres* . . . (1789), pp. 29, 50-51, 62; [Antoine-Louis Séguier], *Façon de voir d'une bonne vieille, qui ne radote pas encore* [ca. end of 1788], pp. 1-2 et passim; Anon., *Fragment d'une lettre écrite à M. Pitt. Par un Anglais* (1789), pp. 1-23; Anon., *Réflexions impartiales sur la grande question qui partage les esprits, concernant les droits du roi et de la nation assemblée en états-généraux* (1789), pp. 6-16.

[27] See above, p. 82.

control over government,[28] but he also defended the English constitution for incorporating the principle of the conflict and balance of parties. This, said Brissot, was the genius of mixed or republican governments.[29] In 1787, when the Duc d'Orléans and the Marquis du Crest were scheming to create a political "opposition," Brissot advised them to copy the leaders of the English opposition party, whose tactics, he said, were to render themselves agreeable to the people, redoubtable to the ministry, and necessary to the king. Brissot expected to see a political system on the English model emerge from the convocation of the Estates-General.[30] Lanjuinais, a notable champion of the Third Estate in both his own province of Brittany and the Constituent Assembly, was another in whose thought the concept of the general will was, as late as October, 1788, mingled with ideas derived from the tradition of Anglophile liberalism.

We reject with equal horror [he wrote] democracy . . . aristocracy . . . and despotism. But we cherish that mixed form so much desired by ancient statesmen, so much applauded by the moderns, wherein from the concourse of king, magnates, and people acting through its representatives will come decisions of a general and constant will.[31]

Other and similar references might be cited.[32]

[28] J.-P. Brissot de Warville (ed.), *Bibliothèque philosophique du législateur, du politique, du jurisconsulte* (10 vols.; Berlin and Paris, 1782-85), III, 254-57.

[29] J.-P. Brissot de Warville, *Tableau de l'état présent des sciences et des arts en Angleterre*, I, No. 1 (Jan., 1784), 32. Otherwise known as *Journal du licée de Londres*.

[30] Brissot to the Marquis du Crest [Aug., 1787], in J.-P. Brissot, *Correspondance et papiers*, ed. Claude Perroud (Paris [1912]), pp. 152-54.

[31] J.-D. Lanjuinais, *Le Préservatif contre l'Avis à mes compatriotes* (Oct., 1788), in Victor Lanjuinais (ed.), *Oeuvres de J.-D. Lanjuinais, pair de France, membre de l'Institut, etc.* (4 vols.; Paris, 1832), IV, 142.

[32] Madame Roland, *De la liberté* [written in 1778], in L.-A. Champagneux (ed.), *Oeuvres de J.-M. Ph. Roland, femme de l'ex-ministre de l'intérieur . . .* (3 vols.; Paris, Year VIII [1799-1800]), III, 170; Madame Roland, *Voyage en Angleterre* [written in 1784], *ibid.*, pp. 213-53; Madame Roland to Bosc, Aug. 13, 1784, in Claude Perroud (ed.), *Lettres de Madame Roland (1780-1793)* (2 vols.; Paris, 1900-1902), I, 455; same to same, Feb. 27 [1786], *ibid.*, p. 567; J.-A.-J. Cérutti, *Les Jardins de Betz* [written in 1785], p. 40, in *Oeuvres diverses de M. Cérutti, ou Recueil de pièces composées avant et depuis la révolution* (2 vols.; Paris, 1792), II; [J.-N. Billaud-Varenne], *Despotisme des ministres de France, ou Exposition des principes et moyens employés par l'aristocratie, pour mettre la France dans les fers* (3 vols.; Amsterdam and Paris, 1789), I, 156, and III, 39-44 [written about 1787]; [Rabaut Saint-Étienne], *À la nation française, sur les vices de son gouvernement; sur la nécessité d'établir une constitution;*

The tendency did not, however, persist. Instead, the doctrine of the popular school became the dominant liberalism, repudiating entirely the Anglophile idea of the division of legislative power in the government and the individualistic, utilitarian premises of the Anglophiles respecting party and political opinion. In the same measure as the newer doctrine succeeded, Anglophile liberalism was, with liberals, discredited. There were several factors in this reversal.

The circumstance that some of the most vigorously Anglophobe writings of the founders of the popular school—who were already great names—were published for the first time in the 1780's is probably of some significance. Rousseau's *Considérations sur le gouvernement de Pologne,* which condemned the irresponsibility of the Parliament of England to the electorate,[33] was published first in 1782, although it had been written ten years prior to that date. One of Mably's earliest political works, *Des droits et des devoirs du citoyen,*[34] which maintained in general that the prerogatives of the crown in England were far too extensive, was published first in 1789 when the constitutional controversy over the structure of the national assembly and the powers of the king was approaching its climax. One of Mably's more recent compositions, *Observations sur le gouvernement et les lois des États-Unis d'Amérique,* which denounced the royal veto and the notion of "virtual" as opposed to that of geographical representation and claimed that English jurisprudence was the sole remaining bulwark of English liberty,[35] had been published first in 1784.

This last-named tract of Mably's had been inspired, as its title

et sur la composition des états-généraux (Nov., 1788 [first published in June, 1788]), p. 30; Duc de Chartres, as quoted in [Métra, J. Imbert, *et al.*], *Correspondance secrète, politique et littéraire, ou Mémoires pour servir à l'histoire des cours, des sociétés et de la littérature en France, depuis la mort de Louis XV* (18 vols.; London, 1787-89), XIV, 342-43 (May 21, 1783); [Jacques Lescène Desmaisons], *Histoire politique de la Révolution en France* (written late in 1788 or early in 1789), II, 150-53 *et passim*.

[33] *Considérations sur le gouvernement de Pologne et sur sa réformation projetée en avril 1772,* in C. E. Vaughan (ed.), *The Political Writings of Jean Jacques Rousseau* (2 vols.; Cambridge, 1915), II, 446.

[34] *Des droits et des devoirs du citoyen* [generally agreed to have been written about 1758], in *Collection complète des oeuvres de l'abbé de Mably* (15 vols.; Paris, 1794-95), XI, 259-518.

[35] *Observations sur le gouvernement et les lois des États-Unis d'Amérique,* ibid., VIII, 350, 382-83.

indicates, by the example of America. America was itself another of the influences that tended to keep apart the Anglophile tradition and the doctrine of the popular school. The admirers of America, some of them no doubt emotionally predisposed in its favor by the circumstances in which the United States secured its independence, were fond of contrasting American political forms and procedures with those of England, to the disadvantage of the latter. Even people who were able to admire both countries at once were not infrequently inclined to favor America. On the whole, the principles of the new American governments fortified the critique of English government as the popular school had hitherto developed it. In the state constitutions of revolutionary America this school discovered that the legislature was more democratic than the Parliament of England and that it was superior to the executive instead of sharing power equally with the executive, as they thought of Parliament and crown sharing it (especially legislative power) in the English government. They sometimes concluded that even civil liberty was more extensive and secure in America than in England.[36] The Federal Constitution of 1787, actually the product of a conservative reaction in the United States, did service for the arguments of both the Anglophile and the popular school. The former could adduce the fact that the document of 1787 provided for an upper house and an executive veto,[37]

[36] *Ibid.;* Brissot, *Bibliothèque philosophique,* III, 254-57; Condorcet, *De l'influence de la révolution d'Amérique sur l'Europe* (1786), in *Oeuvres,* VIII, 16-17; Condorcet, *Lettres d'un bourgeois de New-Haven, ibid.,* IX, *passim;* [Jérôme Pétion de Villeneuve], *Avis aux François sur le salut de la patrie* (1788), pp. 92-94; [William Livingston], *Examen du gouvernement d'Angleterre, comparé aux constitutions des États-Unis. Où l'on réfute quelques assertions contenues dans l'ouvrage de M. Adams, intitulé: Apologie des constitutions des États-Unis d'Amérique, et dans celui de M. Delolme, intitulé: De la constitution d'Angleterre* [trans. Fabre and ed. Dupont de Nemours *et al.*] (London and Paris, 1789), *passim,* including editorial commentary; *Mercure de France,* May 23, 1789, pp. 156-57, reviewing Livingston, *Examen du gouvernement d'Angleterre;* M-J. de Chénier, *Dénonciation des inquisiteurs de la pensée* (Paris, 1789), p. 58; Lafayette to Alexander Hamilton, May 25, 1788, papers of Alexander Hamilton, Library of Congress; Lanjuinais, quoted in the *Journal des débats et des décrets,* No. 13 (Sept. 7, 1789), p. 2.

[37] Rabaut Saint-Étienne, *À la nation française,* pp. 28-32; [François Soulès], *Le Véritable patriotisme* (1788), pp. 13-27, 30-33; Cérutti, *Vues générales sur la constitution françoise, ou Exposé des droits de l'homme dans l'ordre naturel, social et monarchique* (Paris, 1789), p. 157, in *Oeuvres diverses,* I; Anon., *Lettre d'un Suisse aux Français, pour concilier les trois ordres* (Berne, 1789), pp. 26-27; N. Bergasse, *Lettre de M. Bergasse, sur les états-généraux* (1789), pp. 28-33; Évêque-duc de Langres [C.-G. de La Luzerne], *Sur la forme d'opiner aux états-généraux* [1789], pp. 10-11.

while the latter could point out that the upper house was not hereditary and the veto of the executive only suspensive.[38] But the appellation of "American" was appropriated in 1789 by those who, like Lafayette and Brissot, advocated in contravention to the Anglophile party of that date that the proposed French constitution provide for a merely suspensive royal veto and for an upper chamber that was not hereditary.

With respect to political forms and procedures, the principal new idea derived by Frenchmen from the example of the United States was that of the constitutional convention, or rather, the distinction between convention and legislature. In neither the Anglophile tradition nor in the previous doctrine of the popular school had there been any idea of a superlegislature with a special mandate to determine the "fundamental" laws. But the popular school, which now appropriated the concept, did not adduce the lack of it against the Anglophiles until very late, and even then the charge was not vigorously pushed.[39] After all, the concepts of legislature and convention were confounded in the Constituent Assembly itself, and it behooved people who lived in this particular glass house not to throw stones. America, then, as an example of a type or model of government, was simply fitted into and made to bolster a pre-existing set of principles.

Probably the most significant aspect of the influence of America lay in the stimulation that this new utopia afforded to the rationalist proclivities of French thought. Or, to put the matter another way, the influence of America was to make Frenchmen more critical than before of the usefulness of historical examples in general and the British example in particular. In total disregard of the fact that the American constitutions were the outgrowth of colonial

[38] Lafayette, *Mémoires, correspondance et manuscrits du général Lafayette, publiés par sa famille* (6 vols.; Paris, 1837-38), III, 202-3, and IV, 187; Eloise Ellery, *Brissot de Warville. A Study in the History of the French Revolution* (Boston and New York, 1915), pp. 127, 130; Marat to the President of the Estates-General, Aug. 23, 1789, in *Correspondance de Marat*, p. 100; Louis R. Gottschalk, *Jean-Paul Marat. A Study in Radicalism* (London, n.d.), p. 54; [J.-G. Peltier], *La Trompette du jugement. Au sallon d'Hercule, premier septembre 1789* [1789], pp. 26, 30. Cf. publication of the American Federal Constitution in Livingston, *Examen du gouvernement d'Angleterre*.

[39] *Mercure de France*, May 23, 1789, pp. 160-64, reviewing Livingston, *Examen du gouvernement d'Angleterre;* Abbé Sieyès, *Dire de l'abbé Sieyes, sur la question du veto royal, à la séance du 7 septembre 1789* (Paris [1789]), pp. 20-23.

experience, it was observed only that in certain respects they differed from the English constitution (which had formerly been, so Frenchmen thought, the fundamental law of the colonies), and the founding fathers were thought of as having sat themselves down in Arcady to correct a historical pattern, the English pattern, in the light of reason.[40] Why therefore should not Frenchmen do the same? Surely, for this task the eighteenth century, the most enlightened of the Christian era, had wisdom enough and to spare. Originally the popular school had not been much more rationalist or less historical than the Anglophiles, but in the decade just before the French Revolution the rationalist argument became very conspicuous among the disciples of Rousseau and Mably. It was mixed judiciously, however, with the argument from history: history showed what bad results the adoption of English forms of government would entail; reason dictated that the French consult, not a historical example, but their own enlightened intelligence. This rationalist repudiation of the habit of deferring to the example of the English naturally drove the school of Rousseau and Mably still farther from the Anglophile liberal tradition.

Both the rationalism and the Anglophobe bias of the popular school were further reinforced in the 1780's by the addition of the Neo-Physiocrats to their ranks. It will be remembered that the Physiocratic "sect" had split. Some, like the Abbé Baudeau and the Marquis de Mirabeau, continued to profess the doctrine of legal despotism and were compelled by the course of events to side with old-fashioned political conservatives,[41] to whose ideas classic Physiocracy had indeed always borne some relation. Others, like Turgot, the Marquis de Condorcet, and Dupont de Nemours, adopted, in approximation more or less to the ideas of Rousseau, the concept of the sovereignty of the general will. Dupont and Condorcet therefore adhered to the popular party, which in 1789

[40] Cf. R. R. Palmer, "The French Idea of American Independence on the Eve of the French Revolution" (unpublished Ph.D. dissertation, Cornell University, 1934), p. 68, and chap. i, *passim*.

[41] [Abbé Baudeau], *Idées d'un citoyen presque sexagénaire sur l'état actuel du royaume de France, comparées à celles de sa jeunesse* (Paris, 1787), Part III, pp. 17-29; the Marquis de Mirabeau to the Bailli de Mirabeau, June 19, 1787, "Lettres inédites du marquis de Mirabeau (1787-1789)," *Le Correspondant*, CCL (1913), 267; same to same, Aug. 7, 1787, *ibid.*, p. 275; same to same, Feb. 9, 1789, *ibid.*, CCLI (1913), 317; same to same, April 28, 1789, *ibid.*, p. 327.

constituted the political left wing. This did not by any means signify a complete reversal of ideas on their part. Rather, it meant an amalgamation of two versions of the thesis that the lawmakers in any society ought to be an elite—in the case of the Physiocrats, an elite of intelligence; in that of the Rousseauists, an elite of virtue. For the Rousseauist terms "nation" and "general will," while usually carrying vaguely the connotation of large numbers of people, had also the connotation of an elite, a homogeneous group distinguished by special qualifications. If one played down the democratic aspects of Rousseauist doctrine, the elites of virtue and intelligence could easily amount to pretty much the same thing. If one substituted the enlightened intelligence of the nation for the single enlightened despot of the Physiocrats, the union of the two doctrines could be established. Since the notion of a political elite had been one of the main points of divergence between Anglophile liberalism on the one hand and Physiocracy and the doctrine of the school of Rousseau on the other, the addition of the Neo-Physiocrats to the disciples of Rousseau and Mably helped all the more to keep the latter from being confounded with the Anglophile liberals.

Both ideas of an elite appeared in the political tracts that Condorcet began to write about 1785 in order to combat Anglomania. The idea of the elite of virtue predominated in his discussion of the bad effects that he thought had resulted from the division of legislative power in the English constitution. Since this kind of constitution (according to Condorcet) put a premium on party, i.e., faction, and there was no advancement save in attachment to party, party must dominate the considerations of every member of Parliament[42] to the detriment of disinterested legislation. For example, the fact that the English government continued to have to derive the major part of its revenues from tariff and excise duties instead of a land tax, despite the incontestable advantages of having a single tax levied on the income from land, was the work of the politicians. The politicians were the great proprietors of the country, but the point Condorcet emphasized was not their economic interest in avoiding a land tax. It was the patronage which was involved in the collection of tariff and excise duties and which

[42] *Lettres d'un bourgeois de New-Haven*, in *Oeuvres*, IX, 86-88.

they would have lost in the abolition of these indirect taxes.[43] Condorcet pointed out other melancholy instances of the dominance of party interest. The debates in Parliament on parliamentary reform, on the liquidation of the national debt, and the reform of the East India Company were, he complained, so full of sophisms that the real issues had been quite obscured.[44] Making the same point in another way, Condorcet brought out the idea that a government in which legislative authority was divided was a complicated government. Only with simplicity in the political structure could the truth and the public interest prevail.[45]

On the other hand, the idea of an elite of intelligence predominated in Condorcet's disapproval of the extent to which the masses seemed to count in English politics, including elections.[46] The Gordon riots of June, 1780, had made as great an impression on him as they had made on his friend Turgot.[47] Condorcet thought Parliament could have cut away at the roots of the bad influence of the populace by dividing the cities into quarters, introducing public education, and establishing free trade. He also censured members of Parliament for acting on the theory that their own interest lay in deferring to popular prejudices.[48] Condorcet did not recommend that the franchise should be more restricted than it already was in England, but favored a system of indirect election such as applied to the provincial assemblies designed to be established in France by the edict of 1787,[49] agencies which he thought might well form part of the machinery for electing a national assembly.[50]

Condorcet's belief that the upper classes were better qualified to look after the interest of the lower classes than the latter were

[43] *Ibid.*, pp. 89-90.
[44] *Ibid.*, p. 87.
[45] *Ibid.*, p. 75.
[46] *Essai sur la constitution et les fonctions des assemblées provinciales* (1788), *ibid.*, VIII, 156; *Vie de Voltaire* (1789), *ibid.*, IV, 115.
[47] *De l'influence de la révolution d'Amérique sur l'Europe* (1786), *ibid.*, VIII, 48; *Avertissements insérés par Condorcet dans l'édition complète des oeuvres de Voltaire* [1785-89], *ibid.*, IV, 352.
[48] *Lettres d'un bourgeois de New-Haven, ibid.*, IX, 90; *Idées sur le despotisme à l'usage de ceux qui prononcent ce mot sans l'entendre* (1789), *ibid.*, pp. 161-63.
[49] *Essai sur la constitution et les fonctions des assemblées provinciales, ibid.*, VIII, 156-57.
[50] *Ibid.*, pp. 221-58.

themselves did not mean that he favored class representation as such. Indeed, quite the contrary was the case. He disapproved of the English House of Lords, even though, as he believed, membership in it was desired chiefly for its honorific value, just because the House of Lords created and perpetuated a patrician class distinct from the rest of the nation.[51] This association of Anglomania with class interest was a rather new emphasis in the writings of the popular school, but it was one that had suddenly become quite prominent with them. Moreover, it was a highly significant emphasis. It points to another and perhaps the weightiest of the circumstances which prevented the ideas of the school of Rousseau and Mably from becoming absorbed into the older tradition of Anglophile liberalism and which at the same time caused the name of Anglophile to become anathema in the ears of liberals. This circumstance was the appearance, in the latter part of the decade, of a formidable body of opinion that appropriated Anglophile ideology for conservative uses.

This new conservatism was, on the surface, moderate, for it adopted the idea of limited monarchy. But its limited monarchy did not have the republican overtones that had formerly accompanied that idea. Its viewpoint was set forth theoretically in the Swiss legist Delolme's treatise on the government of England, first published in 1770 but not appraised correctly in France until the 1780's. Regarded formerly as nothing more than an essay upon government by contract and the right of revolution,[52] this work was really a glorification of constitutional monarchy, proclaiming the crown to be the keystone of that tripartite structure of King, Lords, and Commons that according to the author so perfectly preserved in England both the liberties of the subject

[51] *Ibid.*, pp. 155-57; *Lettres d'un bourgeois de New-Haven, ibid.*, IX, 81-82.
[52] [Louis Bachaumont et al.], *Mémoires secrets pour servir à l'histoire de la république des lettres en France, depuis MDCCLXII jusqu'à nos jours; ou Journal d'un observateur* . . . (36 vols.; London, 1784-89), VI, 31-33 (Nov. 11, 1771). Cf. Madame Roland, then Mlle Phlipon, to the Cannet sisters, Jan. 5, 1777, in Claude Perroud (ed.), *Lettres de Madame Roland, nouvelle série 1767-1780* (2 vols.; Paris, 1913-15), II, 5-9; [François] Lacombe, *Tableau de Londres et de ses environs, avec un précis de la constitution de l'Angleterre, et de sa décadence* (London and Brussels, 1784), pp. 145-67. The second edition of this last-named work had appeared in 1780; Gabriel Bonno, *La Constitution britannique devant l'opinion française* . . . (Paris, 1932), gives 1777 as the date of the edition he used.

and public order.⁵³ The re-evaluation of Delolme had been accompanied by a re-evaluation of English politics. The conservative and nationalist revival that had taken place in England after the close of the American war contributed no little to this end. In 1784 the king's choice for prime minister, William Pitt the Younger, after weeks of striving to carry on the government against a hostile Whig majority in the House of Commons, had been sustained by the country in a general election. During the next few years the Pitt ministry sponsored a number of constructive commercial and financial policies, some of which it succeeded in putting through Parliament. With the new type of French conservative, English royalty began to enjoy a prestige that prior to this time it certainly had lacked among all parties in France. Although French newspapers carried accounts of the election of 1784 indicating that political morality had been quite wanting therein,⁵⁴ the new Anglophiles paid no attention. They now preferred to believe that the crown in England had extensive powers and that these were not dependent on corruption but derived from the very nature of the constitution itself.⁵⁵ Whereas previous to this time Frenchmen had uniformly believed that the king of England was neither loved nor revered by his subjects, the attitude that Englishmen were thought to have toward their kings now began to seem much less republican. In fact, the veneration of the English for King George III actually appeared as a theme of at least one French pamphlet.⁵⁶ Parliament, too, underwent a kind of metamorphosis. The House of Lords, formerly

---

⁵³ Jean Louis Delolme, *The Constitution of England, or an Account of the English Government; in Which It Is Compared with the Republican Form of Government, and Occasionally with the Other Monarchies in Europe* (new ed.; London, 1777), Bk. II, chaps. x and xviii, *passim*.

⁵⁴ *Courier de l'Europe*, XV, 195 (March 26, 1784); *Journal de Genève*, 1784, II, 79-80; *Journal encyclopédique*, 1784, IV, 179.

⁵⁵ *Mémoires du marquis de Bouillé*, ed. MM. Berville and Barrière ("Collection des mémoires relatifs à la Révolution française," XLV; 2d ed.; Paris, 1822), pp. 23-26; Mallet du Pan, in *Journal de Genève*, 1784, I, 425-27, and in *Journal politique de Bruxelles* (otherwise known as the *Mercure politique*), Jan. 1, 1785, "Tableau politique de l'Europe en 1784," pp. 4-9. At this time both the *Journal de Genève* and the *Journal politique de Bruxelles* were edited by Mallet du Pan. Cf. Mallet du Pan on Delolme in *Mercure de France*, Jan. 17, 1789, pp. 109-22; Jan. 24, 1789, pp. 150-66.

⁵⁶ [Sir Nathaniel William Wraxall], *Coup d'oeil sur l'état politique de la Grande-Bretagne, au commencement de l'année 1787*, trans. from the English (London, 1787), *passim*.

eclipsed in French eyes by the House of Commons, now emerged as a prominent third in the legislative trinity.

In a sense the new conservative Anglomania was not new, for it was related to the old *frondeur* Anglomania of the *grands seigneurs* and the legal aristocracy before the American Revolution. There was a difference, however. Formerly the *frondeurs* had conceived of the crown as their chief enemy. They had desired to limit royal authority in order to revive the long-dead political power of the great nobility and, more specifically, to prevent the monarchy from making the privileged orders assume a proportionate share of the expense of government. Now the issue had broadened into a matter of defending the entire social position of the nobility against the Third Estate, which desired to abolish privilege. The nobility, both greater and lesser, began to think of a constitution on the English model as a means not only of getting political power but of maintaining it and their privileges, too, against the encroachments of the "people." To them the idea of the sovereignty of the nation, now heard on every hand, had ominously democratic connotations. Fear of democracy also led bourgeois conservatives to favor the Anglophile idea of a constitution of checks and balances. Not that the aristocracy and the conservative bourgeoisie had identical expectations about the way in which a constitution on the English model would operate. Whereas aristocratic conservatives hoped to establish an alliance between themselves and the monarch against the Third Estate, middle-class conservatives hoped that the king would hold a balance of power between the Third Estate and the aristocracy.

Throughout the greater part of the decade following the American war there was no open conflict between the Anglophiles, whether of the old liberal or the new conservative persuasion, and the popular school, the school of Rousseau and Mably. These different elements were for a time, in fact, allies devoted to attaining a common end, the destruction of royal absolutism. But after August, 1788, when the government had capitulated to the general demand, led by the parlements, for the convocation of the Estates-General, the privileged orders inaugurated a counterrevolution to prevent the Estates from becoming an effective agency of majority opinion. Spokesmen for the privileged classes pronounced either for the retention of the customary organization in three separate estates or for a bicameral assembly with the clergy and nobility united into an upper house. A number of spokesmen for the conservative bourgeois ideal of a strong monarchy came out also for a bicameral arrangement. The example of the English Parliament was adduced not only to support the bicameral plan but also, sometimes, to defend the three-house organization, on the ground that the principle of the division of legislative power between nobility and commoners was embodied in the one instance as in the other.[57] Although the Third Estate succeeded in transforming (June, 1789) the Estates-General into a unicameral body, the Constituent Assembly, the same issues were carried over into the next phase of the constitutional controversy, that of the late summer of 1789. At this time the debate over the "permanent" constitution then being drafted turned specifically on the organization of the assembly (whether it should be bicameral or unicameral) and on the royal veto. Again the conservative forces took an Anglophile position and again they were defeated. The most that was conceded them was a suspensive royal veto.

The propaganda of the Anglophobe liberals throughout this critical debate in the years 1788-89 made no virtue of consistency. Various approaches were employed to arrive at the one conclusion that whatever the English political system was, its introduction into France would prevent the achievement of equality and freedom.

One approach was to destroy the ground for imitating the English by insisting that England was not really free. No country could be free in which the monarch had so extensive a prerogative, including, especially, the veto power. The royal veto (at least, the

---

[57] Comte d'Antraigues, *À l'ordre de la noblesse du Bas-Vivarais* [Paris, 1789], pp. 23, 41, *et passim;* Comte de Lauraguais, *Dissertation sur les assemblées nationales, sous les trois races des rois de France* (Paris, Oct. 10, 1788), pp. 12-13, 83, 91; Lauraguais, referred to in *Journal général de l'Europe, première partie. Politique, commerce, agriculture,* 1789, I, 20; La Luzerne, *Sur la forme d'opiner aux états-généraux,* pp. 7-29, 92, 106-8; [C.-A.] de Calonne, *Lettre adressée au roi* (London [1789]), pp. 62, 67-68, 137, 282; [J.-J. Duval d'Éprémesnil?], *Réflexions d'un magistrat sur la question du nombre, et celle de l'opinion par ordre ou par tête* [1788], quoted by Servan in *Réflexions d'un magistrat . . . suivies des remarques d'un pauvre tiers incrédule,* in his *Recueil de pièces intéressantes pour servir à l'histoire de la révolution de 1789, en France* (2 vols.; 1789), II, 181-87.

absolute veto, for some of the popular school would accept the suspensive veto) contradicted the principle, fundamental to political liberty, that the king should not have anything but executive authority, that he should be no more than the mandatory of the legislature. To minimize or even to deny the existence of political liberty in England had of course been the line taken by the school of Mably and Rousseau from its beginnings. There was nothing new about their position here except the extreme to which some of them pushed it.[58] In their concern to deny that the English were really free, they came up against an obstacle to which they had never before paid any attention. This was the habit, long established among Frenchmen, of regarding England as the true symbol of *civil* liberty—of freedom of the press, free-

[58] Pétion de Villeneuve, *Avis aux François sur le salut de la patrie*, pp. 88-89; the same, in *Journal des débats*, No. 5 (Sept. 1, 1789), p. 3; Livingston, *Examen du gouvernement d'Angleterre, passim*, including the notes by Dupont de Nemours and others; Helvétius to Lefebvre-Laroche [*sic*] on the constitution of England, Sept. 8, 1768 (apocryphal; see above, chap. i, n. 9, and Appendix), in *Oeuvres complètes d'Helvétius* (14 vols.; Paris, 1795), XIV, 78-87; [A.-E.-N. Fantin des Odoards], *Considérations sur le gouvernement qui convient à la France et sur les moyens de concourir au rétablissement des finances de l'état, en vendant pour deux milliards des biens du clergé. Par un citoyen de Paris, membre du district des Cordeliers* (1789), pp. 83-88; [J.-P. Marat], *Projet de déclaration des droits de l'homme et du citoyen, suivi d'un plan de constitution juste, sage et libre* ... (Paris, 1789), pp. 28-30; Marat to the President of the Estates-General, Aug. 23, 1789, *Correspondance de Marat*, pp. 100-103; Dupont de Nemours, *De la périodicité des assemblées nationales, de leur organisation, de la forme à suivre pour amener les propositions qui pourront y être faites, à devenir des loix; et de la sanction nécessaire pour que ces loix soient obligatoires* (Paris, 1789), pp. 6, 18-22; Duc de la Rochefoucauld, *Opinion de M. le duc de la Rochefoucauld, député de Paris, 7 septembre 1789* [1789], pp. 4, 17, *et passim*; Rabaut Saint-Étienne, *L'Opinion de M. Rabaut St.-Étienne sur quelques points de la constitution* [Paris, 1789], p. 28; [François] de Pange, *De la sanction royale* (Paris, 1789), p. 40; [J.-B.] Salle, *Opinion de M. Salle, député de Lorraine, sur la sanction royale, à la séance du premier septembre 1789* (Paris, 1789), pp. 26-27; [Henri] Grégoire, *Opinion de M. Grégoire, curé d'Embermenil, député de Nanci, sur la sanction royale. À la séance du 4 Septembre* [Paris, 1789?], p. 8 n.; the same in *Procès-verbal de L'Assemblée nationale constituante* (101 vols. [Paris, 1789-91]), III, 2; Lanjuinais, in *Journal des débats*, No. 13 (Sept. 7, 1789), p. 2; De Leipand, *ibid.*, No. 7 (Sept. 2, 1789), p. 5; *Révolutions de Paris, dédiées à la nation et au district des Petits-Augustins*, No. 8 (Sept. 1, 1789), p. 19; [J.-L. Carra], *L'Orateur des états-généraux. Second partie* (Paris, 1789), p. 21; Anon., *L'Aristocratie enchaînée et surveillée par le peuple et le roi; suivi d'un Mémoire des barons nés de Languedoc et de la réponse à leurs prétensions exhorbitantes. Par J. L. G. S.* (Jan. 31, 1789), p. 7; Anon., *L'Anti-sanctionnaire anglois, ou Aiguillon à la constitution* (1789), *passim*; Anon., *Lettre du roi d'Angleterre au roi de France, sur les états-généraux* (1789), p. 5 *et passim*.

dom of person, and so on. Now the school of Mably and Rousseau had always taken the position that in the last analysis political and civil liberty stood or fell together. What if Frenchmen were to argue, in the present crisis, that since civil liberty existed in England, political liberty must exist there, too, and the English constitution be therefore desirable? To head off this line of argument the school of Mably and Rousseau sometimes declared that civil liberty was not so extensive among the English as was generally supposed. They pointed out the existence of imprisonment for debt, in which circumstance the famous Act of Habeas Corpus did not apply. They adduced the use of the press gang for the recruitment of seamen, the partial character of religious toleration, and the fact that the much-vaunted freedom of the press in England was founded, not upon statute, but only upon judicial precedent, which these critics assumed to be less reliable than statute.[59] To the foregoing array of injustices and inadequacies, some of which were stock charges, publicists who entertained free-trade beliefs added that in England economic liberty was incomplete.[60] On the other hand, however, the popular party sometimes presented the view, once common to the Physiocrats and to such Anglophile liberals as Voltaire and Helvétius, that civil liberty was simply the result of enlightenment among those in authority, who had merely to enact a few good laws, and that it had no necessary relation to the structure of the government.[61] Whether the English possessed civil liberty or not was therefore irrelevant to the point at issue.

Adherents of the popular party not only asserted (on occasion) that freedom in England was an illusion. They also asserted (on

[59] Livingston, *Examen du gouvernement d'Angleterre*, notes of Dupont and others, pp. 73-75, 81-84, 185-87; Condorcet, *Idées sur le despotisme*, in *Oeuvres*, IX, 154; Grégoire, *Opinion . . . sur la sanction royale*, pp. 7-8 n.

[60] Livingston, *Examen du gouvernement d'Angleterre*, nn., pp. 74, 79-80; Grégoire, *Opinion . . . sur la sanction royale*, p. 7 n.

[61] Livingston, *Examen du gouvernement d'Angleterre*, notes of Dupont and others, pp. 76-77; [Abbé Lefebvre de la Roche?], "Lettre de M. Helvétius au président de Montesquieu," *Lettres de M. Helvétius au président de Montesquieu et à M. Saurin, relatives à l'aristocratie de la noblesse* (1789), p. 13; Sieyès, *Qu'est-ce que le tiers état?*, pp. 62-63; Salle, *Opinion . . . sur la sanction royale*, p. 27; [Maximilien] Robespierre, *Dire de M. de Robespierre, député de la province d'Artois à l'assemblée nationale, contre le veto royal, soit absolu, soit suspensif* [Sept., 1789], p. 13.

occasion) that equality was, too, or at least they declared that there was an aristocracy in England separate from the rest of the nation and that the aristocracy had preponderance over the commoners in the government. A "direct despotism" prevailed in England, said Condorcet, because the king and the House of Lords both had a power of veto that left the people no means of revoking a law contrary to the popular interest. An "indirect despotism" existed there, he said, because even the House of Commons did not really represent the nation but was itself an essentially aristocratic body dominated by some forty or fifty individuals—peers, ministers, or certain members of the House.[62] Thus Condorcet, among others,[63] gave a new twist to the old contention of the school of Rousseau, that the general will seldom found expression in England. The older form of the criticism had attributed this condition to the infrequency of parliamentary elections and to the fact that the members of the House of Commons were not subjected to the mandate of the constituencies on specific questions. The school of Rousseau and Mably, like most other Frenchmen, had in general accepted the notion that English society was egalitarian. The new version of the criticism, that the House of Commons was unrepresentative in its membership and that the form of the constitution favored an alliance between the crown and the aristocracy at the expense of the rest of the nation, perhaps showed somewhat more insight into the structure of English politics. It was certainly more pertinent to the needs of the party's argument at the beginning of the Revolution, having arisen in answer to the invocation of Anglophile constitutionalism by conservatives who saw therein a means of preserving in France the prerogatives of the privileged orders.

But the popular party did not by any means discard entirely the old idea that the society of England was egalitarian. On the

[62] *Idées sur le despotisme,* in *Oeuvres,* IX, 148-49.

[63] Pétion de Villeneuve, *Avis aux François sur le salut de la patrie,* pp. 92-94; Livingston, *Examen du gouvernement d'Angleterre,* ed. Dupont de Nemours *et al.,* Note II, pp. 84-85, 87-95; Helvétius to Lefebvre-Laroche, Sept. 8, 1768 [apocryphal], *Oeuvres* (1795), XIV, 85; Dupont de Nemours, *De la périodicité des assemblées nationales,* pp. 10-12; Grégoire, *Opinion . . . sur la sanction royale,* p. 8 n.; Lanjuinais, in *Journal des débats,* No. 13 (Sept. 7, 1789), pp. 2-3; Anon., *États-généraux de l'an mil neuf cent quatre-vingt-dix-neuf. Dédiés à l'Assemblée nationale. Par un député des communes* (1789), pp. 8-93; *Journal général de l'Europe,* 1789, V, 98-99.

contrary, they used it, but in conjunction with a thesis they had hitherto consistently opposed: that in England royal despotism was dead. It was now one of their principal approaches, in debating against the Anglophiles, to assume that England was essentially a republican state in which both royal despotism and privilege had been destroyed. In this the chief objective was, clearly, to persuade convinced Anglophile liberals that the introduction of the English constitution of checks and balances into France would not destroy despotism and perhaps privilege there, as such Anglophiles had formerly supposed, but would only perpetuate these evils. (One can sometimes trace the changes of heart that considerations of this nature did induce among Anglophile liberals. During the controversy over the organization of the Estates-General, for example, several spokesmen for the Third Estate who only a short time before had been advocating a constitution on the English model changed their minds[64] or showed definite signs of swinging over to an anti-Anglophile opinion.[65]) The argument went, in summary, as follows: The position and powers of the House of Lords in England did not constitute the same threat to the rights of the nation as a whole as would the existence of a similar body in France, because the English nobility, unlike that of France, had no wish or power to be really distinct from the rest of the nation. Nor did the apparently extensive prerogatives of the English crown confer upon it, actually, the power which those same prerogatives would confer upon the crown in France. In view of France's position as a great continental power, its king had at his disposal a far larger army than the king of England commanded and would therefore be in a much more favorable position to intimidate the legislature, unless he were deprived of all legislative influence.[66] Besides—so at least one publicist declared—the

[64] Cérutti, *Observations rapides sur la lettre de M. de Calonne au roi* (Paris, 1789), pp. 59-63, and *Exhortation à la concorde, envoyée aux états-généraux sous le nom du roi* (1789), pp. 26-27, both in *Oeuvres diverses*, Vol. I; compare [Rabaut Saint-Étienne], *Question de droit public: Doit-on recueillir les voix, dans les états-généraux, par ordres, ou par têtes de délibérans? Par l'auteur des Considérations sur les intérêts du tiers-état* ("En Languedoc," 1789), pp. 48-54, *et passim*, with the same author, *À la nation française*, pp. 28-45.

[65] Compare Lanjuinais, *Réflexions patriotiques sur l'arrêté de quelques nobles de Bretagne, daté du 25 octobre 1788*, in *Oeuvres*, IV, 110-23, with his *Le Préservatif contre l'Avis à mes compatriotes* (Oct., 1788), *ibid.*, p. 142.

[66] [Jean-Joseph Mounier], *Nouvelles observations sur les états-généraux de*

king of England needed the absolute veto in order to defend his prerogative against complete destruction by Parliament, in which the constituent power was combined with the legislative. But in France the king's position would be stronger to begin with, since the legislative and constituent powers would be separate.[67] He therefore did not need the veto.

Although the determination of the popular party to destroy privilege was as great as their desire to eliminate the crown's role in legislation, if not greater, the prerogative of the crown was more often the direct object of the Anglophobes' attack upon Anglophile constitutionalism than was the power of the nobility. The apparent paradox is partly explained by the fact that the popular party was answering specifically the demand of conservative Anglophiles for a strong, if constitutional, monarchy. They reasoned that the king was not reconciled to the downfall of royal absolutism, and that the more power he was allowed, the more he would seek to recover. But they also thought that the question of royal power subsumed the question of privilege. Eighteenth-century Frenchmen, politically conditioned under a regime of absolute monarchy, could not help rating pretty heavily the influence of the monarchy in giving direction to French institutions. As the popular party read the history of France for the previous two hundred years, monarchy and privilege were allied, even though that alliance might have been at times no more than a

---

France (1789), pp. 245-51; [Servan], *Entretien de Monsieur Necker avec Madame la comtesse de Polignac, Monsieur le baron de Breteuil et l'abbé de Vermon* (London, 1789), pp. 68-77; Rabaut Saint-Étienne, *Question de droit public*, pp. 51-54; [G.-J.-B. Target], *IIe suite de l'écrit intitulé: Les États-généraux convoqués par Louis XVI* [Paris, 1789], pp. 2, 39-40; Anon., *Discours de l'orateur des trois ordres, aux états-généraux. Par un député* (1789), pp. 24-25, 30; [Abbé Joseph-André Brun], *Le Point de ralliement des citoyens françois, sur les bases d'une constitution nationale, et sur les pouvoirs des députés* (1789), pp. 136-39; Anon., *Des droits du citoyen, et de leur réunion avec une bonne constitution. Par R***. J**., député particulier du diocese de Lodeve* (1789), pp. 24-27; [Philippe-Antoine Grouvelle], *De l'autorité de Montesquieu dans la révolution présente* (1789), p. 122 and n.; Sieyès, *Qu'est-ce que le tiers état?*, pp. 59-60 n., 60, 63; Anon., *Plan d'une constitution nouvelle, convenable à la nation françoise* [Paris, 1789], nn. pp. 13-16; Robespierre, *Dire . . . contre le veto royal*, p. 13; Joseph Barnave, in *Journal des débats*, No. 7 (Sept. 2, 1789), p. 6; Alexandre de Lameth, *ibid.*, No. 9 (Sept. 3, 1789), p. 5; De Leipand, *ibid.*, No. 7 (Sept. 2, 1789), p. 5.

[67] Abbé Sieyès, *Dire de l'abbé Sieyes, sur la question du veto royal, à la séance du 7 Septembre 1789* (Paris [1789]), pp. 20-23.

modus vivendi. Montesquieu himself had said that monarchy and privilege were natural allies ("no monarch, no nobility"),[68] and liberals were beginning to attack Montesquieu's authority as an Anglophile by asserting that he had been at heart, not an admirer of the "republic hidden under the form of monarchy,"[69] but an aristocratic conservative.[70] The popular party took no stock in any expectation on the part of any of the Anglophiles that in a strong constitutional monarchy the king would hold the balance of power between the aristocracy and the Third Estate. The king would support the aristocracy. The judgment of the popular party regarding the king's intentions was confirmed in their eyes by what seemed to be, especially after June, 1789, when the Estates-General became the unicameral Constituent Assembly, the establishment of an alliance between the court and the aristocracy for the purpose of intimidating the Assembly.

One of the effects, certainly, of this constitutional debate over the prerogatives of the king and the political representation of the aristocracy was the eclipse of the old Anglophile liberalism, which suffered from being confounded with the new Anglophile conservatism. Except with ultraconservatives, who still considered Anglomania a subversive force, Anglophile ideas had become associated entirely with counterrevolution. Conversely, the only doctrine that still had a revolutionary meaning was the Anglophobe doctrine of the sovereignty of the nation.

The revolutionary force of this last-named ideology cannot be explained entirely, however, in terms of the constitutional and social problems of liberty and authority, equality and privilege. If its significance is to be fully appreciated, it must be understood also as the principal vehicle for the expression of nationalist ideas and sentiments in the decade of the beginning of the Revolution. The preceding chapters have described various manifestations of French nationalist sentiment and theory in the period be-

---

[68] *De l'esprit des lois*, Bk. II, chap. iv, in Édouard Laboulaye (ed.), *Oeuvres complètes de Montesquieu* . . . (7 vols.; Paris, 1875-79), III, 115.

[69] *De l'esprit des lois*, Bk. V, chap. xix, *ibid.*, p. 216.

[70] Grouvelle, *De l'autorité de Montesquieu*, pp. 92, 98, *et passim*; [Lefebvre de la Roche?], "Lettre de M. Helvétius au président de Montesquieu . . . ," *Lettres de M. Helvétius au président de Montesquieu et à M. Saurin* . . . , *passim*. Cf. Linguet, *La France plus qu'angloise*, pp. 114-15, in regard to the estimate of Montesquieu as an aristocratic conservative.

tween the Seven Years' War and the close of the War of American Independence. During that period nationalism and liberalism were only beginning to display an affinity. National sentiment was then chiefly an expression of the conservative viewpoint, whereas the movement for reform tended, with one notable exception, to be cosmopolitan in belief and temper. The exception was the Physiocrats, who, as economic liberals and "philosophers" had been the first to exhibit in their doctrine the union of the reform impulse and a self-conscious, mature nationalism of both theory and sentiment. In the 1780's, as political opinion moved to the left, the older conservative nationalism became much less conspicuous, while the demand for reform (political or economic or both) became the way in which French nationalism was most usually and vigorously expressed. Reformers invoked the love of country and the pride of nationality. They wished France to achieve, so they said, the destiny which nature had intended for her, but which the tissue of abuses that constituted the old regime had thus far prevented her from attaining. Without denying the measure of truth in the widely accepted idea that French nationalism was a product of the Revolution, one may observe with just as much, if not more, truth that the Revolution was a product of French nationalism, which partly justified it.

One of the principal factors in this association of nationalism and reform was the War of American Independence and its aftermath. The participation of Frenchmen in making that new America which was one of the principal symbols of liberal ideals in the 1780's seems not only to have contributed to the development of liberal opinion but also to have stimulated national feeling mightily. The success of their war against Britain gave immense satisfaction to the pride of all classes of Frenchmen, who exulted in having humbled the "haughty islanders," preserved the freedom of the seas, and raised their country again to that rank among the powers to which they felt she was entitled.[71] The score being

[71] [J.-B.] Mailhe, *Discours qui a remporté le prix à l'Académie des jeux floraux en 1784, sur la grandeur et l'importance de la révolution qui vient de s'opérer dans l'Amérique Septentrionale* (Toulouse, 1784), pp. 36-37; [L. de Chavannes de la Giraudière], *L'Amérique délivrée, esquisse d'un poëme sur l'indépendance de l'Amérique* (2 vols.; Amsterdam, 1783), *passim* and II, 477 n. 5; Fantin des Odoards, *Histoire de France, depuis la mort de Louis XIV jusqu'à la paix de Versailles de 1783* (8 vols.; Paris, 1789), VIII, 375-77, 409 [written,

evened and honor satisfied, they might feel some glow of geniality toward the former enemy. They might say, in idealistically worded utterances, that they hoped for Anglo-French co-operation in the future instead of a continuance of enmity. French travelers poured across the Channel. Even Lafayette, who had been an ardent hater of the English, wanted to travel in England, and, when entertaining at his house the youthful but already renowned William Pitt, declared that he now felt a great pleasure in meeting Englishmen. But the hopes expressed for Anglo-French co-operation were usually associated with the idea that France was as great a power as England, if not greater, and as notable a leader of civilization;[72] and Lafayette admitted candidly that his own pleasure in seeing Englishmen resulted from their having been defeated by the French. He still felt some hostility. "Without having the self-conceit to treat them as personal enemies," he said, "I cannot forget that they are enemies of French glory and prosperity."[73]

As the decade advanced, the sense of national rivalry was intensified by the apparent disinclination of the English to recognize their defeat and to draw from it the salutary lessons they had been supposed to learn. They had put off their withdrawal from the territory they had surrendered to the United States in the treaty of peace, and elsewhere in the Empire they were still, it seemed, practicing a policy of oppression like that which had brought about the American rebellion. Ireland, despite the grant of "home rule,"

---

apparently, soon after the peace]; Cérutti, *L'Aigle et le hibou, ou l'Ami de la lumière et l'ami des ténèbres, fable* [1783], p. 9, in *Oeuvres diverses*, II; [Lescène Desmaisons], *Qu'est-ce que les parlemens en France?* (The Hague, 1788), p. 56; Courtial, *Ode sur la paix*, reviewed in *Journal des sçavans*, April, 1784, p. 221; Labrat, *Ode sur la paix*, quoted in *Mercure de France*, March 5, 1785, p. 44; Racine, *Discours sur la paix*, reviewed in *L'Année littéraire*, 1784, II, 333; Jean-Baptiste, Baron de Cloots du Val-de-Grace ["Anacharsis Cloots"], *Voeux d'un Gallophile* (new ed. rev.; Amsterdam, 1786), pp. 1-2; Ségur, *Mémoires ou Souvenirs et anecdotes*, II, 30; Lafayette, *Mémoires*, I, 8-9 [written ca. 1783-84], *Journal général de l'Europe*, I, 18 (June 4, 1785).

[72] Cérutti, *L'Aigle et le hibou*, pp. 9, 21, 22, in *Oeuvres diverses*, II; [Dupont de Nemours], *Lettre à la chambre du commerce de Normandie*, pp. 263-65; Métra, *Correspondance secrète*, XVIII, 315-16 (Aug. 18, 1785); *La France et l'Angleterre, dialogue . . .* , quoted and reviewed in *Journal encyclopédique*, 1786, VII, 365-67.

[73] Lafayette to unknown [Oct., 1783], *Mémoires*, II, 160-61. The date 1786 given by the editors is clearly incorrect, for the letter refers to Pitt's visit to Lafayette, and Pitt was in France only in 1783.

did not have true equality with Britain. The government of the East India Company was such as to elicit expressions of pious horror from French journalists. The two India bills sponsored by Charles James Fox and William Pitt, respectively, attracted a good deal of attention. So did the impeachment of the former governor of the territories of the East India Company, Warren Hastings, which, being admired as a notable example of justice rendered by a state to its subjects, did something to counteract the prevalent impression of tyranny in the Empire. But the generally favorable effect of the impeachment was more than offset by the hostility aroused in Frenchmen as a result of English policy toward The Netherlands, where Britain joined Prussia in supporting the stadtholder against the French-supported Dutch Republican and Patriot parties. This action, which in 1787 brought France and England to the verge of war, was stigmatized in France as the sacrifice of liberty within Holland to a predatory British foreign policy that aimed ultimately at nothing less than the humiliation of France.[74] Throughout the decade, with the rivalry of France and

[74] Comte de Mirabeau, *Doutes sur la liberté de l'Escaut réclamée par l'empereur; sur les causes et sur les conséquences probables de cette réclamation* (London [1785]), pp. 8, 21, 75-80; Comte de Mirabeau to a Hollander, Nov., 1787, quoted in J.-P. Brissot, *Mémoires (1754-1793)*, ed. Claude Perroud (2 vols.; Paris [1911]), II, 175-76; Comte de Mirabeau, *Aux Bataves sur le stathouderat* ([Amsterdam?], 1788), *passim*; [Comte de Mirabeau], *Le Despotisme de la maison d'Orange prouvé par l'histoire. Par Karel van Ligtdal* ("In Holland" [1788]), p. 9 *et passim*; J.-P. Brissot de Warville, *Tableau de la situation actuelle dans les Indes orientales, et de l'état de l'Inde en général*, No. 1 (London, 1784), pp. 9-13; Étienne Clavière and J.-P. Brissot de Warville, *De la France et des États-Unis, ou De l'importance de la révolution de l'Amérique pour le bonheur de la France, des rapports de ce royaume et des États-Unis, des avantages réciproques qu'ils peuvent retirer de leurs liaisons de commerce, et enfin de la situation actuelle des États-Unis* (London, 1787), pp. ii-xiii; [Louis-Gabriel Bourdon], *Voyage d'Amérique. Dialogue en vers, entre l'auteur et l'abbé **** (London and Paris, 1786), pp. 124-35; Condorcet, *Lettres d'un bourgeois de New-Haven*, in *Oeuvres*, IX, 44; Lafayette, "Observations sur le commerce entre la France et les États-Unis" [1783], in Louis Gottschalk (ed.), "Lafayette as Commercial Agent," *American Historical Review*, XXXVI (1931), 564-70; Lafayette to Washington, May 14, 1784, in *The Letters of Lafayette to Washington 1777-1799*, ed. Louis Gottschalk (New York, 1944), p. 283; Lafayette to Washington, March 19, 1785, *ibid.*, p. 293; Lafayette to Washington, May 24, 1786, *ibid.*, pp. 311-12; Lafayette to Knox, Feb. 4, 1789, Massachusetts Historical Society; Lescène Desmaisons, *Histoire politique de la révolution en France*, I, 58-59, and II, 6; Livingston, *Examen du gouvernement d'Angleterre*, notes of Dupont and others, p. 98; Helvétius to Lefebvre Laroche [*sic*], Sept. 8, 1768 [apocryphal], *Oeuvres* (1795), XIV, 89-90; Lescure (ed.), *Correspondance secrète*, II, 190 (Oct. 15, 1787), 198 (Nov. 12, 1787); *Analyse des papiers*

Britain always in the background, the close association of the two ideals of the political and martial glory of France and the freedom of the citizen is very noticeable. The most vocal condemnation of Britain's imperial and foreign policy came at this time from liberals. When agitators like the Comte de Mirabeau and Lafayette supported the cause of liberty abroad, as they did in Ireland and in Holland, they were combating the enemy of France as well as the tyranny of governments.

A related set of French grievances against the English, giving rise likewise to nationalist utterances, revolved around British postwar commercial policy. Behind the idea of the freedom of the seas as conceived in France had lain, the reader will recall, the purpose of obtaining easy access to the commerce of England and her empire. After the conclusion of peace the French government had admitted foreign ships to the French sugar islands, but the British had declined to liberalize their own exclusive navigation policy. French shipowners, complaining that foreigners were depriving them of the trade with their own colonies while they had no compensation in trade with the colonies of Britain, loudly attacked both their own government and the English. Frenchmen felt all the more chagrined in that, despite a political alliance and a commercial treaty with the United States, they had been unable to divert to France any considerable share of the trade of the former British colonies, which remained, even without obtaining any concessions in return, the customers primarily of Britain.[75] The conditions of direct trade between France and Britain were still another sore issue. This trade had long been governed by a regime of mutually high duties and prohibitions, only occasionally relaxed, and tempered by a flourishing business in contraband. There was no trade treaty between the two states. An Anglo-French commercial convention had been contemplated in the treaty of peace of 1783, but it appeared that the English were disinclined

---

anglais (1787-89), *passim; Courier de l'Europe*, XXI, 345 (May 22, 1787); *Journal général de l'Europe*, I [1785], "Introduction politique," pp. 13-15; *ibid.*, 1788, I, "Discours préliminaire," p. 44; *ibid.*, II, 313-14.

[75] Métra, *Correspondance secrète*, XVIII, 205-10 (June 30, 1785); *ibid.*, pp. 271-73 (July 28, 1785); Lafayette to James Madison, March 16, 1785, Pennsylvania Historical Society; Lafayette to Elias Boudinot, March 16, 1785, New Jersey Historical Society.

either to begin negotiations for it or to relax their trade restrictions unilaterally. In 1785, in retaliation against the maintenance of British tariff and navigation walls, the French government prohibited completely the importation into France of numerous classes of English goods that it had previously allowed to enter. Then, in 1786, France and Britain concluded the Eden Treaty, establishing a reciprocal low-tariff regime.

Except for doctrinaire free-trade extremists like Condorcet, who thought commercial treaties worse than useless,[76] the free-trade school rejoiced. Not so the manufacturers, who protested because the treaty increased the competition offered by English goods to French textiles and hardwares. A great economic depression that in 1787 spread over France was widely attributed to it, and critics took the government to task for having failed to solicit the views of the industrial interests before settling on its terms.[77] Hostility against the English mounted, too, because of the treaty. It was said that, while inundating France with their goods, they were boycotting French imports into their own country.[78] In certain parts of France it became patriotic to "buy French." At the textile centers of Rouen and Lyon balls were given to which were admitted only such persons as were dressed in materials of French manufacture, referred to as *modes patriotiques*.[79] During the Anglo-French diplomatic crisis of 1787 opinion in Normandy, an industrial area, was reputed to be in favor of war to get rid of the treaty.[80] The Norman Chamber of Commerce asserted that the English had been well aware, during the negotiations, that they were dealing French industry a serious blow, for without protection it would be a very long time before

[76] *Lettres d'un bourgeois de New-Haven*, in *Oeuvres*, IX, 44. Cf. *Journal général de l'Europe*, 1788, I, 305-6.
[77] E. Levasseur, *Histoire du commerce de la France* (2 vols.; Paris, 1911-12), I, 542-44; Frances Acomb (ed.), "Unemployment and Relief in Champagne, 1788," *Journal of Modern History*, XI (1939), 43 nn. 8, 9, and 46 n. 16; *Réponse des négociants de la ville de Grenoble, à MM. les juges-consuls de Montauban, Clermont-Ferrand, Châlons, Orléans, Tours, Besançon, Dunkerque et Saint-Quentin, et à la chambre de commerce de Picardie, de Saint-Mâlo et de l'Isle en Flandre* [1788], p. 10 and n. Cf. *Courier de l'Europe*, XX, 303 (Nov. 10, 1786); *Journal de Genève*, 1786, IV, 381; *Mercure de France*, Oct. 25, 1788, p. 153; *Journal général de l'Europe*, 1788, I, 305; and see nn. 78-82 below.
[78] Bachaumont, *Mémoires secrets*, XXXVI, 3-4 (Sept. 11, 1787).
[79] *Courier de l'Europe*, XXIII, 75 (Feb. 1, 1788).
[80] Bachaumont, *Mémoires secrets*, XXXVI, 118 (Oct. 25, 1787).

French manufactures could compete on equal terms with those of England.[81] They could not adopt[82] the attitude expressed by the director of the École Royale Gratuite de Dessein, who, just before the treaty was to go into effect, urged the students at that institution to redouble their efforts to perfect the national manufactures, whose superior quality would then cause them to be preferred to foreign products.[83] The Norman Chamber explicitly rejected the thesis of the Neo-Physiocrat Dupont de Nemours, who argued that competition with foreign manufactures would serve only to toughen French industry and bring it to maturity.[84]

Dupont's view, which, no less than the opinion of his opponents, was stated with considerable anti-English animus, was really just as nationalist as theirs.[85] Indeed, it was if anything more so, in the sense of being founded on a hardier confidence in the capacity of the country to prosper under the conditions of free world competition.

Physiocratic nationalism pervaded more than the economic sphere. While the Neo-Physiocrats accommodated their political theory to the doctrine of the school of Mably and Rousseau, their nationalism was absorbed into it. To the concept of the sovereignty of the nation developed by the popular school in opposition to the divided-sovereignty concept of Anglophile liberalism, to the emphasis of this school upon the idea of political devotion or the general will as against that self-interest said to have corrupted the "republican monarchy" of England, there were added now all the ingredients of the nationalist outlook of the Physiocrats: their desire to establish an economic basis for the political unity of their country, their faith in the strength of France, both material and spiritual, their consciousness of the leading role of France in the development of contemporary European civilization, and their

---

[81] *Observations de la chambre du commerce de Normandie, sur le traité de commerce entre la France et l'Angleterre* [1787 or early 1788], p. 10 *et passim*.

[82] Chambre du Commerce de Normandie, *Réfutation des principes et assertions contenus dans une lettre qui a pour titre: Lettre à la chambre du commerce de Normandie, sur le mémoire qu'elle a publié relativement au traité de commerce avec l'Angleterre, par M. D. P.* (1788), *passim*.

[83] Bachaumont, *Mémoires secrets*, XXXIII, 265 (Dec. 31, 1786).

[84] Dupont de Nemours, *Lettre à la chambre du commerce de Normandie*, pp. 48-50 *et passim*.

[85] See above, p. 66.

great pride of nationality. This was undoubtedly another major factor in the union of nationalism and reform.

To be sure, the popular school did not have a monopoly of nationalism in the decade prior to the Revolution. Even Anglomania at this time, whether liberal or conservative, contained usually some admixture of nationalist sentiment. The viewpoint that Anglophile arguments expressed was that France had only to put her house in order by imitating the government of England and certain English policies, particularly with regard to financial reconstruction, to attain her maximum strength and greatness.[86] But there still lingered around Anglophile ideas something of the cosmopolitan attitude, some worship of the foreigner and his ways. On the other hand, the popular school not only held, in contrast with the Anglophiles, that party interest should somehow be merged in the general interest, they also held that reform should not consist in what they called the "servile" imitation of another people, who were moreover the traditional enemy of their country. It should consist in surpassing that other people's achievement, by following the pure light of reason.[87] The rationalism of the popular party, which has been remarked on elsewhere in this chapter, had a peculiarly French flavor. A Swiss publicist who was in France in 1789 observed this as he watched the debate in the Constituent Assembly:

They have [he said] so much national vanity, so much pretension, that they will prefer all kinds of stupidities of their own choice to the results

---

[86] Anon., *Lettre d'un Suisse aux Français*, pp. 3, 21, *et passim*; *Réponse des négociants de la ville de Grenoble, à MM. les juges-consuls de Montauban* . . . , pp. 3-10; De Sainte-Albine, *Projet d'une banque nationale à établir en France* (1789), pp. 1-7; [Étienne Clavière], *De la foi publique envers les créanciers de l'état. Lettres à M. Linguet sur le n. CXVI des ses Annales* (London, 1788), pp. 53-54, 127-28, 142-43; Soulés, *Le Véritable patriotisme*, pp. 2-33; Rabaut Saint-Étienne, *À la nation française*, p. 35.

[87] Helvétius to Lefebvre-Laroche, Sept. 8, 1768 [apocryphal], *Oeuvres* (1795), XIV, 78-82; Anon., *Exposé des principes de droit public, qui démontrent que les députés du tiers-état se sont légalement constitués comme représentant la nation. Par l'auteur des Quatres mots, adressés au journaliste des états-généraux* (1789), p. 7; [Louis-Gabriel Bourdon], *Le Patriote, ou Préservatif contre l'anglomanie. Par l'auteur du Voyage d'Amérique, etc.* [1789], *passim*; Dupont, *De la périodicite des assemblées nationales*, pp. 10-12; Pierre-Étienne Dumont to Samuel Romilly, June 21, 1789, in *Memoirs of the Life of Sir Samuel Romilly, Written by Himself; with a Selection from His Correspondence*, edited by his sons (2d ed.; 3 vols.; London, 1840), I, 354-55; Robespierre, *Dire . . . contre le veto royal*, p. 12; [Camille] Desmoulins, *La France libre* (3d ed.; 1789), p. 69.

of British experience. . . . They are agreed that you have two or three fine laws; but it is insupportable that you should have the presumption to say that you have a constitution.[88]

The words of the devotees of the popular faith themselves furnish perhaps the clearest indication of how their nationalist sentiments reinforced their constitutional position. "The representatives of the French nation," said Robespierre, "knowing how to give their country a constitution worthy of her and of the wisdom of this century, were not delegated to copy servilely an institution born in times of ignorance, of necessity and of the strife of opposing factions"[89]—in short, the English constitution. Even more belligerently the journalist Camille Desmoulins exulted: "We shall go beyond these English, who are so proud of their constitution and who mocked at our servitude."[90]

In review, it is evident that the role that England played in French political thought during the eighteenth century was not a simple one. "England," wrote a contemporary in the early days of the Revolution, "is our model and our rival, our guiding light and our enemy."[91] In a measure, that is a text upon which this entire essay is a commentary.

First of all, and for the greater part of the century prior to the Revolution, England was the symbol of everything hostile to the old regime—hostile, that is, to the divine-right monarchy, the authority of an intolerant religion, an excessive *étatisme*, and the principles of hierarchy and privilege. Against this symbol, this influence, the conservatives, many of whom never did cease to regard England as anything but a subversive force, invoked the most effective weapons available to them, French royalism and French nationalism. But after, and even during, the Seven Years' War the example of the English had begun to be deprecated by some liberals, too. Although it was not until the very eve of the Revolution that "republican" England suddenly assumed the

[88] Dumont to Samuel Romilly, June 21, 1789, in Romilly, *Memoirs*, I, 354-55.
[89] *Dire . . . contre le veto royal*, p. 12.
[90] *La France libre*, p. 69.
[91] [J.-P.-L. de Luchet], *Les Contemporains de 1789 et 1700, ou Les Opinions débattues pendant la première législature; avec les principaux événemens de la révolution. Rédigé par l'auteur de la Galerie des états-généraux* (3 vols.; Paris, 1790), I, 56.

lineaments of a monarchy, it was a generation earlier that the example of that country began to be termed a stumbling block to progress. The Physiocrats held that English fiscal and economic policy was grossly wrong, enshrining vicious popular prejudices to which the form of government allowed undue influence. To them, political liberty without enlightenment was vain. The founders of the school of Rousseau and Mably, basing their reflections upon the predominance of the Tory party and the revolt of the Americans against "despotism," concluded that in England political morality was wanting and that political liberty was coming to be, or had never been more than, a fiction.

The adherents of the Anglophile tradition, which remained the dominant liberalism until the period of the War of American Independence, had not troubled much to think through the problem of obtaining and maintaining liberty and economic and social reforms in despite of an absolute monarch unwilling or unable to introduce such measures by royal fiat. Now the almost simultaneous failure of the reformist Turgot ministry in France and success of the Revolution in America were followed by the rapid spread of a conviction among French reformers that absolute monarchy must go, and that, moreover, any government replacing it must be so set up that no special groups or interests could block reforms that would redound to the welfare of the nation as a whole. (For even if the real beneficiaries of the desired reforms were to be the bourgeoisie, reformers *thought* in terms of the nation.) Anglophile constitutionalism, which began suddenly to blossom and which admitted the crown and peerage to participation in the legislative process and organized political opposition to an at least half-legitimate place in government, came to seem, in the eyes of liberals, worse than useless. The Anglophobe doctrine of the school of Rousseau and Mably, with its key concepts of the general will, the sovereignty of that will (which was identified with the nation), and the legislative supremacy of the nation's representatives, excluding the king and any representatives of a special class, became the dominant revolutionary creed, its vigor and aggressiveness strengthened by the conversion to it of the left-wing Physiocrats.

The Anglophobe viewpoint of the liberals reflected not only

their increasing radicalism but their nationalism, which itself reinforced their radicalism. The liberalism of Mably and Rousseau, comprehending the concepts of the general will and the sovereignty of that will, had had a nationalist direction, even if, as nationalism, it had lacked local or historical association, the pride of nationality. This pride of nationality, which infused the whole revolutionary movement of the 1780's, had been attached to the Physiocrats' agrarian nationalism from the beginning. Undoubtedly they had helped to introduce it into the broader movement. Yet they cannot be accounted the only cause of this result. It appears that many a Frenchman who had thrilled to victory in the War of American Independence and who also desired to see a constitution established in France (where in his opinion none deserving of the name existed) entertained a condescending, if not hostile, attitude toward the political institutions of the English, convinced that the political genius of the French, their "reason," was not in need of taking lessons from their late enemies across the Channel.

In the perspective of the eighteenth century as a whole, the decline of Anglophile liberalism appears as one sign, at least, of the passing of the cosmopolitan spirit, the spirit of Voltaire, Helvétius, and Montesquieu. The liberalism of the Anglophobes, on the other hand, was not alone the immediate bringer of the Revolution to France; it was the forerunner of a spirit that would joyfully assume the mission of carrying that Revolution to other nations as well, by force of arms.

APPENDIX

Apocryphal Letters of Helvétius

THE EDITION OF Helvétius's works published in 1795 by his literary executor, the Abbé Lefebvre de la Roche, contains four letters[1] not found in the previous edition published in 1781.[2] Two of these letters appeared in 1789 in the form of a pamphlet entitled *Lettres de M. Helvétius au président de Montesquieu et à M. Saurin, relatives à l'aristocratie de la noblesse*. If the other two were ever published before the edition of 1795, I do not know where. All four appear to be of the same species, but only the letter to Montesquieu, undated and published in 1789, and a letter to Lefebvre de la Roche, dated September 8, 1768, and published for the first time, so far as I know, in 1795, will concern us here; for of the four letters only those two express opinions about England. Specifically, they consist of extremely hostile judgments upon the English constitution, quite at variance with the very Anglophile opinions expressed by Helvétius elsewhere both in his work intended for publication and in his private correspondence.

Helvétius professed the utilitarian thesis that the best government is that which insures the greatest happiness of the greatest number of people. He thought of such government as one that would leave the freest play to individual aims and desires, or to the aims and desires of those classes and parties into which human

[1] *Oeuvres complètes d'Helvétius* (14 vols.; Paris, 1795), XIV, 61-109.
[2] *Oeuvres complettes de M. Helvétius* (5 vols.; London, 1781).

beings were grouped, and considered that social good was a kind of resultant of the clash of many opinions. He admired the English government because he believed that it presented the conditions of liberty essential to the realization of men's happiness.

Helvétius particularly and continually praised English liberty of speech and of the press, which seemed to him the most effective guarantees of the public welfare. "If in the science of government, as in every other," he said, "the light strikes from the clash of contrary opinions, there is no country where the administration can be more enlightened [than it is in England], since there is none where the press is more free."[3] As a footnote to this he added:

In London there is no workman, no chair-carrier, who does not read the papers, who does not suspect the venality of his representatives, and who does not believe in consequence that he should instruct himself in his duties as a citizen. Moreover, no member of Parliament would dare propose a law contrary to the national liberty. If he did, this member, called to account before the people by the opposition party and the public papers, would be exposed to its vengeance.[4]

In *De l'homme*, the work from which the foregoing quotations have been taken, Helvétius said that love of power was the principle of all governments alike,[5] and indicated that in general he favored a government where power would be divided equally among all classes because then the very exercise of power would achieve the greatest good of the greatest number.[6] This idea sounds like a utilitarian version of "mixed government," in other words, a reference to the English parliamentary system. Some years earlier, on returning from a trip to England, Helvétius had written to another Anglophile, Servan:

I have visited England and have been very much pleased with my journey.... There you will see enlightened men and happy people; a government where all the passions are in play, where one thing balances another, and where repose is born of the equilibrium of forces.... By the nature of the government even the vices, if one may say so, are advantageous to England.[7]

[3] *De l'homme*, in *Oeuvres* (1781), IV, 74.
[4] *Ibid.*, p. 123 n. 3.   [5] *Ibid.*, III, 303.   [6] *Ibid.*
[7] Helvétius to Servan, Dec. 19, 1764, in X. de Portets (ed.), *Oeuvres choisies de Servan* (new ed.; 5 vols.; Paris, 1822), I, cxxxiv.

In *De l'homme*, again, Helvétius carried this idea over to approval of the party system. "The opposition," he remarked, "excited by ambition, vengeance, or the love of country, protects the people against tyranny; the court party, animated by the desire of places, favor, or money, sustains the ministry against the sometimes unjust attacks of the opposition."[8]

The letters that Helvétius wrote to his wife from England in 1764 are similarly lyrical. In one of them he praised both liberty and equality as found there.

This is a country of liberty [he wrote]; it seems to me that people here breathe more easily, that the soul and the lungs have more elasticity. . . . This people . . . sees matters more largely than we do. Just recently the daughter of a milord married an actor; you know what a disturbance that would make in Paris; here, it is of no consequence. "What difference does it make?" an Englishman said to me. "Will our fleet be any the less able to blockade your ports when we are at war?" They place no more importance on the hanging of a milord, when he has deserved it. "It is good," they say, "that the people should know that rascals are hanged, of whatever condition they may be."[9]

About the time that Helvétius was composing *De l'homme*, and only four years after he had written the above-mentioned letters to his wife and to Servan, he was supposed to have written the long letter dated September 8, 1768, and addressed to Lefebvre de la Roche. This letter, not reproduced here as it may easily be consulted in Helvétius's works, contains the following particularly un-Helvétian propositions:

1. Through corruption, the executive has achieved control of the government of England and can rule even against the wishes of the nation. In the face of parliamentary factions, however, corruption is virtually a legal and necessary means of carrying on business.

2. The House of Lords is a remnant of feudalism that supports the royal prerogative in return for the perpetuating of its own privileges, and it shares with the crown and at the expense of the people the advantages thus obtained.

[8] *De l'homme*, in *Oeuvres* (1781), IV, 133 n. 26.
[9] Helvétius to Mme Helvétius, April, 1764, in Antoine Guillois (ed.), "Correspondance d'Helvétius avec sa femme," *Le Carnet historique et littéraire*, VI (July-Dec., 1900), 481.

3. Energy sufficient to maintain the public welfare is to be found in England only in an opposition party that is often too slow in awaking to danger. However, the fundamental principle of government should not be an eternal struggle between opposing powers, but unity of sentiment and action.

4. When the English constitution was formed, it was the best that could have been made, but since that time the English have stopped progressing.

5. It is true that the writings that have flowed from a free press in England have indemnified humanity for the wrongs that the English have done to it, but while profiting from the study of the English example, the French should not think of transporting the English constitution to the Continent.

The disparity between these ideas and those that have been described as belonging to Helvétius according to other and genuine sources is self-evident. The ideas are not only un-Helvétian, they are not characteristic of 1768. The whole letter, as the last point stated above suggests, is a somewhat hysterical argument against the imminent introduction of the English constitution into France. No one in 1768 was worried over such a contingency. It is true that the parlements were then being charged, or would soon be charged, with aping the Parliament of England, but there was no question of introducing a whole new constitution, and in general the literature of the parlementary controversy of 1770-71 has quite another tenor from that of the letter in question. On the other hand, this letter contains a pattern of ideas very common in the pamphlets of 1789 with writers who saw in the constitutional Anglomania of that year a fortress of the defenders of aristocratic privilege and royal preponderance against the interest of the nation as a whole.

The same remarks can be made about the letter to Montesquieu, which maintains that the combinations of powers described in the analysis of the English constitution in the *Esprit des lois* only separate and complicate the interests of individuals instead of uniting them. Further, this letter can be classed with other pamphlets of 1788-89 attacking Montesquieu as an aristocratic conservative. Keim, the biographer of Helvétius, noted that the letter to Montesquieu seemed to anticipate the ideas of 1789,[10] though he did not deny its authenticity. He apparently did not know that it had been published as a pamphlet in 1789.

In form, both of the letters discussed here, the letter to Montesquieu and the one to Lefebvre de la Roche, are not truly epistolary. They read like pamphlets.

Since the edition of Helvétius published in 1795 was the work of Lefebvre de la Roche, and since he was content that one of these letters should stand in it as having been addressed to himself, he must have been either the author or an accomplice. The substance of that letter, as well as the one addressed to Montesquieu, could easily have been his own political views, for the Abbé Morellet, who knew him well, says that in the summer of 1789 Lefebvre de la Roche was an ardent supporter of the left wing,[11] the anti-English devotees of the doctrine of popular sovereignty.

[10] Albert Keim, *Helvétius, sa vie et son oeuvre* . . . (Paris, 1907), p. 158.
[11] *Mémoires (inédits) de l'abbé Morellet, suivis de sa correspondance avec M. le comte R***, ministre des finances à Naples* ("Collection des mémoires relatifs à la Révolution française," LIV-LV; 2 vols.; Paris, 1823), I, 381.

BIBLIOGRAPHY

The greater number of the primary sources listed in the following bibliography are those to which there are footnote references. But a considerable number of sources that it was not convenient to cite in footnotes have also provided material for this study, notably, for example, in its Anglophile aspects, which have been treated in less detail than the Anglophobe developments. It has been thought proper to include such sources in the bibliography. Similarly in the listing of secondary works, all those that were useful in the preparation of this study are indicated, whether or not they have been cited in the footnotes.

In many cases the edition listed is not the earliest edition of a given source. Where there are footnote references to such works, the footnotes inform the reader of the earliest date of publication, so far as it is known. No attempt has been made to indicate fictitious imprints. In general, variations of spelling have been retained.

The outline of the bibliography is as follows:

I. Bibliographies and Catalogues
II. Primary Sources
    A. Manuscripts
    B. Printed Materials
        1. Official or Semiofficial Publications
        2. Periodicals
        3. Nouvelles à la main
        4. Collected Works
        5. Works Separately Published
            a. Books and Pamphlets—Author Anonymous
            b. Books and Pamphlets—Author Known
            c. Correspondence
            d. Memoirs and Journals
            e. Plays
III. Secondary Works
    A. Books
    B. Articles
    C. Works of Reference

I. Bibliographies and Catalogues

Bibliothèque Nationale. Département des imprimés. *Catalogue de l'histoire de France.* 11 vols. Paris, 1855-79.

———. *Catalogue de l'histoire de la Grande-Bretagne.* Paris, 1878. Lithographed.

Cornell University. *Catalogue of the Historical Library of Andrew Dickson White.* 2 vols. Ithaca, 1889-94.

Lanson, Gustave. *Manuel bibliographique de la littérature française moderne.* New ed. Paris, 1931.

Pinson, Koppel S. *Bibliographical Introduction to Nationalism.* New York, 1935.

Tourneux, Maurice. *Bibliographie de l'histoire de Paris pendant la Révolution française.* 5 vols. Paris, 1890-1913.

II. Primary Sources

A. MANUSCRIPTS[1]

Letter of Lafayette to James McHenry, February 15, 1781. Henry E. Huntington Library, MH 156.

Letter of Lafayette to Henry Laurens, July 6, 1783. South Carolina Historical Society.

Letter of Lafayette to Franklin [October 13, 1783]. American Philosophical Society, Franklin Papers, XLII, No. 140.

Letter of Lafayette to the President of Congress, December 26, 1783. Library of Congress, Papers of the Continental Congress, 156.

Letter of Lafayette to Henry Knox, January 8, 1784. Massachusetts Historical Society.

Letter of Lafayette to "My dear sir" [Colonel Wadsworth?], March 7, 1784. Connecticut Historical Society.

Letter of Lafayette to James Madison, March 16, 1785. Pennsylvania Historical Society.

Letter of Lafayette to Elias Boudinot, March 16, 1785. New Jersey Historical Society.

Letter of Lafayette to McHenry, October 26, 1786. Library of Congress, James McHenry Collection.

Letter of Lafayette to Col. William Smith, January 16, 1787. MS in the possession of H. A. DeWindt.

Letter of Lafayette to Alexander Hamilton, October 15, 1787. Library of Congress, Papers of Alexander Hamilton.

[1] Photostatic copies from the collection of Professor Louis Gottschalk were used in place of the originals.

Bibliography

Letter of Lafayette to Hamilton, May 25 [24?], 1788. Library of Congress, Papers of Alexander Hamilton.

Letter of Lafayette to Knox, February 4, 1789. Massachusetts Historical Society.

Letter of B. [or P.] Langan to Sir John Johnson, November 15, 1784. Newberry Library, American Historical MSS in the Ayer Collection.

Letter of Sir Edward Newenham to Lafayette, March 22, 1784. American Philosophical Society, Franklin Papers, XXXI, Part 2, No. 118.

B. PRINTED MATERIALS

1. Official or Semiofficial Publications

ASSEMBLÉE NATIONALE [CONSTITUANTE]. *Journal des débats et des décrets.* Nos. 1-862. 10 vols. 1789-91.

———. *Procès-verbal de l'Assemblée nationale constituante* . . . Nos. 1-782. 101 vols. [Paris, 1789-91].

HISTORICAL MANUSCRIPTS COMMISSION. *Fourteenth Report,* Appendix, Part 1. *The Manuscripts of His Grace the Duke of Rutland, K. G., Preserved at Belvoir Castle,* Vol. III. London, 1894.

2. Periodicals

Affaires de l'Angleterre et de l'Amérique. 15 vols. Antwerp, 1776-79.

Analyse des papiers anglais. 4 vols. November 14, 1787–November 19, 1789.

Annales politiques, civiles, et littéraires du dix-huitième siècle. 19 vols. London, Brussels, Paris, 1777-92. (Generally known as *Annales de Linguet.*)

L'Année littéraire; ou, Suite des lettres sur quelques écrits de ce temps. Amsterdam, Paris, 1754-90.

Courier de l'Europe. 32 vols. London, 1777-92.

Éphémérides du citoyen, ou Chronique de l'esprit national. 69 vols. Paris, 1765-72. (Subtitle from 1767 is *Bibliothèque raisonnée des sciences morales et politiques.*)

Gazette de France. Paris, 1762-92.

Journal anglais, contenant les découvertes de la science, des arts libéraux et mécaniques, les nouvelles philosophiques, littéraires, économiques et politiques, des trois royaumes et des colonies qui en dependent. 7 vols. Paris, 1775-78.

Journal de Paris. 87 vols. Paris, 1777-1811.

Journal de politique et de littérature, contenant les principaux événemens de toutes les cours, les nouvelles de la république des lettres, etc. Brussels, 1774-78. (Generally known as *Journal politique de Bruxelles,* under which title it became, from 1778, the political setion of the *Mercure de France.*)

Journal des beaux-arts et des sciences. Paris, 1768-82.

Journal des sçavans. Paris, 1665-1864.

Journal encyclopédique. Liége, Bouillon, 1756-93.

Journal général de l'Europe. Première partie. Politique, commerce, agriculture. Herve, 1785-92.

Journal historique et littéraire. Luxembourg, 1773-94.

Journal historique et politique des principaux événemens des différentes cours de l'Europe. 79 vols. Geneva, 1772-92. (Generally known as *Journal de Genève.*)

Mercure de France. Paris, 1724-91.

Révolutions de Paris. 17 vols. Paris, 1789-94.

3. Nouvelles à la main

[BACHAUMONT, LOUIS, AND CONTINUATORS]. *Mémoires secrets pour servir à l'histoire de la république des lettres en France, depuis MDCCLXII jusqu'à nos jours; ou Journal d'un observateur.* . . . 36 vols. London, 1784-89.

Correspondance secrète, inédite, sur Louis XVI, Marie-Antoinette, la cour et la ville, de 1777 à 1792. Edited by M. de Lescure. 2 vols. Paris, 1866.

GRIMM [F.-M., BARON DE], ET AL. *Correspondance littéraire, philosophique et critique par Grimm, Diderot, Raynal, Meister, etc. revue sur les textes originaux.* . . . Edited by Maurice Tourneux. 16 vols. Paris, 1877-82.

LA HARPE, J.-F. DE. *Correspondance littéraire, adressée à son A. I. Mgr le grand-duc, aujourd'hui empereur de Russie; et à M. le comte André Schowalow, chambellan de l'impératrice Catherine II, depuis 1774 jusqu'à 1791.* Vols X-XIII of *Oeuvres de La Harpe.* 16 vols. Paris, 1820-21.

[MÉTRA, J. IMBERT, ET AL.]. *Correspondance secrète, politique et littéraire, ou Mémoires pour servir à l'histoire des cours, des sociétés et de la littérature en France, depuis la mort de Louis XV.* 18 vols. London, 1787-89.

4. Collected Works

CÉRUTTI, J.-A.-J. *Oeuvres diverses de M. Cérutti, ou Recueil de pièces composées avant et depuis la révolution.* 2 vols. Paris, 1792.

CHAMFORT, N.-S. ROCH DE. *Oeuvres complètes de Chamfort.* Edited by P.-R. Auguis. 5 vols. Paris, 1824-25.
CONDORCET, MARQUIS DE. *Oeuvres de Condorcet.* Edited by A. Condorcet O'Connor and M. F. Arago. 12 vols. Paris, 1847-49.
DIDEROT, DENIS. *Oeuvres complètes de Diderot, comprenant tout ce qui a été publié à diverses époques et tous les manuscrits inédits conservés à la bibliothèque de l'Ermitage.* Edited by J. Assézat. 20 vols. Paris, 1875-77.
HELVÉTIUS, C.-A. *Oeuvres complettes [sic] de M. Helvétius.* New edition, corrected and enlarged. 5 vols. London, 1781.
———. *Oeuvres complètes d'Helvétius.* [Edited by Lefebvre de la Roche.] 14 vols. Paris, 1795.
LANJUINAIS, J.-D. *Oeuvres de J.-D. Lanjuinais, pair de France, membre de l'Institut, etc. . . .* Edited by Victor Lanjuinais. 4 vols. Paris, 1832.
LINGUET, S.-N. *Oeuvres de M. Linguet.* 6 vols. London, 1774.
MABLY, ABBÉ DE. *Collection complète des oeuvres de l'abbé de Mably.* 15 vols. Paris, Year III (1794-95).
MONTESQUIEU, BARON DE. *Oeuvres complètes de Montesquieu avec les variantes des premières éditions, un choix des meilleurs commentaires et des notes nouvelles.* Edited by Édouard Laboulaye. 7 vols. Paris, 1875-79.
MORELLET, ABBÉ. *Mélanges de littérature et de philosophie du 18ᵉ siècle.* 4 vols. Paris, 1818.
NECKER, JACQUES. *Oeuvres complètes de M. Necker.* Edited by Baron de Staël. 15 vols. Paris, 1820-21.
NECKER, MADAME. *Mélanges extraits des manuscrits de Mme Necker.* 3 vols. Paris, 1798.
———. *Nouveaux mélanges extraits des manuscrits de Mme Necker.* 2 vols. Paris, 1801.
ROLAND, MADAME. *Oeuvres de J.-M. Ph. Roland, femme de l'ex-ministre de l'intérieur. . . .* Edited by L.-A. Champagneux. 3 vols. Paris, Year VIII (1799-1800).
ROUSSEAU, J.-J. *The Political Writings of Jean Jacques Rousseau.* Edited by C. E. Vaughan. 2 vols. Cambridge, 1915.
SERVAN, J.-M.-A. *Oeuvres choisies de Servan.* New enlarged edition. Edited by X. de Portets. 5 vols. Paris, 1822-25.
TURGOT, A.-R.-J. *Oeuvres de Turgot et documents le concernant avec biographie et notes.* Edited by Gustave Schelle. 5 vols. Paris, 1913-23.
VOLTAIRE. *Oeuvres complètes de Voltaire.* New edition. 52 vols. Paris, 1877-85.

5. Works Separately Published

a. Books and Pamphlets—Author Anonymous

L'Anti-sanctionnaire anglois, ou Aiguillon à la constitution. N.p., 1789.

L'Aristocratie enchaînée et surveillée par le peuple et le roi; suivi d'un Mémoire des barons nés de Languedoc et de la réponse à leurs pretensions exhorbitantes. Par J. L. G. S. N.p., January 31, 1789.

L'Aristocratie financière, avec un moyen patriotique de s'en faire une ressource pour les besoins de l'état. N.p. [178–].

Coup d'oeil sur la Grande-Bretagne. London, 1776.

Coup d'oeil utile, s'il fixe l'attention de mes concitoyens. Par M. P. D. C. N.p., 1788.

De la république et de la monarchie. N.p. [1789].

Derniere relation de ce qui vient de se passer à Rennes; ou Apologie des sentiments et de la conduite des gens du Tiers-Etat de la ville de Rennes. N.p. [1789].

Des droits du citoyen, et de leur réunion avec une bonne constitution. Par R***. J**., député particulier du diocese de Lodeve. N.p., 1789.

Discours de l'orateur des trois ordres, aux états-généraux. Par un député. N.p., 1789.

Discours de M. le premier président de la chambre des communes du caffé de Dubuisson, successeur de Procope, sur les affaires actuelles de l'état. N.p. [1771?].

Entretien de M. le comte de Mirabeau et de M. Duval d'Espresmenil. N.p. [1789].

Épitre à Monsieur Necker, directeur général des finances, par un ami de la vérité, bon citoyen, bon patriote et bon sujet, l'écho du public impartial. N.p. [1788].

États-généraux de l'an mil neuf cent quatre-vingt-dix-neuf. Dédiés à l'Assemblèe Nationale. Par un député des communes. N.p., 1789.

Exposé des droits des colonies britanniques, pour justifier le projet de leur indépendance. Amsterdam, 1776.

Exposé des principes de droit public, qui démontrent que les députés du tiers-état se sont légalement constitués comme représentant la nation. Par l'auteur des Quatre mots, adressés au journaliste des États-Généraux. N.p., 1789.

Extrait d'une lettre, en date de Londres, du 3 mai 1771. N.p. [1771].

Le Fin mot de l'affaire. N.p. [1771?].

Fragment d'une lettre écrite à M. Pitt. Par un Anglais. N.p., 1789.

Fragment de Polybe; et quelques extraits de Spelman sur la meilleure forme de gouvernement possible, traduits en françois. N.p. [1789?].

Les Francs. N.p., 1785.
Je m'en rapporte à tout le monde, ou Réflexions impartiales sur les affaires actuelles. London, 1788.
Lettre à M. d'Epremesnil, à l'occasion de la reprise des fonctions du parlement. N.p., 1788.
Lettre d'un Anglois à Paris. London, 1787.
Lettre d'un homme à huit cents soixante-quatre nobles Bretons. N.p., 1789.
Lettre d'un jeune homme à son ami, sur les Français et les Anglais, relativement à la frivolité reprochée aux uns, et la philosophie attribuée aux autres; ou Essai d'un parallele à faire entre ces deux nations. Amsterdam and Paris, 1779.
Lettre d'un Suisse aux Français, pour concilier les trois ordres. Berne, 1789.
Lettre de M. C** à M. de St**** à Rouen. Servant de réponse à la lettre du parlement de Normandie au roi, en date du 8 février, sur l'état actuel du parlement de Paris. N.p. [1771].
Lettre du roi d'Angleterre au roi de France, sur les états généraux. N.p., 1789.
Lettre sur l'état actuel du crédit du gouvernement en France. N.p., 1771.
Lettres de M. le marquis de *** à un Français retiré à Londres. Amsterdam, 1788.
Mémoire du peuple françois au roi. N.p. [1788].
Le Négociant citoyen, ou Essai dans la recherche des moyens d'augmenter les lumieres de la nation sur le commerce et l'agriculture. Par M. C. C. A. Amsterdam and Paris, 1764.
Nouvelles observations sur la seconde lettre de M^r. de Pinto, à l'occasion des troubles de l'Amérique septentrionale. Pour servir de suite aux Observations d'un homme impartial sur la premiere lettre de M^r. *****. London, 1776.
Observations d'un homme impartial sur la Lettre de M^r. S. B. docteur en médecine à Kingston, au sujet des troubles qui agitent actuellement toute l'Amérique septentrionale. London, 1776.
Observations sur les remontrances du clergé. Du 15 juin 1788. N.p. [1788].
Ouvrage d'un citoyen, gentilhomme et militaire, ou Lettres sur la noblesse . . . à MM. les notables. London, 1787.
Plan d'une constitution nouvelle, convenable à la nation françoise. N.p. [1789].

Le Plus fort des pamphlets. L'ordre de paysans aux états-généraux. N.p., 1789.

Réflexions d'un citoyen sur l'édit de décembre 1770. N.p. [1770 or 1771].

Réflexions impartiales sur la grande question qui partage les esprits, concernant les droits du roi et de la nation assemblée en états-généraux. N.p., 1789.

Réflexions sur la question de savoir si on opinera par ordre ou par tête. N.p. [1789].

Les Rêveries patriotiques du comte L*** de G******. Versailles, 1789.

Le Songe d'un jeune Parisien. N.p. [ca. 1770].

La Tête leur tourne. N.p. [ca. 1770-71].

Les Vices découverts, ou Avis à mes concitoyens, sur quelques objets importans, relatifs à l'état présent des affaires. "En France," 1789.

La Voix du peuple, ou Les Anecdotes politiques du bon-homme Richard, sur les affaires du temps. Paris, 1789.

b. Books and Pamphlets—Author Known

[ABEILLE, LOUIS-PAUL]. *Faits qui ont influé sur la cherté des grains, en France et en Angleterre.* N.p., 1768.

[———]. *Principes sur la liberté du commerce des grains.* Amsterdam and Paris, 1768.

———. *Réflexions sur la police des grains en France et en Angleterre.* See entry below under Dupont de Nemours: *De l'exportation et de l'importation des grains.*

[ACCARIAS DE SERIONNE, JACQUES]. *Les Intérêts des nations de l'Europe, dévelopés relativement au commerce.* 2 vols. Leyden, 1766.

ADAMS, JOHN. *A Defence of the Constitutions of Government of the United States of America, against the Attack of M. Turgot, in His Letter to Dr. Price, Dated the Twenty-second Day of March, 1778.* Reprinted in Vol. IV, pp. 271-588, Vol. V, and Vol. VI, pp. 3-220 of *The Works of John Adams, Second President of the United States.* Edited by Charles Francis Adams. 10 vols. Boston, 1856.

ALBON, COMTE D'. *Discours sur l'histoire, le gouvernement, les usages, la littérature et les arts, de plusieurs nations de l'Europe.* 4 vols. Geneva and Paris, 1782.

ANTRAIGUES, COMTE D'. *À l'ordre de la noblesse du Bas-Vivarais.* N.p. [1789].

[————]. *Mémoire sur les états généraux, leurs droits, et la maniere de les convoquer.* N.p., 1788.
BAILLIO. *Le Coup de grace des aristocrates, ou Essai sur la régénération nationale.* "Au palais royal" [Paris], 1789.
[BARBEU-DUBOURG, JACQUES]. *Petit code de la raison humaine, ou Exposition succincte de ce que la raison dicte à tous les hommes pour éclairer leur conduite et assurer leur bonheur.* Par M. B. D. N.p., 1789.
BASSET DE LA MARELLE [LOUIS]. *La Différence du patriotisme national chez les François et chez les Anglois. Discours lu à l'Académie des Sciences Belles-Lettres et Arts de Lyon.* Lyon, 1762.
BAUDEAU, ABBÉ [NICOLAS]. *Avis au peuple sur son premier besoin.* New edition. Amsterdam and Paris, 1774.
————. *Éclaircissements demandés à M. N**, sur ses principes économiques, et sur ses projets de législation; au nom des propriétaires fonciers et des cultivateurs françois.* N.p., 1775.
[————]. *Idées d'un citoyen presque sexagénaire sur l'état actuel du royaume de France, comparées à celles de sa jeunesse.* Paris, 1787.
[————]. *Idées d'un citoyen sur l'administration des finances du roi.* Amsterdam, 1763.
————. *Première introduction à la philosophie économique ou analyse des états policés.* 1767 [1771]. Edited by A. Dubois. Paris, 1910.
————. *Principes de la science morale et politique sur le luxe et les loix somptuaires.* 1767. Edited by A. Dubois. Paris, 1912.
[BAUDOUIN DE GUÉMADEUC]. *L'Espion dévalisé.* London, 1782.
[BEAUMARCHAIS, PIERRE-AUGUSTIN CARON DE?, OR C. GUILLOTON-BEAULIEU?] *Influence du despotisme de l'Angleterre sur les deux mondes.* Boston [1780].
BEAUMARCHAIS. *Observations sur le Mémoire justificatif de la cour de Londres.* London and Philadelphia, 1779.
[————]. *Le Voeu de toutes les nations, et l'intérêt de toutes les puissances dans l'abaissement et l'humiliation de la Grande-Bretagne.* N.p., 1778.
BERGASSE [NICOLAS]. *Lettre de M. Bergasse, sur les états généraux.* N.p., 1789.
————. *Rapport du comité de constitution sur l'organisation du pouvoir judiciaire, présenté à l'Assemblée nationale.* Paris, 1789.
[BILLAUD-VARENNE, J.-N.]. *Despotisme des ministres de France, ou Exposition des principes et moyens employés par l'aristocratie, pour*

mettre la France dans les fers. 3 vols. Amsterdam and Paris, 1789.

[BLONDE?]. Le Parlement justifié par l'impératrice reine de Hongrie, et par le roi de Prusse; ou Seconde lettre, dans laquelle on continue à répondre aux écrits de M. le Chancelier. N.p. [1771]. Reprinted in Les Efforts de la liberté et du patriotisme, contre le despotisme du sieur de Maupeou, chancelier de France, ou Recueil des écrits patriotiques publiés pour maintenir l'ancien gouvernement français, III, 198-254. [Edited by M. F. Pidansat de Mairobert.] London, 1775.

BOUCHER D'ARGIS [A.-J.] Observations sur les loix criminelles de France. Amsterdam and Paris, 1781.

BOURBOULON [pseud.?]. Réponse du sieur Bourboulon, officier employé dans les finances de Mgr. le comte d'Artois, au Compte rendu au roi, par M. Necker, directeur-général des finances. London, 1781.

[BOURDON, LOUIS-GABRIEL]. Le Patriote, ou Préservatif contre l'anglomanie. Par l'auteur du Voyage d'Amerique, etc. N.p. [1789].

[———]. Voyage d'Amérique. Dialogue en vers, entre l'auteur et l'abbé ***. London, 1786.

BRISSOT DE WARVILLE, J.-P. (ED.). Bibliothèque philosophique du législateur, du politique, du jurisconsulte. 10 vols. Berlin and Paris, 1782-85.

[———]. Dénonciation au public d'un nouveau projet d'agiotage.... London, 1786.

[———]. L'Indépendance des Anglo-Américains démontrée utile à la Grande-Bretagne. Lettres extraits du Journal d'agriculture, avril et mai 1782. N.p., n.d.

———. Journal du licée de Londres, ou Tableau de l'état présent des sciences et des arts en Angleterre. Paris, 1784.

———. Réponse de Jacques-Pierre Brissot à tous les libellistes qui ont attaqué et attaquent sa vie passée. Paris, August 10, 1791.

———. Tableau de la situation actuelle des Anglois dans les Indes orientales, et de l'état de l'Inde en général. London, 1784.

[———]. Testament politique de l'Angleterre. N.p., 1780.

———. Théorie des loix criminelles. 2 vols. Berlin, 1781.

BRISSOT DE WARVILLE [J.-P.], AND CLAVIÈRE, ÉTIENNE. De la France et des États-Unis, ou De l'importance de la révolution de l'Amérique pour le bonheur de la France, des rapports de ce royaume et des États-Unis, des avantages réciproques qu'ils peuvent retirer *de leurs liaisons de commerce, et enfin de la situation actuelle des États-Unis.* London, 1787.

[————]. *Lettre à l'auteur du Mercure politique par les auteurs du traité intitulé: De la France et des États-Unis.* Bouillon, 1787.

[BROWN, JOHN]. *Les Moeurs angloises, ou Appréciation des moeurs et des principes qui caractérisent actuellement la nation britannique.* [Translated from the English by P. Chais.] The Hague, 1758.

[BRUN, ABBÉ JOSEPH-ANDRÉ]. *Le Point de ralliement des citoyens françois, sur les bases d'une constitution nationale, et sur les pouvoirs des députés.* N.p., 1789.

BURKE, EDMUND. *Thoughts on the Causes of the Present Discontents.* Reprinted in *The Works of the Right Honorable Edmund Burke,* I, 435-537. 12 vols. Boston, 1865.

CALONNE [CHARLES-ALEXANDRE] DE. *Lettre adressée au roi, par M. de Calonne, le 9 février 1789.* London [1789].

[CARACCIOLI, L.-A. DE]. *Les Entretiens du palais-royal.* 2 vols. Utrecht and Paris, 1787.

————. *Voyage de la raison en Europe.* Reprinted in *Voyages imaginaires,* XXVII, 139-478. [Edited by Garnier.] Amsterdam and Paris, 1787. (Erroneously attributed on title page to the *Marquis* de Caraccioli.)

————. *The Travels of Reason in Europe.* Translated from the French of the Marquis [sic] Caraccioli. London, 1780.

CARBONNEL. *Le Lys ou Le Rêve d'un roi, fable qui n'en est pas une.* Granada and Paris, 1779.

[CARRA, J.-L.]. *L'Orateur des états-généraux. Seconde partie.* Paris, 1789.

[————]. *Systeme de la raison, ou Le Prophete philosophe.* London, 1782.

CASAUX, MARQUIS DE. *Questions à examiner, avant l'assemblée des états généraux.* N.p., 1788.

CHASTELLUX, MARQUIS DE. *De la félicité publique, ou Considérations sur le sort des hommes dans les différentes époques de l'histoire.* New edition. 2 vols. Paris, 1822.

[CHAUDON, LOUIS-MAYEUL]. *Anti-dictionnaire philosophique, pour servir de commentaire et de correctif au Dictionnaire philosophique, et aux autres livres qui ont paru de nos jours contre le christianisme.* ... Fourth edition. 2 vols. Paris, 1775.

[CHAVANNES DE LA GIRAUDIÈRE, L. DE]. *L'Amérique délivrée, esquisse d'un poëme sur l'indépendance de l'Amérique.* 2 vols. Amsterdam, 1783.

[CHAVEAU-LAGARDE, N.]. *Théorie des états-généraux, ou La France régénerée.* Paris [1789].

CHÉNIER, M.-J. DE. *Dénonciation des inquisiteurs de la pensée.* Paris, 1789.

[CLAVIÉRE, ÉTIENNE]. *De la foi publique envers les créanciers de l'état. Lettres à M. Linguet sur le n. CXVI de ses Annales. Par M***.* London, 1788.

CLOOTS DU VAL-DE-GRACE, JEAN BAPTISTE, BARON DE. *Voeux d'un Gallophile.* New edition. Amsterdam, 1786.

[CONTANT D'ORVILLE]. *Les Nuits angloises, ou Recueil de traits singuliers, d'anecdotes, d'événements remarquables, de faits extraordinaires, de bisarreries, d'observations critiques et de pensées philosophiques, etc., propre à faire connoître le génie et le caractere des Anglois.* 4 vols. Paris, 1771.

[COPPONS, DE]. *Critique de la théorie et pratique de M. Necker, dans l'administration des finances de la France.* 2 vols. N.p., 1785.

[COYER, ABBÉ GABRIEL-FRANÇOIS]. *Nouvelles observations sur l'Angleterre par un voyageur.* Paris, 1779.

[DELEYRE]. *Tableau de l'Europe, pour servir de supplément à l'Histoire philosophique et politique des établissements et du commerce des Européens dans les deux Indes.* Amsterdam, 1774.

[DE LISLE DE SALES]. *Essai sur la liberté de la presse.* In [De Lisle de Sales], *Paradoxes par un citoyen.* Amsterdam, 1775.

DELOLME, JEAN LOUIS. *The Constitution of England, or an Account of the English Government; in Which It Is Compared with the Republican Form of Government, and Occasionally with the Other Monarchies in Europe.* [Translated from the French.] New edition. London, 1777.

DESMOULINS, [CAMILLE]. *La France libre.* Third edition. N.p., 1789.

[DEVAINES, J.]. *Lettres de la comtesse de . . . au chevalier de . . .* N.p. [1789].

DIDEROT, DENIS. *Observations sur l'instruction de S. M. I. aux députés pour la confection des lois (1774).* Edited by Paul Ledieu. Paris, 1921.

DUBOIS DE LAUNAY, ABBÉ. *Coup d'oeil sur le gouvernement anglois.* N.p., 1786.

[DUBUAT-NANÇAY, COMTE DE]. *Les Maximes du gouvernement monarchique, pour servir de suite aux Éléments de la politique.* 4 vols. London, 1778.

[———]. *Remarques d'un Français, ou Examen impartial du livre de M. Necker sur l'administration des finances de la France, pour servir de correctif et de supplément à son ouvrage.* Geneva, 1785.

DUPONT DE NEMOURS [P.-S.]. *De l'exportation et de l'importation des grains. 1764.* L.-P. Abeille. *Premiers opuscules sur le commerce des grains. 1763-64.* Edited by Edgard Depitre. Paris, 1911.

DUPONT DE NEMOURS [P. S]. *De la périodicité des assemblées nationales, de leur organisation, de la forme à suivre pour amener les propositions qui pourront y être faites, à devenir des loix; et de la sanction nécessaire pour que ces loix soient obligatoires.* Paris, 1789.

[———]. *Idées sur les secours à donner aux pauvres malades dans une grande ville.* Philadelphia and Paris, 1786.

[———]. *Lettre à la chambre du commerce de Normandie; sur le mémoire qu'elle a publié relativement au traité de commerce avec l'Angleterre.* Rouen and Paris, 1788.

[———]. *Mémoires sur la vie et les ouvrages de M. Turgot, ministre d'état.* Philadelphia, 1782.

———. *Projet d'articles relatifs à la constitution de l'Assemblée nationale, à la forme de son travail, à la proposition, à la préparation et à la sanction des loix; remis sur le bureau de l'Assemblée nationale dans la séance du vendredi 4 septembre.* Paris [1789].

[DUSAULX.]. *Observations sur l'histoire de la Bastille, publiée par M. Linguet, avec des remarques sur le caractere de l'auteur, suivies de quelques notes sur sa maniere d'écrire l'histoire politique, civile et littéraire.* London, 1783.

[FANTIN DES ODOARDS, A.-E.-N.]. *Considérations sur le gouvernement qui convient à la France et sur les moyens de concourir au rétablissement des finances de l'état, en vendant pour deux milliards des biens du clergé. Par un citoyen de Paris, membre du district des Cordeliers.* N.p., 1789.

———. *Histoire de France, depuis la mort de Louis XIV jusqu'à la paix de Versailles de 1783.* 8 vols. Paris, 1789.

[FERRAND, A.-F., COMTE]. *Essai d'un citoyen.* N.p. [1789].

GAILLARD [G.-H.]. *Histoire de la rivalité de la France et de l'Angleterre.* 3 vols. Paris, 1771.

GALIANI, ABBÉ FERDINAND. *Dialogues sur le commerce des blés.* Reprinted in *Scrittori classici italiani di economica politica,* XII, XIII, 5-192. Milan, 1803.

[GEE, JOHN]. *Coup d'oeil rapide sur les progrès et la décadence du commerce et des forces de l'Angleterre, ouvrage attribuée à un membre du parlement.* [Translated freely from the English by J.-P. Frenais.] N.p., 1768.

[GIN, P.-L.-C.]. *Les Vrais principes du gouvernement françois, démontrés par la raison et par les faits, par un François.* Geneva, 1777.

[GOUDAR, ANGE]. *L'Autorité des rois de France est indépendante de tout corps politique; elle étoit établie avant que les parlemens fussent créés.* Amsterdam, 1788.

[———]. *L'Espion chinois; ou, L'Envoye secret de la cour de Pekin, pour examiner l'état présent de l'Europe. Traduit du chinois.* 6 vols. Cologne, 1764.

———. *L'Espion françois à Londres, ou Observations critiques sur l'Angleterre et sur les Anglois.* 2 vols. London, 1780.

[GOURCY, ABBÉ CHARLES DE]. *Des droits et des devoirs du citoyen dans les circonstances présentes, avec un jugement impartial sur l'ouvrage de M. l'abbé de Mably. Par un citoyen ami des trois ordres....* N.p., 1789.

GRÉGOIRE [HENRI]. *Opinion de M. Grégoire, curé d'Embermenil, député de Nanci, sur la sanction royale. À la séance du 4 septembre.* N.p. [1789].

GRENOBLE. *Réponse des négociants de la ville de Grenoble, à MM. les juges-consuls de Montauban, Clermont-Ferrand, Châlons, Orléans, Tours, Besançon, Dunkerque et Saint-Quentin, et à la chambre de commerce de Picardie, de Saint-Malô et de l'Isle en Flandre.* N.p. [1788].

[GROSLEY, P.-J.]. *Londres.* 3 vols. Lausanne, 1770.

[GROUVELLE, PHILIPPE-ANTOINE]. *De l'autorité de Montesquieu dans la révolution présente.* N.p., 1789.

[GUDIN DE LA BRUNELLERIE]. *Aux manes de Louis XV, et des grands hommes qui ont vécu sous son régne, ou Essai sur les progrès des arts et de l'esprit humain, sous le régne de Louis XV.* Deux-Ponts, 1776.

HELVÉTIUS, C.-A. See below under Lefebvre de la Roche.

[HOLBACH, BARON D']. *Éthocratie ou Le Gouvernement fondé sur la morale.* Amsterdam, 1776.

[———]. *La Morale universelle, ou Les Devoirs de l'homme fondés sur sa nature.* 3 vols. Amsterdam, 1776.

[———]. *La Politique naturelle ou Discours sur les vrais principes du gouvernement. Par un ancien magistrat.* 2 vols. London, 1773.

[———]. *Système social ou Principes naturels de la morale et de la politique. Avec un examen de l'influence du gouvernement sur les moeurs.* 3 vols. London, 1773.

[Huet de Froberville, J.-B.]. *Catéchisme des trois ordres, pour les assemblées d'élection. Par un gentilhomme françois.* N.p., January, 1789.

Hume, David. *Essays Moral, Political, and Literary.* Edited by T. H. Green and T. H. Grose. 2 vols. London, 1875.

—————. *The History of England, from the Invasion of Julius Caesar to the Revolution in 1688.* New edition. 6 vols. New York, 1879.

Joly de St. Valier. *Histoire raisonnée des opérations militaires et politiques de la dernière guerre, suivie d'observations sur la révolution qui est arrivée dans les moeurs et sur celle qui est sur le point d'arriver dans la constitution d'Angleterre.* Liége, 1783.

Lacombe [François]. *Tableau de Londres et des environs, avec un précis de la constitution de l'Angleterre, et de sa décadence.* London and Brussels, 1784.

[La Coste, de]. *Voyage philosophique d'Angleterre, fait en 1783 et 1784.* 2 vols. London, 1786.

Lacretelle, [P.-L.?]. *De la convocation et de la prochaine tenue des états généraux en France.* N.p. [1788?].

Lafayette, Marquis de. *Observations sur le commerce entre la France et les États-Unis.* Published in Louis R. Gottschalk (ed.), "Lafayette as Commercial Expert," *American Historical Review,* XXXVI (1931), 561-70.

La Luzerne, Cardinal de, Évêque-duc de Langres. *Sur la forme d'opiner aux états-généraux.* N.p. [1789].

[La Rochefoucauld, Duc de (ed.)]. *Constitutions des treize états-unis de l'Amérique.* Philadelphia and Paris, 1783.

—————. *Opinion de M. le duc de la Rochefoucauld, député de Paris. 7 septembre 1789....* N. p. [1789].

Lauraguais, Comte de. *Discours de M. le comte de Lauraguais à la chambre de la noblesse du Vermandois, le 18 mars 1789.* N.p. [1789].

—————. *Dissertation sur les assemblées nationales, sous les trois races des rois de France.* Paris, October 10, 1788.

[Lefebvre de la Roche?]. *Lettres de M. Helvétius au président de Montesquieu et à M. Saurin, relatives à l'aristocratie de la noblesse.* N.p., 1789.

[Lefèvre de Beauvray, Pierre]. *Dictionnaire social et patriotique, ou Précis raisonné de connoissances relatives à l'économie morale, civile et politique.* Par M. C. R. L. F. D. B. A. A. P. D. P. Amsterdam, 1770.

[LE ROY DE BARINCOURT]. *La Monarchie parfaite, ou L'Accord de l'autorité d'un monarque avec la liberté de la nation qu'il gouverne; discours.* Geneva and Paris, 1789.

[LESCÈNE DESMAISONS, JACQUES]. *Histoire politique de la révolution en France, ou Correspondance entre Lord D*** et Lord T***.* 2 vols. London, 1789.

[———]. *Qu'est-ce que les parlemens en France?* The Hague, 1788.

LE TROSNE [G.-F.], or LE TRÔNE. *De l'administration provinciale, et de la réforme de l'impôt.* 2 vols. Basel and Paris, 1788.

———. *De l'intérêt social, par rapport à la valeur, à la circulation, à l'industrie, et au commerce intérieur et extérieur; ouvrage élémentaire, dans lequel on discute quelques principes de M. l'abbé de Condillac.* Paris, 1777.

———. *De l'ordre social, ouvrage suivi d'un traité élémentaire sur la valeur, l'argent, la circulation, l'industrie et le commerce intérieur et extérieur.* Paris, 1777.

———. *La Liberté du commerce des grains, toujours utile et jamais nuisible.* Paris, November 1, 1765.

———. *Suite de la dispute sur la concurrence de la navigation étrangere pour la voiture de nos grains; ou Lettre de M. Le Trosne, avocat du roi au bailliage d'Orléans, en réponse à la lettre datée de Quimper, insérée dans la Gazette du commerce du 11 mars 1765, et les trois suivantes.* Paris, 1765.

LINGUET [SIMON-NICOLAS]. *La France plus qu'angloise, ou, Comparaison entre la procédure entamée à Paris le 25 septembre 1788 contre les ministres du roi de France, et le procès intenté à Londres en 1640, au comte de Strafford, principal ministre de Charles premier, roi d'Angleterre. Avec des réflexions sur le danger imminent dont les entreprises de la robe menacent la nation et les particuliers.* Brussels, 1788.

[———]. *Onguent pour la brulure, ou Observations sur un réquisitoire imprimé en tête de l'arrêt du parlement de Paris du 27 septembre 1788, rendu contre les Annales de M. Linguet. . . .* London, 1788.

———. *Point de banqueroute, plus d'emprunts, et, si l'on veut, bientôt plus de dettes en réduisant les impots à un seul.* N.p. [1789].

———. *Seroit-il trop tard? Aux trois ordres.* N.p., 1789.

[LIVINGSTON, WILLIAM]. *Examen du gouvernement d'Angleterre, comparé aux constitutions des États-Unis. Où l'on réfute quelques assertions contenues dans l'ouvrage de M. Adams, intitulé: Apologie des constitutions des États-Unis d'Amérique, et dans celui de M. Delolme, intitulé: De la constitution d'Angleterre. Par un cultivateur de New-Jersey. Ouvrage traduit de l'anglois, et accompagné de notes.* [Translated by Fabre; notes by Dupont de Nemours, Condorcet, and Gauvin Gallois.] London and Paris, 1789.

[LUCHET, J.-P.-L. DE]. *Les Contemporains de 1789 et 1790, ou les opinions débattues pendant la première législature; avec les principaux événemens de la révolution. Rédigé par l'auteur de la Galerie des états-généraux.* 3 vols. Paris, 1790.

[————]. *Paris en miniature, d'après les desseins d'un nouvel Argus.* Amsterdam, 1784.

[————]. *Le Vicomte de Barjac ou Mémoires pour servir à l'histoire de ce siècle.* 2 vols. Dublin and Paris, 1784.

[LYTTLETON, GEORGE, LORD]. *Letters from a Persian in England to His Friend at Ispahan.* Third edition. London, 1735.

[MACPHERSON, JAMES]. *Les Droits de la Grande Bretagne, établis contre les prétentions des Américains. Pour servir de réponse à la déclaration du congrès général.* Translated from the English by Fréville. The Hague, 1776.

MAILHE [J.-B.]. *Discours qui a remporté le prix à l'Académie des jeux floraux en 1784, sur la grandeur et l'importance de la révolution qui vient de s'opérer dans l'Amérique septentrionale..* Toulouse, 1784.

[MALESHERBES, LAMOIGNON DE]. *Second mémoire sur le mariage des protestans.* London, 1787.

MANDRILLON, J. *Fragmens de politique et de littérature, suivis d'un voyage à Berlin, en 1784....* Paris and Brussels, 1788.

[MARAT, JEAN-PAUL]. *The Chains of Slavery, a Work Wherein the Clandestine and Villainous Attempts of Princes to Ruin Liberty Are Pointed Out, and the Dreadful Scenes of Despotism Disclosed: to Which Is Prefixed an Address to the Electors of Great Britain, in Order to Draw Their Timely Attention to the Choice of Proper Representatives in the Next Parliament.* London, 1774.

————. *Le Pamphlets de Marat.* Edited by Charles Vellay. Paris, 1911.

————. *Polish Letters.* Translated from the original unpublished manuscript. 2 vols. N.p. [1905].

[———]. *Projet de déclaration des droits de l'homme et du citoyen, suivi d'un plan de constitution juste, sage et libre. Par l'auteur de l'Offrande à la patrie.* Paris, 1789.

[MERCIER, LOUIS-SÉBASTIEN]. *L'An deux mille quatre cent quarante. Reve s'il en fut jamais.* London, 1773.

[———]. *Notions claires sur les gouvernements.* 2 vols. Amsterdam, 1787.

———. *Songes et visions philosophiques.* Reprinted as Vol. XXXII of *Voyages imaginaires.* [Edited by Garnier.] Amsterdam and Paris, 1788.

[———]. *Tableau de Paris.* New edition. 4 vols. Amsterdam, 1782-83.

[MERCIER DE LA RIVIÈRE]. *L'Intérêt général de l'état, ou La Liberté du commerce des blés, démontrée conforme au droit naturel; au droit public de la France; aux loix fondamentales du royaume; à l'intérêt commun du souverain et de ses sujets dans tous les temps: avec la Réfutation d'un nouveau système, publié en forme de Dialogues sur le commerce des blés.* Amsterdam and Paris, 1770.

[———]. *L'Ordre naturel et essentiel des sociétés politiques.* 1767. Edited by Edgard Depitre. Paris, 1910.

[METTERNICH DE COLOGNE, CHEVALIER]. *Lettres historiques, politiques et critiques, sur les événemens, qui se sont passés depuis 1778 jusqu'à présent. Recueillies et publiées par un homme de lettres qui n'est d'aucune académie, ni pensionné par aucun roi, république, visir ou ministre quelconques.* 18 vols. London, 1788-94.

[MIGNONNEAU]. *Considérations intéressantes sur les affaires présentes. Par M***.* Second edition. London and Paris, 1788.

MILLOT, ABBÉ [C.-F.-X.]. *Élémens de l'histoire d'Angleterre, depuis la conquête des Romains, jusqu'au regne de Georges II.* Third edition. 3 vols. Paris, 1776.

MIRABEAU, COMTE DE. *Aux Bataves sur le stathouderat.* [Amsterdam?], 1788.

———. *Considérations sur l'ordre de Cincinnatus, ou Imitation d'un pamphlet anglo-américain. . . . Suivies de plusieurs pieces relatives à cette institution . . . et de la traduction d'un pamphlet du docteur Price, intitulé: Observations on the Importance of the American Revolution . . . accompagnée de réflexions et de notes du traducteur.* London, 1785.

[———]. *Des lettres de cachet et des prisons d'état. Ouvrage posthume, composé en 1778.* 2 vols. Hamburg, 1782.

[————]. *Le Despotisme de la maison d'Orange prouvé par l'histoire. Par Karel van Ligtdal.* "En Hollande" [1788].

————. *Discours de M. le comte de Mirabeau sur la sanction royale.* N.p. [1789].

————. *Doutes sur la liberté de l'Escaut réclamée par l'empereur; sur les causes et sur les conséquences probables de cette réclamation.* London [1785].

[————]. *Essai sur le despotisme.* Second edition. London, 1776.

————. *Observations d'un voyageur anglais, sur la maison de force, appelée Bicêtre, suivies de réflexions sur les effets de la sévérité des peines, et sur la législation criminelle de la Grande-Bretagne. Imité de l'anglais....* N.p., 1788.

————. *Seizieme lettre du comte de Mirabeau à ses commettans.* N.p., July 3 and 4, 1789.

————. *Sur la liberté de la presse. Imité de l'anglais, de Milton.* London, 1789.

[MIRABEAU, MARQUIS DE]. *L'Ami des hommes, ou Traité de la population.* New edition. 2 vols. N.p., 1758.

[————]. *Les Économiques. Par L. D. H.* 4 vols. Amsterdam and Paris, 1769-71.

[————]. *Lettres sur la législation ou L'Ordre légal, dépravé, rétabli et perpétué. Par L. D. H.* 3 vols. Berne, 1775.

[————]. *Philosophie rurale, ou Économie générale et politique de l'agriculture, réduite à l'ordre immuable des loix physiques et morales, qui assurent la prospérité des empires.* 3 vols. Amsterdam, 1763.

[————]. *Théorie de l'impot.* N.p., 1761.

MONTESQUIEU, BARON DE. *Pensées et fragments inédits de Montesquieu.* Edited by Baron Gaston de Montesquieu. 2 vols. Bordeaux, 1901.

MOORE, JOHN, M. D. *A View of Society and Manners in France, Switzerland, and Germany: with Anecdotes Relating to Some Eminent Characters.* 2 vols. Seventh edition. London, 1789.

[MOREAU, J.-N.]. *Entendons-nous, ou Le Radotage du vieux notaire, sur la Richesse de l'état.* N.p. [Amsterdam, 1763].

————. *Principes de morale, de politique et de droit public, puisés dans l'histoire de notre monarchie, ou Discours sur l'histoire de France.. Dédiés au roi.* 21 vols. Paris, 1777-89.

MORELLET, ABBÉ [ANDRÉ]. *Mémoire sur la situation actuelle de la compagnie des Indes.* Second edition. Paris, 1769.

[————]. *Observations sur le projet de former une assemblée nationale sur le modele des états généraux de 1614.* N.p. [1788].

[————]. *Réfutation de l'ouvrage qui a pour titre Dialogues sur le commerce des bleds.* London, 1770.

MOUNIER [JEAN-JOSEPH]. *Considérations sur les gouvernements et principalement sur celui qui convient à la France.* Versailles, 1789.

————. *Motifs présentés dans la séance de l'assemblée nationale du 4 septembre 1789, au nom du comité de constitution, sur divers articles du plan du corps législatif, et principalement sur la nécessité de la sanction royale.* N.p. [1789].

————. *Nouvelles observations sur les états-généraux de France.* N.p., 1789.

NORMANDIE, CHAMBRE DU COMMERCE DE. *Observations de la chambre du commerce de Normandie, sur le traité de commerce entre la France et l'Angleterre.* N.p. [1787 or early 1788].

————. *Réfutation des principes et assertions contenus dans une lettre qui a pour titre: Lettre à la chambre du commerce de Normandie, sur le mémoire qu'elle a publié relativement au traité de commerce avec l'Angleterre, par M. D. P.* N.p., 1788.

[PANCHAUD]. *Réflexions sur l'état actuel du crédit public de l'Angleterre et de la France.* N.p., November, 1781.

PANGE [FRANÇOIS], CHEVALIER DE. *De la sanction royale.* Paris, 1789.

[PELTIER, J.-G.]. *La Trompette du jugement. Au sallon d'Hercule, premier septembre 1789.* N.p. [1789].

[PÉTION DE VILLENEUVE, JÉRÔME]. *Avis aux François sur le salut de la patrie.* N.p., 1788.

[PETIOT, ABBÉ]. *Réflexions sur la liberté individuelle, et celle de la presse.* N.p. [1789].

[PINTO, ISAAC DE]. *Lettre de Mr. ***** à Mr. S. B., docteur en médecine à Kingston, au sujet des troubles qui agitent actuellement toute l'Amérique septentrionale.* The Hague, 1776.

————. *Réponse de M. J. [sic] de Pinto aux Observations d'un homme impartial, sur sa lettre à M. S. B. . . . au sujet des troubles qui agitent actuellement toute l'Amérique septentrionale.* The Hague, 1776.

————. *Seconde lettre de M. de Pinto, à l'occasion des troubles des colonies, contenant des réflexions politiques sur les suites de ces troubles, et sur l'état actuel de l'Angleterre.* The Hague, 1776.

PRICE, RICHARD. *Observations on the Nature of Civil Liberty, the Principles of Government, and the Justice and Policy of the War* with America. To Which Is Added an Appendix, Containing a State of the National Debt, an Estimate of the Money Drawn from the Public by the Taxes, and an Account of the National Income and Expenditure since the Last War. London, 1776.

[QUESNAY, FRANÇOIS]. *Physiocratie, ou Constitution naturelle du gouvernement le plus avantageux au genre humain.* Edited by Dupont [de Nemours]. Leyden and Paris. 1768.

———. *Tableau oeconomique.* First printed in 1758 and now reproduced in facsimile for the British Economic Association. London, 1894.

[RABAUT SAINT-ÉTIENNE]. *À la nation française, sur les vices de son gouvernement; sur la nécessité d'établir une constitution; et sur la composition des états-généraux.* N.p., November, 1788.

[———]. *Justice et nécessité d'assurer en France un état légal aux protestans.* Augsburg [?], n.d. [1784?].

———. *L'Opinion de M. Rabaut St.-Étienne sur quelques points de la constitution.* N.p. [1789].

[———]. *Question de droit public: Doit-on recueillir les voix, dans les états-généraux, par ordres, ou par têtes de délibérans? Par l'auteur des Considérations sur les intérêts du tiers-état.* "En Languedoc," 1789.

RAPIN-THOYRAS [PAUL] DE. *Histoire d'Angleterre.* 10 vols. The Hague, 1724-27.

[RAYNAL, G.-T.-F.]. *Histoire du parlement anglais, depuis son origine en l'an 1234 jusqu'en l'an VII de la république française; suivie de la grande charte. Par Louis Bonaparte.* ... Paris, 1820. (The original work of Raynal was published first in 1748.)

———. *Histoire philosophique et politique des établissemens et du commerce des Européens dans les deux Indes.* 4 vols. Geneva, 1780.

———. *Révolution de l'Amérique.* London, 1781.

ROBESPIERRE [MAXIMILIEN]. *Dire de M. de Robespierre, député de la province d'Artois à l'assemblée nationale, contre le veto royal, soit absolu, soit suspensif.* N.p. [Sept., 1789].

ROBINET [J.-B.-R.] (ed.). *Dictionnaire universel des sciences morale, économique, politique et diplomatique; ou Bibliothèque de l'homme-d'état et du citoyen.* 3 vols. London, 1777-83.

[———]. *Lettres sur les débats de l'assemblée nationale, relatifs à la constitution.* 1re partie. Second edition. Paris, 1789.

[RUTLEDGE or RUTLIDGE, JAMES]. *Essai sur le caractere et les moeurs des François comparés à ceux des Anglois.* London, 1776.

[————]. *Essais politiques sur l'état actuel de quelques puissances. Par M. R. C. B.* London, 1777.

SACY [C.-L.-M.] DE. *L'Honneur françois, ou Histoire des vertus et des exploits de notre nation, depuis l'établissement de la monarchie jusqu'à nos jours.* 12 vols. Paris, 1770-84.

[SAIGE]. *Catéchisme du citoyen, ou Élémens du droit public françois, par demandes et réponses; suivi de Fragmens politiques par le même auteur.* "En France," 1788.

[SAINT-SUPPLIX, S.-A. COSSÉ, BARON DE]. *Le Consolateur, pour servir de réponse à la Théorie de l'impot, et autres écrits sur l'oeconomie politique.* Brussels and Paris, 1763.

SAINTE-ALBINE, DE. *Projet d'une banque nationale à établir en France.* N.p., 1789.

[SAINTE-CROIX, BARON DE]. *Histoire des progrès de la puissance navale de l'Angleterre suivie d'observations sur l'acte de navigation, et de pieces justificatives.* 2 vols. Yverdon, 1782.

[————]. *Observations sur le traité de paix conclu à Paris le 10 février 1763 . . . relativement aux intérêts de ces puissances dans la guerre présente.* Amsterdam, 1780.

SALLE [i.e., SALLES, J.-B.]. *Opinion de M. Salle, député de Lorraine, sur la sanction royale, à la séance du premier septembre 1789.* Paris, 1789.

[SAPT, DE]. *L'Ami du prince et de la patrie, ou le bon citoyen.* Paris, 1770.

[SÉGUIER, ANTOINE-LOUIS]. *Façon de voir d'une bonne vieille, qui ne radote pas encore.* N.p. [ca. end of 1788].

[SÉNAC DE MEILHAN, GABRIEL]. *Considérations sur l'esprit et les moeurs.* London, 1787.

[————]. *Considérations sur les richesses et le luxe.* Amsterdam and Paris, 1787.

[SERRES] DE LA TOUR. *Appel au bon sens, dans lequel M. de la Tour soumet . . . les détails de sa conduite. . . .* N.p. [178–].

[SERVAN, J.-M.A.]. *Apologie de la Bastille. Pour servir de réponse aux Mémoires de M. Linguet sur la Bastille. . . . Par un homme en pleine campagne.* Kehl and Lausanne, 1784.

[————]. *Avis salutaire au tiers-état; sur ce qu'il fut, ce qu'il est, et ce qu'il peut être. Par un jurisconsulte allobroge.* N.p., 1789.

[————]. *Discours sur les progrès des connaissances humaines en général, de la morale et de la législation en particulier, lu dans une assemblée publique de l'Académie de Lyon. Par M. S**, ancien magistrat.* N.p., 1781.

[————]. *Entretien de Monsieur Necker avec Madame la comtesse de Polignac, Monsieur le baron de Breteuil et l'abbé de Vermon.* London, 1789.

[————]. *Recueil de pieces intéressantes pour servir à l'histoire de la révolution de 1789, en France.* 2 vols. N.p., 1789.

[————]. *La Seconde aux grands.* N.p. [1789].

[————]. *La Troisième aux grands, pour servir à l'histoire de la révolution depuis la convocation des états-généraux, jusqu'à la prise de la Bastille inclusivement.* Paris [1789].

SIEYÈS, ABBÉ. *Dire de l'abbé Sieyes, sur la question du veto royal, à la séance du 7 septembre 1789.* Paris [1789].

————. *Qu'est-ce que le tiers état?* Edited by Edmé Champion. Paris, 1888.

SOULÈS, FRANÇOIS. *Histoire des troubles de l'Amérique anglaise.* 2 vols. London, 1785.

[————]. *Le Véritable patriotisme.* N.p., 1788.

[TARGET, G.-J.-B.]. *IIe suite de l'écrit initulé: Les États-Généraux convoqués par Louis XVI.* N.p. [1789].

TURPIN [FRANÇOIS-RENÉ]. *Histoire des révolutions d'Angleterre, pour servir de suite à celles du père d'Orléans.* New edition. 2 vols. Paris, 1793.

[VIVANT DE MEZAGUE]. *A General View of England . . . Argumentatively Stated; from the Year 1600, to 1762; in a Letter to A. M. L. C. D. by M. V. D. M. Now Translated from the French, first Printed in 1762.* London, 1766.

VOLTAIRE. *Lettres philosophiques ou Lettres anglaises.* Edited by Raymond Naves. Paris [1939].

[WRAXALL, SIR NATHANIEL WILLIAM, BART.]. *Coup d'oeil sur l'état politique de la Grande-Bretagne, au commencement de l'année 1787. Traduit de l'anglois sur la sixième édition.* London, 1787.

c. Correspondence

BERNIS, CARDINAL DE. *Correspondance de Voltaire et du cardinal de Bernis depuis 1761 jusqu'à 1777.* Edited by Citizen Bourgoing. Paris, Year VII (1798-99).

BOISGELIN DE CUCÉ. "Lettres de M. de Boisgelin, archevêque d'Aix, à la comtesse de Gramont (1776-1789)," edited by A. Cans, *Revue historique*, LXXIX (1902), 316-23; LXXX (1902), 65-77, 301-17.

BRISSOT, J.-P. *Correspondance et papiers.* Edited by Cl. Perroud. Paris [1912].

BUFFON, LECLERC DE. *Correspondance inédite de Buffon à laquelle ont été réunies les lettres publiées jusqu'à ce jour.* Edited by Henri Nadault de Buffon. 2 vols. Paris, 1860.

CHASTELLUX, MARQUIS DE. Letters to Hume, edited by J.-S.-T. Grieg in "Notes et documents," *Revue de littérature comparée*, XII (1932), 829-37.

———. "Lettres inédites de Chastellux à Wilkes," edited by G. Bonno, *Revue de littérature comparée*, XII (1932), 619-23.

COLLÉ, CHARLES. *Correspondance inédite de Collé, faisant suite à son journal.* . . . Edited by Honoré Bonhomme. Paris, 1864.

DIDEROT, DENIS. *Lettres à Sophie Volland.* . . . Edited by André Babelon. 3 vols. Paris [1930].

DU DEFFAND, MADAME. *Correspondance complète de Mme du Deffand avec la duchesse de Choiseul, l'abbé Barthélemy et M. Craufurt.* Edited by the Marquis de Sainte-Aulaire. New edition. 3 vols. Paris, 1877.

ÉPINAY, MADAME D'. *Gli ultimi anni della signora d'Épinay: Lettere inedite all' abate Galiani (1773-1782).* Edited by Fausto Nicolini. Bari, 1933.

———. *La Signora d'Épinay e l'abate Galiani: Lettere inedite (1769-1772).* Edited by Fausto Nicolini. Bari, 1929.

GALIANI, ABBÉ FERDINAND. *Lettres de l'abbé Galiani à Madame d'Épinay, Voltaire, Diderot, Grimm, le baron d'Holbach, Morellet, Suard, d'Alembert, Marmontel, la vicomtesse de Belsunce, etc.* Edited by Eugène Asse. 2 vols. Paris, 1881.

HELVÉTIUS, C.-A. "Correspondance d'Helvétius avec sa femme," edited by Antoine Guillois, *Le Carnet historique et littéraire, revue mensuelle rétrospective et contemporaine*, VI (July-Dec., 1900), 424-46, 481-98.

LAFAYETTE, MARQUIS DE. *The Letters of Lafayette and Jefferson.* Edited by Gilbert Chinard. Baltimore, 1929.

———. *The Letters of Lafayette to Washington 1777-1799.* Edited by Louis Gottschalk. New York, 1944.

LESPINASSE, MLLE DE. *Lettres de Mlle de Lespinasse.* . . . Edited by Eugène Asse. Paris, 1876.

LISLE, CHEVALIER DE. "Les Correspondants du prince. Le chevalier de Lisle," *Annales Prince de Ligne*, V (1924), 47-91.

MARAT, J.-P. *La Correspondance de Marat.* Edited by Charles Vellay. Paris, 1908.

MIRABEAU, MARQUIS DE. "Lettres inédites du marquis de Mirabeau

(1787-1789)," *Le Correspondant,* CCL (1913), 253-79, 674-702, 1142-59; CCLI (1913), 313-37.

MORELLET, ABBÉ. *Lettres de l'abbé Morellet de l'Académie française à Lord Shelburne depuis marquis de Lansdowne, 1772-1803.* Edited by Lord Edmond Fitzmaurice. Paris, 1898.

ROLAND, MADAME. *Lettres de Madame Roland. Nouvelle série 1767-1780.* Edited by Claude Perroud. 2 vols. Paris, 1913-15.

——. *Lettres de Madame Roland (1780-1793).* Edited by Claude Perroud. 2 vols. Paris, 1900-1902.

ROUSSEAU, J.-J. *Correspondance générale de J.-J. Rousseau.* Edited by Théophile Dufour. 20 vols. Paris, 1924-34.

SABRAN, COMTESSE DE. *Correspondance inédite de la comtesse de Sabran et du chevalier de Boufflers 1778-1788.* Edited by E. de Magnieu and Henri Prat. Paris, 1875.

SPARKS, JARED (ed.). *The Diplomatic Correspondence of the American Revolution. . . .* 12 vols. Boston, 1830.

SUARD, J.-B. "Lettres inédites de Suard à Wilkes," edited by Gabriel Bonno, *University of California Publications in Modern Philology,* XV (1932), 161-280.

WALPOLE, HORACE. *The Yale Edition of Horace Walpole's Correspondence.* Vols. III-VIII, *Horace Walpole's Correspondence with Madame Du Deffand.* Edited by W. S. Lewis and Warren Hunting Smith. 6 vols., separately numbered. New Haven, 1939.

WILKES, JOHN. *The Correspondence of the Late John Wilkes with His Friends, Printed from the Original MSS. . . .* Edited by John Almon. 5 vols. London, 1805.

d. Memoirs and Journals

BAILLY, J.-S. *Mémoires de Bailly . . .* "Collection des mémoires relatifs à la Révolution française," Vols. VIII-X. Edited by MM. Berville and Barrière. 3 vols. Paris, 1821-22.

BOUILLÉ, MARQUIS DE. *Mémoires du marquis de Bouillé . . .* Second edition. "Collection des mémoires relatifs à la Révolution française" [Vol. XLV]. Edited by MM. Berville and Barrière. Paris, 1822.

BRISSOT, J.-P. *Mémoires (1754-1793).* Edited by Claude Perroud. 2 vols. Paris [1911].

CLERMONT-GALLERANDE, MARQUIS DE. *Mémoires particuliers pour servir à l'histoire de la révolution qui s'est opérée en France en 1789.* 3 vols. Paris, 1826.

CROŸ, DUC DE. *Journal inédit du duc de Croÿ 1718-1784.* Edited by the Vicomte de Grouchy and Paul Cottin. 4 vols. Paris, 1906-7.

DUTENS [LOUIS]. *Mémoires d'un voyageur qui se repose; contenant des anecdotes historiques, politiques et littéraires, relatives à plusieurs des principaux personnages du siècle.* 3 vols. Paris, 1806.

ESTERHAZY, COMTE. *Mémoires du cte Valentin Esterhazy.* Edited by Ernest Daudet. Paris, 1905.

FAVART, C.-S. *Mémoires et correspondance littéraires, dramatiques et anecdotiques de C.-S. Favart.* Edited by A.-P.-C. Favart. 3 vols. Paris, 1808.

GARAT, DOMINIQUE-JOSEPH. *Mémoires historiques sur la vie de M. Suard, sur ses écrits, et sur le XVIIIe siècle.* 2 vols. Paris, 1820.

GEORGEL, ABBÉ. *Mémoires pour servir à l'histoire des événemens de la fin du XVIIIe siècle depuis 1760 jusqu'en 1806-1810, par un contemporain impartial.* Edited by M. Georgel. 6 vols. Paris, 1820.

GROSLEY [P.-J.]. *Vie de M. Grosley, écrite en partie par lui-même.* Edited by Abbé Maydieu. London and Paris, 1787.

LAFAYETTE, MARQUIS DE. *Mémoires, correspondance et manuscrits du général Lafayette.* Edited by his family. 6 vols. Paris, 1837-38.

LA ROCHEFOUCAULD-LIANCOURT, FRANÇOIS, DUC DE. *A Frenchman in England 1784, Being the Mélanges sur l'Angleterre of François de la Rochefoucauld.* Edited from the MS by Jean Marchand and translated by S. C. Roberts. Cambridge, 1933.

MALLET DU PAN. *Mémoires et correspondance de Mallet du Pan pour servir à l'histoire de la Révolution française.* Edited by A. Sayous. 2 vols. Paris, 1851.

MALOUET, P.-V. *Mémoires de Malouet.* Edited by his grandson, Baron Malouet. 2 vols. Paris, 1868.

Mémoires et correspondances historiques et littéraires inédits 1726 à 1816. Edited by Charles Nisard. Paris, 1858.

MILLOT, ABBÉ. *Mémoires de l'abbé Millot (1726-1785).* Reprinted from the *Nouvelle revue rétrospective*, February-April, 1898. Edited by Léonce Pingaud. Paris, n.d.

MONTBAREY, PRINCE DE. *Mémoires autographes de M. le prince de Montbarey.* 3 vols. Paris, 1826-27.

MOREAU, JACOB-NICOLAS. *Mes souvenirs.* Edited by Camille Hermelin. 2 vols. Paris, 1898-1901.

MORELLET, ABBÉ. *Mémoires (inédits) de l'abbé Morellet, suivis de sa correspondance avec M. le comte R***, ministre des finances à*

Naples. "Collection des mémoires relatifs à la Révolution française," Vols. LIV-LV. 2 vols. Paris, 1823.
ROLAND, MADAME. *Mémoires de Madame Roland.* New critical edition. Edited by Claude Perroud. 2 vols. Paris, 1905.
ROMILLY, SIR SAMUEL. *Memoirs of the Life of Sir Samuel Romilly, Written by Himself; with a Selection from His Correspondence.* Second edition. Edited by his sons. 3 vols. London, 1840.
ROUSSEAU, J.-J. *Les Confessions de J.-J. Rousseau.* New edition. Paris [1881].
SÉGUR, COMTE DE. *Mémoires ou Souvenirs et anecdotes.* Third edition. 3 vols. Paris, 1827.
WEBER [LALLY-TOLLENDAL?]. *Mémoires de Weber, concernant Marie-Antoinette* ... "Collection des mémoires relatifs à la Révolution française," Vols. XI-XII. Edited by MM. Berville and Barrière. 2 vols. Paris, 1822.
YOUNG, ARTHUR. *Travels in France during the Years 1787, 1788, and 1789.* Edited by Constantia Maxwell. Cambridge, 1929.

e. Plays

BELLOY, [P.-L. B.] DE. *Le Siège de Calais, tragédie dédiée au roi.* Paris, 1765.
———. *The Siege of Calais. A Tragedy. From the French of Mr. de Belloy.* London, 1765.
FAVART, C.-S. *L'Anglois à Bordeaux.* Reprinted in *Répertoire général du théatre français,* XLV, 299-359. Paris, 1818.
SAURIN. *L'Anglomane, ou L'Orpheline léguée, comédie.* Reprinted in *Répertoire général du théatre français,* XLVI, 248-305. Paris, 1818.

III. SECONDARY WORKS

A. BOOKS

ALENGRY, FRANCK. *Condorcet guide de la Révolution française, théoricien du droit constitutionnel et précurseur de la science sociale.* Paris, 1903.
ASCOLI, GEORGES. *La Grande Bretagne devant l'opinion française au XVIIe siècle.* Travaux et mémoires de l'Université de Lille. Droit-Lettres. Nouvelle série, fascicule 13. 2 vols. in 1. Paris, 1930.
AULARD, ALPHONSE. *The French Revolution, a Political History.* Translated from the French of the third edition by Bernard Miall. 4 vols. New York, 1910.
BARNES, DONALD GROVE. *A History of the English Corn Laws from 1660-1846.* London, 1930.

BLEACKLEY, HORACE. *Life of John Wilkes.* London, 1917.
BONNO, GABRIEL. *La Constitution britannique devant l'opinion française de Montesquieu à Bonaparte.* Paris, 1932.
———. *La Culture et la civilisation britanniques devant l'opinion française de la paix d'Utrecht aux Lettres philosophiques (1713-1734).* Transactions of the American Philosophical Society. New Series. Vol. XXXVIII, Part 1. Philadelphia, June, 1948.
CARCASSONNE, E. *Montesquieu et le problème de la constitution française au XVIIIe siècle.* Paris [1927].
CARRÉ, HENRI. *La Noblesse de France et l'opinion publique au XVIIIe siècle.* Paris, 1920.
———. *Le Règne de Louis XV (1715-1774),* Vol. VIII, Part II of *Histoire de France depuis les origines jusqu'à la Révolution.* Edited by Ernest Lavisse. Paris, 1909.
CARRÉ, H., SAGNAC, P., AND LAVISSE, E. *Le Règne de Louis XVI (1774-1789),* Vol. IX, Part I of *Histoire de France depuis les origines jusqu'à la Révolution.* Edited by Ernest Lavisse. Paris, 1910.
CRU, R. LOYALTY. *Diderot as a Disciple of English Thought.* New York, 1913.
CUSHING, MAX PEARSON. *Baron d'Holbach. A Study of Eighteenth Century Radicalism in France.* New York, 1914.
DEDIEU, JOSEPH. *Montesquieu et la tradition politique anglaise en France. Les Sources anglaises de l' "Esprit des lois."* Paris, 1909.
DOWELL, STEPHEN. *A History of Taxation and Taxes in England from the Earliest Times to the Present Day.* 4 vols. London, 1884.
ELLERY, ELOISE. *Brissot de Warville. A Study in the History of the French Revolution.* Boston, 1915.
ESMEIN, A. *Cours élémentaire d'histoire du droit français à l'usage des étudiants de première année.* Fifteenth edition. Edited by R. Génestal. Paris, 1925.
FAŸ, BERNARD. *The Revolutionary Spirit in France and America. A Study of Moral and Intellectual Relations between France and the United States at the End of the Eighteenth Century.* Translated from the French by Ramon Guthrie. New York [1927].
GLASSON, E. *Le Parlement de Paris. Son rôle politique depuis le règne de Charles VII jusqu'à la Révolution.* 2 vols. Paris, 1901.
GOTTSCHALK, LOUIS R. *Jean Paul Marat. A Study in Radicalism.* London, n.d.
———. *Lafayette Comes to America.* Chicago [1935].
———. *Lafayette Joins the American Army.* Chicago [1937].

———. *Lafayette and the Close of the American Revolution.* Chicago [1942].
GREEN, F. C. *Eighteenth-Century France. Six Essays.* London and Toronto [1929].
GUADEMET, EUGÈNE. *L'Abbé Galiani et la question du commerce des blés à la fin du règne de Louis XV.* Paris, 1899.
GUERRIER, M.-W. *L'Abbé de Mably moraliste et politique.* . . . Paris, 1886.
HATIN, EUGÈNE. *Histoire politique et littéraire de la presse en France avec une introduction historique sur les origines du journal et la bibliographie générale des journaux depuis leur origine.* 8 vols. Paris, 1859-61.
HAUSER, HENRI. *Le Principe des nationalités. Ses origines historiques.* Paris, 1916.
HAYES, CARLETON J. H. *Essays on Nationalism.* New York, 1926.
———. *The Historical Evolution of Modern Nationalism.* New York, 1931.
HAZARD, PAUL. *La Pensée européenne au XVIIIe siècle de Montesquieu à Lessing.* 3 vols. Paris, 1946.
HYSLOP, BEATRICE FRY. *French Nationalism in 1789 according to the General Cahiers.* New York, 1934.
JOHANNET, RENÉ. *Le Principe des nationalités.* New edition. Paris, 1923.
KEIM, ALBERT. *Helvétius, sa vie et son oeuvre d'après ses ouvrages, des écrits divers et des documents inédits.* Paris, 1907.
KEIR, D. L. *The Constitutional History of Modern Britain, 1485-1937.* London, 1938.
KENT, C. B. ROYLANCE. *The English Radicals. An Historical Sketch.* London, 1899.
KOHN, HANS. *The Idea of Nationalism. A Study in Its Origins and Background.* New York, 1944.
LAMY, ÉTIENNE. *Un Défenseur des principes traditionnels sous la Révolution. Nicolas Bergasse, avocat au parlement de Paris, député du tiers état de la sénéchaussée de Lyon aux états-géneraux (1750-1832).* Paris, 1910.
LAS VERGNAS, R. *Le Chevalier Rutlidge, "gentilhomme anglais," 1742-94.* Paris, 1932.
LAVAQUERY, ABBÉ E. *Le Cardinal de Boisgelin 1732-1804.* 2 vols. Paris [1920-21].
———. *Necker fourrier de la Révolution 1732-1804.* Paris [1933].

LAVISSE, ERNEST. *General View of the Political History of Europe.* Translated by Charles Gross. New York [1891].

LEFEBVRE, GEORGES. *Quatre-vingt-neuf.* Paris, 1939.

LEIGHTON, RICHARD M. "The Tradition of the English Constitution in France on the Eve of the Revolution." Unpublished Ph.D. dissertation, Cornell University, 1941.

LEVASSEUR, E. *Histoire du commerce de la France.* Vol. I. Paris, 1911.

LOCKITT, C. H. *The Relations of French and English Society (1763-1793).* London, 1920.

MALLET, BERNARD. *Mallet du Pan and the French Revolution.* London, 1902.

MARION, MARCEL. *Histoire financière de la France depuis 1715.* 6 vols. Paris, 1914-31.

MARTIN, KINGSLEY. *French Liberal Thought in the Eighteenth Century.* Boston, 1929.

MATHIEZ, ALBERT. *The French Revolution.* Translated by Catherine Alison Phillips. New York, 1928.

MORNET, DANIEL. *Les Origines intellectuelles de la Révolution française (1715-1787).* Paris, 1933.

PALMER, ROBERT ROSWELL. "The French Idea of American Independence on the Eve of the French Revolution." Unpublished Ph.D. dissertation, Cornell University, 1934.

PROTEAU, PIERRE. *Étude sur Morellet considéré comme auxiliaire de l'école physiocratique et examen de ses principaux ouvrages économiques.* Laval, 1910.

REDSLOB, ROBERT. *Die Staatstheorien der französischen Nationalversammlung von 1789. Ihre Grundlage in der Staatslehre der Aufklärungszeit und in den englischen und amerikanischen Verfassungsgedanken.* Leipzig, 1912.

RIPERT, HENRI. *Le Marquis de Mirabeau (l'Ami des hommes), ses théories politiques et économiques.* Paris, 1901.

RIVIÈRE, H.-F. *Précis historique et critique de la législation française sur le commerce des céréales et des mesures d'administration prises dans les temps de cherté.* Paris, 1859.

ROYAL INSTITUTE OF INTERNATIONAL AFFAIRS. *Nationalism.* A Report by a Study Group of Members of the Royal Institute of International Affairs. London, 1939.

SABINE, GEORGE H. *A History of Political Theory.* New York [1937].

SAGNAC, PHILIPPE. *La Fin de l'ancien régime et la Révolution américaine (1763-1789).* "Peuples et civilisations," Vol. XII. Edited by Louis Halphen and Philippe Sagnac. Paris, 1947.

———. *La Formation de la société française moderne.* 2 vols. Paris, 1945-46.

SCHUYLER, ROBERT LIVINGSTON. *The Britannic Question and the American Revolution.* Reprinted from the *Political Science Quarterly*, XXXVIII (1923), 104-14. New York, 1923.

———. *Parliament and the British Empire. Some Constitutional Controversies concerning Imperial Legislative Jurisdiction.* New York, 1929.

——— (ed.). *Josiah Tucker. A Selection from His Economic and Political Writings.* New York, 1931.

THOMSON, MARK A. *A Constitutional History of England 1642 to 1801,* Vol. IV of *A Constitutional History of England.* Edited by R. F. Treharne. London [1938].

THOMPSON, J. M. *The French Revolution.* New York, 1945.

VEITCH, GEORGE STEAD. *The Genesis of Parliamentary Reform.* London, 1913.

WEULERSSE, GEORGES. *Le Mouvement physiocratique en France de 1756 à 1770.* 2 vols. Paris, 1910.

WHITFIELD, ERNEST A. *Gabriel Bonnot de Mably.* London, 1930.

B. ARTICLES

ACCARIAS, JOSEPH. "Un Publiciste dauphinois du 18e siècle . . . ," *Académie Delphinale, Bulletin, Série 4,* III (1889), 487-533.

ACOMB, FRANCES (ED.). "Unemployment and Relief in Champagne, 1788," *Journal of Modern History,* XI (1939), 41-48.

AULARD, ALPHONSE. "Patrie, patriotisme avant 1789," *La Révolution française,* LXVIII (1915), 193-224.

———. "Patrie, patriotisme sous Louis XVI et dans les cahiers," *La Révolution française,* LXVIII (1915), 301-39.

BRITSCH, AMÉDÉE. "L'Anglomanie de Philippe-Égalité, d'après sa correspondance autographe (1778-1785)," *Le Correspondant,* CCCIII (1926), 280-95.

FEBVRE, LUCIEN. "Langue et nationalité en France au XVIIIe siècle," *Revue de synthése historique,* XLII (Dec., 1926), 19-40.

HYSLOP, BEATRICE F. "Recent Work on the French Revolution," *American Historical Review,* XLVII (April, 1942), 488-517.

LASKI, H. J. "The English Constitution and French Public Opinion, 1789-94," *Politica,* III (1938), 27-42.

MATHIEZ, ALBERT. "Pacifisme et nationalisme au dix-huitième siècle," *Annales historiques de la Révolution française*, XIII (1936), 1-17.
———. "La Place de Montesquieu dans l'histoire des doctrines politiques du XVIIIe siècle," *Annales historiques de la Révolution française*, VII (1930), 97-112.
PALMER, ROBERT R. "The National Idea in France before the Revolution," *Journal of the History of Ideas*, I (1940), 95-111.
SAGNAC, PHILIPPE. "L'Idée de la nation en France (1788-1789)," *Revue d'histoire politique et constitutionnelle*, I (1937), 158-63.
SHAFER, BOYD C. "Bourgeois Nationalism in the Pamphlets on the Eve of the French Revolution," *Journal of Modern History*, X (1938), 31-50.
WILLIAMS, DAVID. "French Opinion concerning the English Constitution in the Eighteenth Century," *Economica*, X (1930), 295-308.

C. WORKS OF REFERENCE

Biographie universelle, ancienne et moderne; ou, Histoire, par ordre alphabétique, de la vie publique et privée de tous les hommes qui se sont fait remarquer par leurs écrits, leurs actions, leurs talents, leurs vertus ou leurs crimes. . . . [Edited by J.-F. Michaud]. New edition. 45 vols. Paris, 1870-73.
BOURSIN, E., AND CHALLAMEL, AUGUSTIN. *Dictionnaire de la Révolution française.* Paris, 1893.
BARBIER, ANTOINE-ALEXANDRE. *Dictionnaire des ouvrages anonymes.* Third edition, revised and enlarged by MM. Olivier Barbier, René and Paul Billard. 4 vols. Paris, 1882.
BRUNET, GUSTAVE, ET AL. *Dictionnaire des ouvrages anonymes suivi des Supercheries littéraires dévoilées. Supplément à la dernière édition de ces deux ouvrages (édition Daffis).* Paris, 1889.
CHÉRUEL, A. *Dictionnaire historique des institutions, moeurs et coutumes de la France.* 2 vols. Paris, 1855.
Dictionary of National Biography from the Earliest Times to 1900. Edited by Sir Leslie Stephen and Sir Sidney Lee. 22 vols. Oxford, 1921-22.
HATIN, EUGÈNE. *Bibliographie historique et critique de la presse périodique française, ou Catalogue systématique et raisonné de tous les écrits périodiques de quelque valeur publiés ou ayant circulé en France depuis l'origine du journal jusqu'à nos jours.* . . . Paris, 1866.

MARION, MARCEL. *Dictionnaire des institutions de la France aux XVIIe et XVIIIe siècles.* Paris, 1923.

Nouvelle biographie universelle depuis les temps les plus reculés jusqu'à nos jours. . . . Edited by M. Hoefer. 46 vols. Paris, 1852-66.

QUÉRARD, J.-M. *La France littéraire, ou Dictionnaire bibliographique des savants, historiens et gens de lettres de la France, ainsi que les littérateurs étrangers qui ont écrit en français, plus particulièrement pendant les XVIIIe et XIXe siècles.* 12 vols. Paris, 1827-64.

———. *Les Supercheries littéraires dévoilées.* . . . Third edition, revised and enlarged by M. Olivier Barbier. 3 vols. Paris, 1869-70.

INDEX

A

Affaires de l'Angleterre et de l'Amérique, 83-85
Agriculture, 9, 48, 59, 60, 63, 65-66
America, as a symbol, 88, 100-101
L'Anglois à Bordeaux, 55-56
Anglomania, vii-viii, viii n. 1, ix, 5, 12, 14, 14 n. 13, 15-16, 27, 38-40, 68 n. 46, 78-80, 89, 96-113, 120, 121, 122-23, 125-26
Anglophile liberal tradition, see Anglomania
Anglophiles, see Anglomania
Anglophobe, use of term, ix
Anti-Anglophile, use of term, ix
Army, 35, 61, 111
Ascoli, Georges, viii n. 1
Atheism, 25
Aulard, Alphonse, 52 n. 1

B

Balance of powers, see Checks and balances
Bankers, 91
Baudeau, Abbé Nicolas, 46-47, 101
Bayle, Pierre, 62
Beaumarchais, P.-A. Caron de, 76
Belloy, P.-L. B. de, 56
Bicameralism, viii, 99-100, 107; see also Checks and balances, House of Lords
Bill of Rights, English, 5
Bolingbroke, Henry Saint-John, Viscount, 31, 62
Bonno, Gabriel, viii n. 1
Bossuet, Bishop, 62
Boucher d'Argis, A.-J., 92-93
Bourgeoisie, 7, 9, 46-47, 56, 86-87, 106, 122

Brissot de Warville, J.-P., 6 n. 4, 82, 96-97, 100
Brittany, 97

C

Catholics, treatment accorded to, 24, 27, 45, 103, 109
Censorship, 16, 25; see also Liberty
Checks and balances, viii, 4, 12, 14, 22, 43, 46, 97, 98, 99, 103, 104, 106, 122, 127; see also Bicameralism, House of Lords, Royal prerogative, Constitution, English
Civil liberty, see Liberty, Jurisprudence, Press, freedom of, Religious toleration
Colonies, 9, 50, 60, 69, 117
Comédie Française, 58
Commerce, 8, 9, 46, 63, 66, 70-71, 73, 103, 109; see Economic policy, Economic status, Navigation Acts, Treaty of 1786
Compte rendu au roi, 90-92
Condorcet, Marquis de, 7, 68 n. 46, 101, 102-4, 118
Conservatism, 16-17, 19-29, 27-28, 74-78, 89-90, 104-6
Conservatives, see Conservatism
Constituent Assembly, 82, 97, 100, 107, 113, 120
Constituent power, 100, 112
Constitution, English, 22, 42, 75, 90, 91-92, 104-5, 121, 122, 126-27; see also Checks and balances, Liberty, Parliament, Republic, Republican, Fundamental law
Constitution, French, 14, 25, 28, 64, 75, 95, 121, 123; see also Monarchy, Fundamental law

Constitutions, American, 69-70, 75, 83-84, 88, 96-97, 99-101
Contraband trade, 23, 117
Convention, constitutional, *see* Constituent power
Corn laws, 47-49
Corps intermédiaires, *see* Intermediary powers
Corruption, political, 4-5, 10, 22, 29, 31, 41, 45, 75, 84, 126
Cosmopolitanism, 51, 54, 62-63, 67-68, 87, 120, 123
Counterforces, *see* Checks and balances
Counterrevolution, 106, 113
Crime, 8, 26, 93
Cromwell, Oliver, 6
Croÿ, Duc de, 58, 77

D

Debt, public, 47, 49, 59, 60, 85, 91-92, 103
Declaration of Independence, American, 69, 83-84, 88
Dedieu, Joseph, viii n. 1
Deficit, French, 91
Delolme, J.-L., 104-5
Democracy, political, 34, 99, 106
Depression of 1787, 118
Derogation of noblesse, *see* Nobility
Desmoulins, Camille, 121
Despotism, 6, 10, 16, 22-23, 69-70, 71, 77, 80, 83, 110-11, 122; *see also* Freedom of the seas, Royal prerogative
Diderot, Denis, 16, 17, 30, 37, 67
Divine right, theory of, 19, 24
Doubling of the Third, 96
Dubois de Launay, Abbé, 90
Du Crest, Marquis, 97
Du Deffand, Madame, 74 n. 14
Dupont de Nemours, P.-S., 64, 66, 101, 119

E

East India Company, British, 103, 116
École Royale Gratuite de Dessein, 119
Economic policy, British, 8-9, 12-13, 46-50, 59, 109, 117-19, 122
Economic policy, French, 16, 48, 50, 117-19
Economic status of Britain and France, comparative, 8-9, 50, 59-61, 60-61, 65-66, 85
Eden Treaty, *see* Treaty of 1786
Education, 40-41, 42, 103

Elections, 26, 34, 35, 103, 105
Electorate, *see* Representation
Elites, 45, 102-3
Enlightenment, 6, 12, 65, 67-68, 101, 109, 122
Equality, 6-7, 9, 12, 15, 26, 45-46, 107, 110-11, 113, 126
Estates-General, 14, 93-94, 95-96, 97, 106, 107, 111
Étatisme, 121
Evidence, concept of, 42-43

F

Faction, 5, 24, 36-38, 102, 122, 126
Fanaticism, 6, 11, 24
Favart, C.-S., 55
Faÿ, Bernard, 72-73, 83-84, 87-88
Febvre, Lucien, 53 n. 2
Fénelon, Archbishop, 62
Feudalism, 7, 46, 126
Finance, public, 91, 94, 120, 122; *see also* Debt, public, Deficit, Taxation
Fléchier, Bishop, 62
Fox, Charles James, 116
Franchise, *see* Representation, Democracy, political
Franco-American alliance, 72, 117
Franklin, Benjamin, 83
Freedom of the seas, 73, 77, 79-80, 87, 114, 117
Fréron, Élie, 28
Frondeurs, 13, 15-16, 31, 80-81, 83, 106
Fundamental law, 5, 14, 64, 69-70, 75, 100

G

Galiani, Abbé, 77
Gardes Françaises, 15
General will, 14 n. 13, 17, 38, 39-40, 67, 96-97, 102, 110, 120, 122-23, 127; *see also* Nation
George III, King of England, 19, 105
Gottschalk, Louis, xii, 15 n. 17
Gournay, Vincent de, and his school, 12-13, 47
Grimm, Baron, 58-59

H

Habeas corpus, writ of, *see* Jurisprudence
Hanoverian succession, 36
Hastings, Warren, 116
Hauser, Henri, 52 n. 1
Hayes, C. J. H., 52 n. 1
Hazard, Paul, 53 n. 2

Index

Helvétius, C.-A., xi, 12, 12 n. 9, 37, 109, 123, 124-28
Heresy, 25, 87
Highways, 8, 26, 85
Holbach, Baron d', 17, 30, 31, 37, 41
Honor, 10, 21, 54, 61-62, 62 n. 23, 86, 115
House of Commons, 7, 15, 32, 35, 38, 105-6, 110, 111
House of Lords, 7, 15, 38, 104, 105-6, 110, 126
Hume, David, 28, 44-45
Hyslop, Beatrice, 52 n. 1

I

Imperial rivalry of France and Britain, 9, 61, 65-66, 73, 77, 83, 85, 87, 117; see also Freedom of the seas, Nationalism, *Revanche*, sentiment of
Imperialism, British, 9, 10, 40, 49-50, 59-60, 71-73, 77, 79, 115-16
Imprisonment for debt, 23
India, 72
Industrial development, 9, 10, 66, 118-19
"Influence" of the crown, 31, 33-35, 69; see also Corruption, political, Royal prerogative
Intermediary powers, 8, 22, 23, 95
International law, 65, 73
Ireland, 24, 59, 71-72, 115-16, 117

J

Jeanne d'Arc, 20
Johannet, René, 53 n. 2
Jurisprudence, English, 3, 27, 42, 45, 92, 98, 109
Jury trial, see Jurisprudence, English

K

Keim, Albert, 127-28
King of England, attitude of subjects toward, 19-21, 22, 105
King of France, attitude of subjects toward, 20-21, 52 n. 1, 53 n. 2, 57-58, 66, 106, 121
King's Friends, 31, 32, 33
Kohn, Hans, 52 n. 1

L

Laboring classes, 6, 23, 26, 27-28, 41, 41-42, 59-60; see also Poor, Populace
Lafayette, Marquis de, 6 n. 4, 15-16 n. 17, 72, 100, 115, 117

La Harpe, J.-F. de, 58
Lanjuinais, J.-D., 97
La Rochefoucauld, Duc de (seventeenth-century writer), 62
Laski, H. J., viii n. 1
Lauzun, Duc de, 15
Lavisse, Ernest, 52 n. 1
Lefebvre, Georges, viii n. 1
Lefebvre de la Roche, Abbé, 124, 126, 128
Legal despotism, 17, 42-43, 63, 66
Leighton, Richard M., viii n. 1
Le Trosne, G.-F., 44, 65-66
Liberalism, ix, 5-6, 9-10, 12, 15, 30-50, 72, 78-80, 81-83, 87, 88, 113, 114-21
Liberalism, economic, 13, 17, 47, 50, 65, 70-71, 83, 114, 118
Liberty, 3, 4, 5, 6, 10, 11, 12, 15, 22, 24, 26, 30, 31-32, 45, 69-70, 73, 75, 82-83, 99, 104, 107, 108-9, 122, 125-26, 127
License, 24-25, 75; see also Liberty, Faction
Linguet, S.-N., xi, 23-24, 24 n. 17, 76, 95
Lit de justice, 13, 94, 95
Local government, English, 7-8
Locke, John, vii, 5, 10
London, 19, 33
Louis XIV, vii, 54, 62
Louis XV, 15
Louis XVI, 13-14, 15, 24 n. 17
Lyon, textile interests of, 118

M

Mably, Abbé de, 17, 30, 35, 36, 37-38, 40, 70, 81-82, 98, 123
Magna Carta, 5, 19, 96
Mandate of constituents, 34, 110; see also Representation
Marat, Jean-Paul, 17, 30, 37, 41-42
Maréchaussée, see Military police
Marx, Karl, 46
Mathiez, Albert, 53 n. 2
Maupeou Parlement, 13-14, 94; see also Parlements
Mercantilism, see Economic policy
Mercier, L.-S., 86-87
Mercier de la Rivière, 43
Middle class, see Bourgeoisie
Middlesex County, constituency of John Wilkes, 32-33
Military police, 8

Millot, Abbé C.-F.-X., 28
Mirabeau, Comte de, 82-83, 117
Mirabeau, Marquis de, 44, 101
Mission, national, 62, 65, 67, 73, 87, 115, 119, 123
Mixed government, 4, 76, 97, 125
Monarchy, 6, 21, 22, 23, 25-26, 28-29, 36, 46, 47, 52 n. 1, 53 n. 2, 57-58, 64, 66, 95, 104-6, 112-13, 121, 122
Montesquieu, Baron de, 4, 8, 15, 22-23, 62, 95, 113, 123, 124, 127-28
Moore, John, M. D., 58
Moreau, J.-N., 95-96
Morellet, Abbé, 13, 16, 50 n. 70, 68, 72-73, 78-79, 128

N

Nation, 12, 14 n. 13, 39, 51, 53, 69, 102, 106, 110, 113, 119, 127; *see also* General will
National character, English, 5, 10-11, 21, 55, 64, 71, 72
National character, French, 25, 55, 64-65
Nationalism, ix, 20, 51-52, 52-53, 52 n. 1, 53 n. 2, 54-67, 72, 83-87, 114-21; *see also* Imperial rivalry, Mission, national, *Revanche*, sentiment of
Natural laws, 42-43, 45, 46, 65
Natural rights, 39-40, 70-71
Navigation Acts, 50, 73, 117-18; *see also* Economic policy
Navy, 61, 85
Necker, Jacques, 90-92
Neo-Physiocrats, 17, 43, 101-2, 119
Netherlands, The, vii, 116-17
Newton, Sir Isaac, 10
Noailles, Maréchal de, 58
Nobility, 6-7, 15-16, 46-47, 80-81, 86, 106-7, 112-13; *see also* Frondeurs, Parlements
Normandy, Chamber of Commerce of, 118-19
North Briton, No. 45, 31-32

O

Opposition party, *see* Faction, Whigs, Radicals
Orléans, Duc d', 97

P

Pacifism, 79
Paine, Thomas, 83-84
Palmer, R. R., 53 n. 2

Paris, 33
Parlements, 13-14, 29, 32-33, 45, 93-95, 106, 127
Parliament, English, 7, 8, 10, 12, 22, 23, 26, 29, 31, 33, 35, 38, 39, 47-48, 69, 70, 94, 98, 99, 102, 103, 112, 127; *see also* House of Commons, House of Lords
Parliamentary absolutism, 5, 5 n. 3, 35
Patrie, 53, 54, 58
Patriot party (Dutch), 116
Patriotisme, 53-54
Patronage, political, 7, 31, 33-34, 102-3
Peasants, *see* Laboring classes
Peerage, English, 7, 15, 35; *see also* House of Lords
Philosophes, 12, 13, 14, 16, 17, 27, 31, 54, 62, 67, 78
Physiocrats, xi, 13, 16, 17, 42-43, 63-67, 101-2, 109, 114, 122, 123
Pitt, William (the Elder), 44-45
Pitt, William (the Younger), 105, 115, 115 n. 73
Political liberty, *see* Liberty, Checks and balances, General will, Representation
Poor, the, 28, 41-42, 92
Populace, 8, 19, 45, 103
Popular school, *see* Rousseau and Mably, school of
Population, 60, 61, 85
Press, freedom of, 3, 24-25, 37, 109; *see also* Censorship, Liberty
Press gang, 23, 85, 109
Price, Richard, 64, 83-84
Privilege, 6-7, 8, 26, 46, 106, 110, 112-13, 121, 126-27; *see also* Equality, Intermediary powers, Nobility, Monarchy
Progress, idea of, 68, 81, 121
Property, right of, 8, 46, 71
Provincial assemblies, 7, 103
Prussia, 116
Public opinion, ix-x, 43-44, 45, 64-65, 122, 125

Q

Quakers, 25
Quesnay, François, 17, 44, 45

R

Radicals, 31, 34-35
Rationalism, vii, 42, 67, 100-102, 120; *see also* Enlightenment, Utopianism

Redslob, Robert, viii n. 1
Religious toleration, 3, 109, 121; see also Catholics, treatment accorded to, Fanaticism
Representation, 34, 35, 38, 39, 98, 99, 103, 104, 110; see also General will, House of Commons, Democracy, political
Republic, 4, 6, 28-29, 44, 46-47, 121
Republican, 4, 6, 10, 44, 89-90, 97, 119
Republican party (Dutch), 116
Resources, see Economic status
Revanche, sentiment of, 59, 61-62, 66, 73, 80-81, 83, 85, 86
Revolution, American, 29, 69-72, 87-88, 106, 116, 122; see also Colonies, War of American Independence
Revolution of 1688, vii, 5, 6, 36, 76, 95
Revolution, French, vii, viii, ix, 4, 39, 54, 114, 123
Revolution, Puritan, 6, 24, 95
Revolution, right of, 5, 5 n. 3, 39, 70, 75-76, 104
Rivalry, national, see Nationalism, Imperial rivalry
Robespierre, Maximilien, 121
Rouen, textile interests of, 118
Rousseau, Jean-Jacques, 17, 30, 36, 38, 42, 98, 123
Rousseau and Mably, school of, 17, 30-42, 38, 96-113, 108, 120, 122-23
Royal Institute of International Affairs, 52 n. 1
Royal prerogative, 33-36, 38, 99-100, 107, 111-13, 126; see Veto, royal

S

Sagnac, Philippe, 53 n. 2
Saurin, 124
Scotland, 59
Séguier, A.-L., 25
Ségur, Comte de, 15, 80
Servan, J.-M.-A., 86, 125
Seven Years' War, viii, ix, 12-13, 18, 47, 50, 54, 55, 59, 114, 121
Shafer, Boyd C., 52 n. 1
Shelburne, Lord, 73, 78
Le Siège de Calais, 56-59
Sources, discussion of, x-xii
Sovereignty, see General will, Nation

Steele, Sir Richard, 62
Suicide in England, 10
Switzerland, vii

T

Taxation, 23, 27, 49, 59, 70, 85, 92, 102-3; see also Finance, public
Third Estate, 86, 96, 97, 106-7, 111, 113
Thompson, J. M., 52 n. 1
Tillotson, Archbishop, 62
Tories, 36, 122; see also King's Friends
Travelers, English, 10-11
Treaty of 1763 (Peace of Paris), 55
Treaty of 1783, 115, 117
Treaty of 1786 (Eden Treaty), 117-19
Tucker, Josiah, 50
Turgot, A.-R.-J., Baron de l'Aulne, 17, 44, 45, 64-65, 81-82, 101, 122

U

Unicameralism, viii, 96, 104, 107, 126; see also Vote by head
Utilitarianism, 37, 98, 124-25
Utopianism, vii, 3, 44, 88, 100-101

V

Veto, royal, viii, 35, 98, 99-100, 107-8, 110; see also Royal prerogative
Virtue, political, 4, 10, 40-41, 52, 70, 81, 122; see General will
Voltaire, x, 12, 16, 28, 42, 62, 68, 68 n. 46, 79, 109, 123
Vote by head, 96, 107, 111; see Unicameralism
Vote by order, 96, 107; see Bicameralism

W

Walpole, Sir Robert, 44
War of American Independence, 12, 16, 18, 29, 42-43, 63, 69-88, 114, 122, 123
Warrants of arrest, 23, 31; see Jurisprudence, Liberty
Weulersse, Georges, 46
Whig political theory, 5, 5 n. 3
Whigs, 31, 33-35, 36, 68, 78
Wilkes, John, 19, 31-33
William III, King of England, 36
Williams, David, viii n. 1

AUGSBURG COLLEGE & SEMINARY
George Sverdrup Library
MINNEAPOLIS 4, MINNESOTA